Optimize Your School

This book is dedicated to my bride of 50 years, Sandy Jenkins. She has supported my work in amazing ways, even though the thought of another book wasn't the most exciting thing she ever heard.

Optimize Your School

It's All About the Strategy

Lee Jenkins

Foreword by Michael Fullan

CORWIN
A SAGE Company

FOR INFORMATION:

Corwin

A SAGE Company

2455 Teller Road

Thousand Oaks, California 91320

(800) 233-9936

www.corwin.com

SAGE Publications Ltd.

1 Oliver's Yard

55 City Road

London EC1Y 1SP

United Kingdom

SAGE Publications India Pvt. Ltd.

B 1/I 1 Mohan Cooperative Industrial Area

Mathura Road, New Delhi 110 044

India

SAGE Publications Asia-Pacific Pte. Ltd.

3 Church Street

#10-04 Samsung Hub

Singapore 049483

Printed in the United States of America

ISBN 978-1-4833-8289-0

Senior Acquisitions Editor: Jessica Allan

Senior Associate Editor: Kimberly Greenberg

Editorial Assistant: Cesar Reyes

Production Editor: Melanie Birdsall

Copy Editor: Diane DiMura

Typesetter: C&M Digitals (P) Ltd.

Proofreader: Eleni-Maria Georgiou

Indexer: Sheila Bodell

Cover Designer: Michael Dubowe

Marketing Manager: Amy Vader

This book is printed on acid-free paper.

15 16 17 18 19 10 9 8 7 6 5 4 3 2 1

Contents

Visit the companion website at
http://resources.corwin.com/jenkinsoptimize
for additional resources.

List of Figures

Foreword

Ever since I saw Lee Jenkins' striking graph of teachers' perceptions of "loss of enthusiasm" by students over the grades levels—declining from 95 percent enthusiasm in kindergarten to 37 percent in Grade 9, I became hooked on what we could do to make school engaging for students. Fortunately, Lee Jenkins himself has pursued this matter and develops a strong set of strategies that he incorporates in his comprehensive new book, *Optimize Your School: It's All About the Strategy.*

Jenkins first sets the stage by showing that continuous improvement is not a matter of attitude but rather one of *strategy.* He then begins to unpack continuous strategic improvement within the classroom, especially concerning the role of students. Then comes the critical role of "instructional leadership" in which he pinpoints strategies worth testing. Underpinning instructional development are the basics of "human resources" and "finance and operations." Managerial effectiveness is essential for optimized systems.

Once the basics are set, Jenkins turns his attention to systematic continuous improvement in the classroom (teachers as experts), in the principalship, and in relation to leadership principles essential for guiding the whole process. All through the process and in a wrap of Chapter 18, Jenkins shows that data, results, and related impact measures are integral to optimized school systems.

What makes *Optimize Your School* especially valuable is the combination of assets it provides: It is comprehensive in coverage; it addresses explicitly all the subject areas; it contains ideas, tools, and strategic advice. It is at once lofty in its overview and precise in its application. As Jenkins weaves his way to a comprehensive strategy, I found it especially helpful that he enumerates "what not to do." In an early chapter on strategy, for example, he lists eleven unsuccessful strategies, all of which ring true in my own work on what we know about change (things like adding pressure, pouring on more incentives, and so on).

Before getting to solutions he discusses three big education "wasters": time, money, and enthusiasm. He then spends most of his time on steps that do work to increase enthusiasm, engagement, and results. Start with the classroom, he advises, and keep it front and center. He provides numerous ideas for students and teachers to set and chart their learning directions. All of this is based on setting high standards and engaging in 21st century learning experiences that develop essential skills for problem solving and learning. There is plenty in the book on leadership—by students, by teachers, and by principals. Jenkins always directs the discussion to sorting out what works and what doesn't work. This gives readers an understanding of why certain traditional strategies don't work and points clearly to productive lines of action. I especially like Chapter 13 which is devoted to "how to evaluate the HR department," a much neglected topic and one that could represent high leverage payoff.

Jenkins ends the book with a challenge in which he shows how top-down and bottom-up forces are both needed and can interact to produce best outcomes.

In short, there is something for all learners in *Optimize Your School*—for their own actions, and what they can do collectively.

Michael Fullan
Author and Consultant
Special Advisor on Education to the Premier of Ontario

Preface

Once every so often, an idea comes along that changes everything. Leadership with continuous strategic improvement in order to optimize your school is one such idea. Continuous improvement is a record or doing better than ever before. The evidence is almost always displayed on a graph—a right-brain view of the organization. The strategic is left brain—it is the testing of hypotheses to see what will bring about more and more improvement until the organization is perfect (which is never). Optimization occurs when all aspects of the school are working efficiently and effectively together. Success is everywhere.

Continuous strategic improvement changes how money is managed, how time is utilized, how the HR department analyzes its results, and how instructional leaders plan and analyze annual learning results. Most important, however, is that continuous strategic improvement changes classroom operations. The use of continuous improvement leadership theories have been studied for eighty years or more. There is a rich history of continuous improvement in some industries that will be referenced throughout this book. The two major contributions of this book are (1) applying this industry success to education and (2) focusing upon the scientific process—the strategic aspect. Readers will learn how to apply strategic thinking to continuous improvement through root cause analysis, countermeasures, testing hypotheses, utilizing best practices properly, and having ways to optimize everybody's best thinking, creativity, and intelligence.

Chapters 1 to 4 provide readers the basic understandings of continuous strategic improvement. The processes described in this book will provide education leaders the tools and language to match what is in their heart. Educators often find that popular leadership practices do not match how they want to lead and treat others.

Chapters 5 and 15 explain continuous strategic improvement in the classroom. By far the most important place to implement continuous strategic improvement is in the classroom. The most apparent difference is the presence of intrinsic motivation, far more than extrinsic motivation.

When students are pressuring the teacher to teach more rather than the other way around, the results are amazing. The classroom description is followed by three chapters devoted to standards and instruction. In the standards chapter, Student Experts: The Standards (Chapter 6), I discuss how to use standards, including the Common Core State Standards. This is followed by my advice regarding teaching practices (Chapter 7). The chapter on instruction, Strategies Worth Testing, is based upon the research from John Hattie (Chapter 11). Once the process for testing instructional hypotheses is established, Hattie's research provides a great guide for staffs as they determine which hypotheses to test.

Further chapters provide details for leadership in curriculum, accountability, personnel, finance, operations, and uses of data. My hope is that the specifics in each chapter are close enough to your reality that you can slightly adjust to make continuous strategic improvement work in all aspects of your school system. At first glance, the ideas presented in this book will seem overwhelming—just too much. In one sense this is true; it will take multiple years to implement the concepts presented. As you study the process, however, the word you will come to use is *simplicity*. One and only one strategy is described in this book. Then this strategy is applied everywhere: in classrooms, finance, personnel, instructional planning, and operations. When continuous strategic improvement is implemented in school systems, the staff will have the security of knowing the strategy to be utilized to improve everything. They will not worry about being hit over the head with three to five new initiatives in August. They will know their brains and personality are needed and will no longer be stored in the coat closet for nine months.

Chapter 17 has little or no new content. It is written as a reflection upon major themes in this book. Too often, in our haste, we move onto the next project without taking time to reflect upon what we just finished. Because reflection is often what people remember, this chapter is provided. Chapter 18 adds a few statistical nuggets and Chapter 19, Conclusion and Challenge, weaves the optimization themes together into one final picture. The choice is clear: surrender or optimize.

At one time in my career, my responsibility included observing education professor candidates as they taught a lesson. Some of the candidates were 100 percent practical while others were 100 percent theoretical. The professors we hired were a third type: 10 to 15 percent theoretical and 85 to 90 percent practical. I observe the same variation today in education products. Some books are 100 percent practical, while others are researched theory with little or no "how to." *Optimize Your School* is 10 to 15 percent theory and 85 to 90 percent how to. I don't want readers of my books to think, "Why would I want to do that?" or at the other end of the spectrum, "Sounds good, but now what do I do?" Fullan (2011) wrote, "Clarity of purpose is a crucial foundation, but how you get there is craft." Readers of *Optimize Your School* will know both the why (clarity of purpose) and the how (craft).

Enjoy your read.

Lee Jenkins
Lee@LBellJ.com
Scottsdale, Arizona

Acknowledgments

Ron Nash and Michael Fullan received e-mails from me asking, "What do you think of publishing with Corwin?" They both had the same response. They told me how happy they were with Corwin and then wrote notes off to Corwin editors with strong recommendations for my work. Thus, my journey with Jessica Allan, Corwin Senior Acquisitions Editor, began by sending her a few chapters, proposed table of contents, and introduction. I would describe her as patient and decisive, plus a person whose opinion and expertise I greatly admire. We worked through chapter organization, suggested additional chapters, title, subtitle, cover design, and numerous other details. Without these three leaders, *Optimize Your School* would only be a dream, not a reality.

Others in Corwin provided very competent help: Cesar Reyes with permissions and cover design, Melanie Birdsall as the senior project editor, and Diane DiMura as copy editor. Their personalities made it very easy to comply with requests for minute details. And then there's the marketing department which is necessary, for you, the reader to even know this book exists. Amy Vader is a most knowledgeable, responsive member of the Corwin team.

Glenn Noreen was the first person to read the first (very) rough manuscript and provided me with detailed advice and encouragement. Others, including Paul Berggren, Rick Fauss and Bill Watkins, read portions and likewise helped me improve the final document. Jeff Liker, author of the *Toyota Way* books, reviewed the manuscript to be sure I referenced Toyota correctly. Ron Rutowski read over the butterfly reference and tweaked the paragraphs to be sure they were 100 percent accurate. The blind reviews were most helpful. The compliments on the quality of the book set the stage for the necessary improvements. I couldn't find one suggestion that I thought, "Oh, that's crazy." No, they were spot on!

I have mentioned or quoted the work of a number of people, teachers in particular. What I want the reader to remember is that teachers have little power to hire a speaker to come conduct staff development in their district. Behind each of these teachers is an incredible administrator who set the stage for all of us to learn together. I mention a few here:

Shirley Simmons, Beth Spears, and Joe Siano in Norman, Oklahoma

Barb Friesth, Carol Jessen, and Joelene Dredge, staff development leaders in Nebraska Educational Service Units 7, 8, and 2

William Hatfield, Laura Walker, and Jason Hayes of Massac County Schools, plus Linda Davis, Brad Misner, and Bret Gowin from Egyptian District—all of these southern Illinois administrators who were helpful in figuring out the process for aligning and stabilizing the curriculum

Steven Woodside, principal of Columbus (NE) High School and Darin Kelberau, Director of Curriculum, Instruction, and Assessment in Fremont, Nebraska

Jane Stavem, Lincoln (NE) Public Schools

Matt Blomstedt, Katie Bieber, Russ Masco, and Frieda Lange of the Nebraska Department of Education who are responsible for the referenced 4' × 4' radar chart and for helping make *all-time-best* (ATB) as common a term as Individualized Education Program (IEP)

Julie Otero, Superintendent in Centura District, Nebraska

Julie Salley, staff development in Paradise Valley School District, Phoenix, Arizona

And last of all, I want Diana Deming Cahill and Judy Cahill to know how much their father and grandfather still influence my life twenty-three years after I heard ninety-two-year old W. Edwards Deming conduct a four-day seminar. Their work to further his wisdom and legacy are needed more now than ever.

PUBLISHER'S ACKNOWLEDGMENTS

Corwin gratefully acknowledges the contributions of the following reviewers:

Cynthia Church
Principal G. Stanley Hall
Elementary School
Glendale Heights, IL

Amanda Mayeaux
Career Management Specialist
Iberville Parish Schools
Plaquemine, LA

Delsia Easley
Principal Gadsden City Schools,
W. E. Striplin Elementary
Gadsden, AL

James L. Morrison
Financial Analyst/Adjunct Instructor
University of Oklahoma,
College of Liberal Studies
Norman, OK

About the Author

**Lee Jenkins** is a full-time author, consultant, and speaker with his Scottsdale, Arizona, firm, From LtoJ® Consulting Group, Inc. His earlier career was in the public schools of California as a district superintendent, assistant superintendent, principal, math coordinator and teacher. In addition, he was a professor/administrator for Oregon State University for five years.

Lee's best seller is *Permission to Forget: And Nine Other Root Causes of America's Frustration with Education* (the 10th anniversary edition published in 2013). Other continuous improvement titles are *Improving Student Learning* (2003) and *From Systems Thinking to Systemic Action* (2008). He started his writing career with math manipulative books, including *It's a Tangram World* (1971), *Fraction Tiles* (1972), *Let's Pattern Block It* (1973), *The Balance Book* (1974), and *Coin Stamp Mathematics* (1976).

Lee continues to be significantly influenced by the teaching of W. Edwards Deming. The impetus for his current work began in 1992 with a four-day, in person Dr. Deming seminar. He received a PhD from Claremont Graduate University, a master's degree from California State University, San Jose, and a bachelor's degree from Point Loma Nazarene University.

Lee's speaking engagements have taken him to most US states, Canada, India, Guatemala, Peru, Brazil, and Chile. He offers keynotes, breakout sessions, and one- to three-day seminars. On his website, www.LtoJConsulting.com, a full keynote, plus segments of breakouts and seminars, are posted.

Lee and his wife Sandy have celebrated their 50th wedding anniversary, have two sons, seven grandchildren, and one great-grandchild. He writes, "Living in Scottsdale, Arizona, has been awesome, having moved there in 2001 to be near the Phoenix airport." Lee's e-mail is Lee@LBellJ.com.

Introduction

If everybody did their best, 95% of the problems would remain.

—W. Edwards Deming (1992)

Optimize Your School weaves together four leadership themes: (1) 4th-Level Leadership, (2) Top-Down/Bottom-Up Leadership, (3) Continuous Improvement, and (4) Servant Leadership. The application of these four themes apply equally well to the classroom; the principal's office; the district's human resources, instruction, and finance offices; and the board and superintendent's decisions.

4TH-LEVEL LEADERSHIP

Level 1: I'll just do the job by myself.

Level 2: I'm in charge; do it the way I tell you.

Level 3: I'll meet with you in the beginning of the year to agree upon your objectives. Then I'll meet with you again near the end of the year to see if you met your objectives.

Level 4: We are a team working together toward optimizing everybody's talent and 100 percent of our responsibilities.

goal *

TOP-DOWN/BOTTOM-UP LEADERSHIP

Jeffrey Liker and James K. Franz (2011) developed a matrix for all types of organizations (see Figure 1). Their matrix is not exclusively for schools. I include their matrix here to communicate to readers where I see the basic issues with schools today; they are firefighting, dealing with the same problems over and over. Almost all schools are hampered by poor strategies and processes. The staffs are dedicated and talented but cannot move ahead because of the strategies and processes. I share this observation at the beginning of this book because I want readers to know I am not trying to fix, manipulate, or incentivize the staffs. I am writing to help fix decades of failed processes. That said, Chapter 13 is about personnel. People can improve. However, even the personnel chapter is about strategy and process for the human resources department.

For years education had a bottom-up leadership theory. Decentralization was the prevailing structure. Each school selected its own staff, curriculum, and materials. Employees were generally happy, but society became unhappy as other countries by-passed America. Top-down was the perceived solution. We even went so far as to mandate a Soviet-style structure; every classroom was to be on the same page on the same day. Society still isn't pleased and the employees are discouraged and angry. Top-down is not a successful theory of leadership. Top-down/bottom-up, however, is a successful theory of leadership.

| **Figure 1** | Liker's Organizational Matrix |

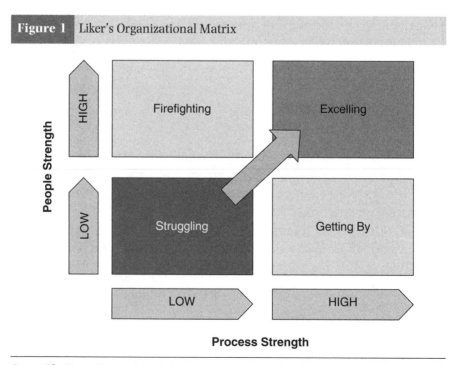

Source: The Toyota Way to Continuous Improvement (p. 40), by J. Liker and J. K. Franz, 2011, New York, NY: McGraw-Hill.

CONTINUOUS IMPROVEMENT LEADERSHIP

The major differences between typical leadership and continuous improvement leadership are the absence of quotas and internal competition. People are held accountable for improvement and work together as a team to create that improvement. Numeric goals, with continuous improvement, are to outperform prior accomplishments. People do not waste time agreeing upon an arbitrary number to meet in the future. The number is simply better than ever before. The time is better spent agreeing upon improvement strategies.

SERVANT LEADERSHIP

John Maxwell's "dos and do nots" begin Chapter 1. These basic attitudes are essential for both 4th-level leadership, top-down/bottom-up leadership, and continuous improvement leadership. Without servant leadership, none of the three other themes make sense and optimization will not occur.

SCHOOLS ARE AT ONE OF FOUR LEVELS

Schools are at one of four levels: (1) at risk of surviving, (2) getting along, (3) excelling, or (4) optimized. At-risk schools have a multiple-year record of failure. They are plagued by rotating leadership and often have more advisors than staff members. Getting-along schools are neither improving nor backsliding; their results are better than other schools, so people generally leave them alone. Excelling schools have high success rates, some of the best achievement results in the area, and are considered superb by most people. Optimized schools can prove all students improved and that most students exceeded state standards. In addition, they have captured the 25 to 33 percent of each school year that is currently utilized for review and reapportioned the time for the arts or acceleration. Liker and Meier (2006) wrote, "Companies . . . reduce the time significantly, but there is no plan for using the freed up time, and the setup times slowly creep back to the original level." The same is true for schools. If the time saved by removing "Permission to Forget" is not reallocated to the arts or to acceleration, the gains will slowly disappear.

Continuous strategic improvement and the practical advice contained in this book will give leaders the knowledge to move their schools from at risk to getting along to excelling and even onto optimization. This will take everybody working together toward a common aim, top-down/bottom-up behavior, a record of getting better and better, and a plethora of servant leaders in the classroom and administrative offices.

GRAPHIC ORGANIZERS

Throughout this book, two graphic organizers are provided to help readers have a picture of the text progression. The first is a fishbone and the second is a 2 × 2 matrix. The Optimization Fishbone was designed to create a sense of motion toward an aim. The aim here is optimization of the school system and thus many aspects of this book are included on the fishbone. In the beginning, the fishbone will be partial with a completed fishbone in the later portions of the book. The Optimization Matrix will also gradually develop and display elements of optimization, and its opposite, sub-optimization.

Figure 2 is the blank Optimization Fishbone. Figure 3 is the blank Optimization Matrix.

Effective:

Efficient:

will

for

SYSTEM

Sub-Optimize   Optimize

PEOPLE

Optimize

Sub-Optimize

PART I

Continuous Strategic Improvement for Optimization

1

Continuous Improvement

Placing Wheels on Servant Leadership

> *We are never satisfied with where we are and always improve our business by putting forth our best ideas and efforts.*
>
> —Jeffrey Liker and Michael Hoseus, 2008

V isit any bookstore, wander off to the leadership/management books and look for the John Maxwell titles. You will probably find a dozen different titles. My understanding of the essence of Maxwell's teaching is included in his four "do nots" and three "dos." Much of the wisdom in all of his writing provides great advice for leaders on how to avoid the four "do nots" and how to make the three "dos" an integral part of their daily lives.

In the age of education accountability, it is very important for leaders to internalize these four "do nots" and three "dos." The strategies *not to use* are

1. Force

2. Intimidation

3. Exchange (incentives)

4. Manipulation

The three strategies *to use* are

1. Persuasion

2. Energizing Others

3. Honoring and Serving Others (Maxwell, 2002)

PLACING THE WHEELS ON SERVANT LEADERSHIP

I am convinced that most school leaders desire to honor and serve others but have become frustrated with the results. These administrators started their administrative assignments convinced that persuasion, energizing others and honoring and serving others was all that was needed. I, the leader, will do all I can to help staff members with what they need or want. The "leadership" in servant leadership went missing; only the servant survived. Everybody seemed happy; that is until the test scores were printed in the newspaper.

Our former **bottom-up** servant became a **top-down** bully. Day to day pacing guides were inspected, test preparation became a school subject, and best practice programs were purchased and implemented with forced fidelity. Everybody was unhappy (including the top-down, former servant). Top-down may have moved the school from "struggling to survive," to "getting along" in the short term, but the pain inflicted upon students and staff was far too high a price to pay.

Continuous strategic improvement is a leadership strategy that helps leaders with that rare, delicate balance of top-down and bottom-up together. The leaders have their responsibilities and so do the staff members. Administrators can follow their heart to be a **servant leader** and, at the same time, meet accountability requirements. "Finland had achieved rigor without ruin," (Ripley, 2013, p. 158) and the United States can also.

> *Administrators can follow their heart to be a servant leader and, at the same time, meet accountability requirements.*

THE DO NOTS

The dilemma for education leaders is that accountability legislation is based on the "Do Not" list. Force is front and center in this legislation; raise test scores or we will fire you. Along the journey to your firing, we will intimidate you by ranking your schools. We will reserve the most severe intimidation for the bottom 5 percent of the schools with the most poverty. **Exchange** is another name for "incentives." The legislation states that if you do what we wrote in the laws we'll exchange your cooperation for a bucket of cash. If you don't do what we say, we'll remove some of the money you already have.

Manipulation is not in the legislation, but fearful educators do resort to manipulation. Of course, it is not labeled *manipulation*; it is labeled *test preparation*. Learning is second place to becoming an expert at taking tests. The issue is how to manipulate the test taking process so students can create the impression they have learned more than they actually have learned.

SERVANT LEADERSHIP VERSUS FEAR

Maxwell's four "do nots" and three "dos" can be organized under two headings: management by fear and servant leadership. Deming's (1986) well-known 14 points for leaders lists Point 8 as simply, "Drive out fear." My only time to hear Deming was in 1992. At that four-day conference, he added a clever insight stating, "Fear is the darkroom where negatives develop." When leaders want to replace fear with care, what are they to do? Bosses can admonish their staffs and they can model caring, serving leadership. However, it is a leadership strategy of continuous strategic improvement that cements care into the fabric of organizations.

Optimize Your School is written as a how-to book. It answers the questions, "How do I treat my students, teachers, and other employees the way I want to be treated AND, at the very same time, meet the accountability requirements that society deserves? Can I actually focus on persuasion, energizing others, and honoring and serving my students and staff PLUS meet accountability expectations?" The answer is yes. Improvement "comes to the steady people who keep working at getting better. If you have a quick fix mindset, then you need to shift to continuous improvement" (Maxwell, 2013, p. 30). As the chapters unfold in this book, it will become apparent that *Optimize Your School* puts the wheels on servant leadership.

The remainder of this chapter contrasts the "do nots" with the "dos," as they are implemented in school systems. This is accomplished by writing about continuous and improvement as separate topics. Chapter 2 inserts strategic into continuous improvement. *Continuous strategic improvement*, the combined term, will be used for the remainder of the book.

CONTINUOUS

Education in the United States is a yo-yo. We go back and forth, up and down, over and under with a few incredibly awe-inspiring tricks from place to place. Some of these incredible advances deserved to be deployed nationwide, but most of these "stars have turned out be comets" (Bogle, 2009, p. 144). The pressure on education is for short-term gains now! Continuous is not even a consideration.

> *Education in the United States is a yo-yo. We go back and forth, up and down, over and under with a few incredibly awe-inspiring tricks from place to place.*

CONTINUOUS EXPLAINED

It would seem unnecessary to explain continuous; it simply means on and on and on, not over and over. Continuous can be on and on from hour to hour, day to day, week to week, month to month, and year to year. For education, what matters is a mindset of on and on versus a final report with an accomplished stamp across the top. We are never done.

Figure 1.1 shows the scoreboard visible at almost all sporting venues. There is no debate regarding what numbers go on the left and the right sides of the scoreboard. The scoreboard is a cultural icon deeply rooted into the norms of our society. Traditional education also has two places for numbers with recent accountability legislation adding a third scoreboard for schools: ranking. Figure 1.2 displays the current scoreboard for education.

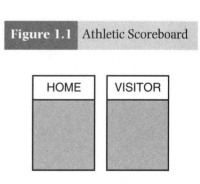

Figure 1.1   Athletic Scoreboard

Figure 1.2   Typical Education Scoreboard

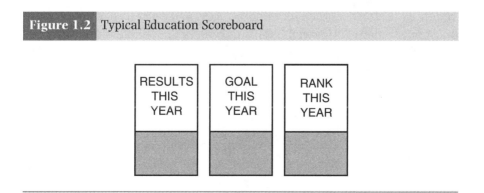

> *The quota is an arbitrary number pulled out of the air and ranking does not tell anyone if improvement has occurred.*

The schools and the school districts are compared to the quota and the ranking for the year. The quota is an arbitrary number pulled out of the air and ranking does not tell anyone if improvement has occurred. Nothing is continuous. We go back and forth, up and down, over and under, and sometimes have a brilliant yo-yo. The left side of the yo-yo is labeled *annual quota* and the right side is labeled *rank*. The yo-yo string is the power structure, but the question is "Who holds the string?"

Political and educational leaders hold the string. The good news is that they too can capture the joy of continuous. Having proof of getting better is so much more enjoyable than being manipulated to "meet the numbers," which is one of the worst business practices being applied to education.

EDUCATION'S IDEAL SCOREBOARD

When continuous improvement becomes the norm, then the scoreboard will look like Figure 1.3. Schools and their districts will be compared to their former selves and not to others. "Your starting point doesn't matter. Everyone who has gotten to where he is, started where he was" (Maxwell, 2013, p. 82). With ranking, only one school can be a winner; the rest are all losers. However, with this scoreboard, it is possible for all schools to be winners, which is defined as doing better than ever before. In Nebraska in 2013, 55 percent of the school districts in the state outperformed their prior **all-time-best**. Another 10 percent tied their former all-time-best. Think about what could happen in the United States if every school and every district knew they were

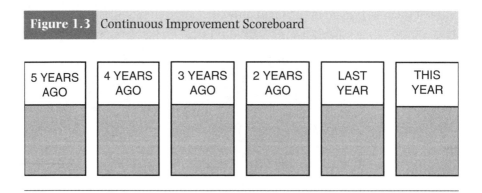

Figure 1.3 Continuous Improvement Scoreboard

5 YEARS AGO	4 YEARS AGO	3 YEARS AGO	2 YEARS AGO	LAST YEAR	THIS YEAR

accountable to outperform their prior best, instead of meeting a quota or outperforming their neighbors.

BUSINESS WORST PRACTICE

The business stories about "meeting the numbers" abound. Essentially, the business leaders set in motion activities to meet quarterly goals at the expense of the long-term health of the corporation. These leaders are not thinking continuous;

> *The essence of continuous requires stubborn persistence.*

they are thinking quarter by quarter by quarter. Bogle (2009) wrote, "Once you decide whether you expect to be in business for a short time or a long time, most of the right decisions are easy" (p. 172). In other words, do you want to be continuously in business or are you massaging the numbers to obtain a promotion? Bogle also wrote, "When corporations fail to meet their numeric targets the hard way—over the long term, by raising productivity; by improving old products and creating new ones; by providing services on a more friendly, more timely, and more efficient basis; and by challenging the people of the organization to work more effectively together (and those are the ways that our best corporations achieve success)—they are compelled to do it in other ways: that often subtract value from you, from me, and from society" (p. 110).

CONTINUOUS DEMANDS PERSISTENCE

The essence of continuous requires stubborn persistence. Calvin Coolidge stated, "Nothing in the world can take the place of persistence. Talent will not; nothing is more common than unsuccessful men with talent" (Bogle, 2009, p. 173).

In addition to persistence, continuous requires stability of leadership, not a continual search for the next superstar. "Our ongoing research into what it takes to prevail in turbulent environments shows a distinct negative correlation between building great companies and going outside for a CEO" (Collins, 2009, p. 95).

How long is continuous? The best answer I've found is from Jim Collins (2009): "Most 'overnight success' stories are about twenty years in the making" (p. 94). Management by fear does not create anything that is continuous. Force, intimidation, exchange, and manipulation are all used by bullies to gain short-term goals. Continuous is not even considered.

> *Management by fear does not create anything that is continuous.*

IMPROVEMENT

Improvement is "getting better." It is different than meeting quotas; improvement is doing better than ever before. Yes, one more student, than ever before, meeting standards, is improvement. It can be for students, teachers, support staff, schools, school districts (divisions in Canada), states (provinces in Canada), and countries.

The scoreboard for improvement is vastly different than the normal education scoreboards.

> *No time is wasted pulling a number out of the air; the real numeric goal is set by the prior ATB.*

The year, with the best record ever, is outlined just like the backboards at basketball games. The basketball backboard has a lighted outline so that officials can tell precisely if a shot was made before the buzzer. The results are clear for all to see. Likewise the scoreboard for education must be clear for all to see. This clear view serves two purposes: designating the all-time-best (ATB) (thanks to Heather Sparks, Oklahoma City teacher, for this term) and setting the goal for next year which is, quite simply, more improvement. No time is wasted pulling a number out of the air; the real numeric goal is set by the prior ATB.

In Figure 1.4, the current year is not the all-time-best; schools did not have an ATB in all subjects and all grade levels. Businesses do not have a profit for every product and schools will not be 100 percent successful. If the ATB was two years ago, then the goal is still to outperform this ATB, even though it was two years ago, as shown in Figure 1.5.

Figure 1.4   This Year's Scoreboard

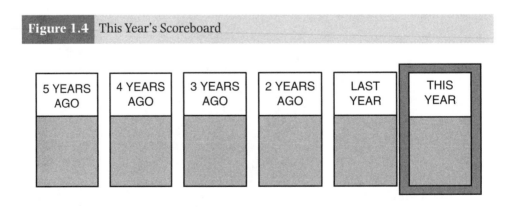

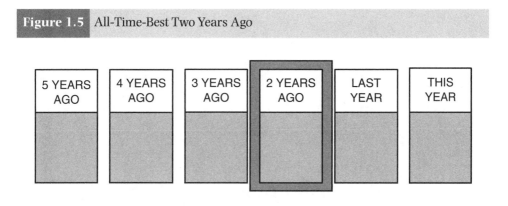

Figure 1.5   All-Time-Best Two Years Ago

NUMERIC GOALS (QUOTAS)

A new numeric goal of only one better seems so weak. People scoff, "Is that all you expect of your people . . . what a miserable leader you are!" I was a beginning teacher in the 1960s and still remember the administrators bringing the teachers together to write 5 *percent* improvement goals because "measureable objectives" was the current management buzzword. Does anybody think that education has improved 5 percent every year for the past fifty years? People should be honored for success, not for "macho" establishing of high goals. Liker and Franz (2011) wrote that "it is more useful to define excellence as a pursuit rather than an absolute value. If we improve, we're closer to excellence than we were before" (p. 6). We teachers were not admonished to improve; we were directed to write 5 percent, absolute value, goals. In fifty years of education reform, most attempts to improve have failed. Exceptions are mathematics education, girls' athletics, and probably a couple of other areas.

The statistics of trends is really different than the statistics of "Did you reach your goal?" Figure 1.6 displays the results from the National Assessment of Educational Progress (NAEP) for 4th-grade mathematics. The data are presented for every assessment since its inception in 1978.

Fourth graders posted the highest scores ever on the NAEP exam in 2013. The average mathematics score for the fourth graders in 2013 was higher than the scores in any previous assessment year. Students scored 1 point higher in 2013 than in 2008 and 29 points higher than in 1978.

Other national results show higher or tied for highest scores in 2013 than for any prior year for White, Black, Native American, Asian, and Hispanic students. Further, both male and female students scored their best

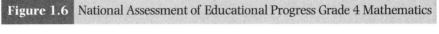

Figure 1.6 National Assessment of Educational Progress Grade 4 Mathematics

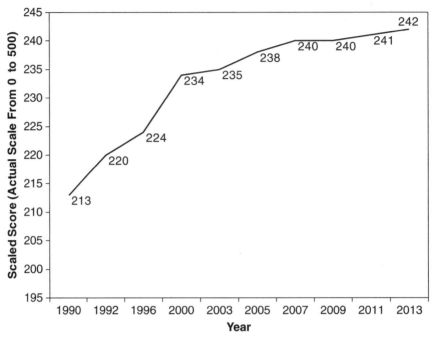

ever. It is very heartening that NAEP gives its headline to improvement data, but disheartening that this leadership is not being disseminated throughout all the US Department of Education and beyond. Maybe the reason for the lack of continuous improvement thinking in the US Department of Education is the lack of continuous improvement in industry. Liker and Franz (2011) wrote, "Would it surprise you to hear that in our collective visits to literally hundreds of companies the last 10 years, we have never seen honest-to-goodness continuous improvement outside of Toyota" (p. 1).

Reflection

What data is available where you work that is long term, such as the math NAEP example? What data is available only for this year and last year?

FORMAL STATISTICS

Since the definition of *improvement* is "getting better," it would seem that formal statistics are not needed. In many instances, this is correct. One does not need formal statistics to recognize that the fourth graders in the

United States had an all-time-best or to know if your school did better than ever before. The only real problem is that in far too many locales, the only numbers you can find are for this year and last year.

At other times, however, this question does need to be answered: "Could the positive trend we see be the result of luck (smarter students moved in) or did the school actually improve because of its initiatives?" Chapter 18 provides an introduction to the more formal aspects of continuous improvement statistics and use of data.

LEADING CONTINUOUS IMPROVEMENT

Leading continuous improvement will never be easy. As will be obvious to readers of this book, set-up time for continuous improvement is necessary. Leaders cannot dictate that we are a continuous improvement school system and then be too important for their own improvement. Deming (1992) stated, "You are never too old to learn or too important to learn." Liker (2004) wrote that continuous improvement "causes some short-term pain and cost . . . It takes discipline to maintain, which is beyond the capacity of many . . . because they don't understand the challenges and pain of continuous improvement. In the long run, the challenges and pain and short-term costs almost always produce dramatically better results" (p. 101).

> If the leader of the school system believes that it is the job of the employees to improve without any leadership, then continuous improvement efforts will fail.

If the leader of the school system believes that it is the job of the employees to improve without any leadership, then continuous improvement efforts will fail. Liker and Franz (2011) wrote that "the only hope of seriously marching toward the ideal of continuous improvement is to have passionate executives leading the charge. They are simply not there in very many organizations" (p. 3). Donald Wheeler and David Chambers (1992) wrote, "It is only when management supports, in both word and deed, the goal of continual improvement, that it will begin to see the increases in both quality and productivity" (p. 12).

Leading continuous improvement involves a number of mindsets for leaders that are reflected upon in an ABC format in Chapter 17. Throughout the reflections is the concept of improvement versus meeting specifications; there is always a better way. Joyce Orsini (2013) writes, "It is necessary in this world to outdo specifications, to move continually toward better and better performance of the finished product" (p. 22). In education, the similar notion is trying to meet **AYP (adequate yearly progress)** instead of having a record of continuous improvement. Larry Webber and Michael Wallace (2007) wrote, "As long as the conformance to specifications is regarded as the main objective for any operation, it will be impossible to sustain any real process improvements" (p. 143). A second mindset, which will occur throughout this book, is that of problem solving. "Problem solving is different from the connotation of **firefighting**. In firefighting, we are running around putting our finger in the dike and hoping that the dam will not collapse. In true problem solving, we are deeply trying to understand the root cause of the problem so that we can ultimately prevent the problem from occurring again" (Liker & Franz, 2011, p. 12). "The most important thing is how your own people develop their ability to lead continuous improvement . . . In many organizations that we work with, something happens that derails the process. That something always involves the lack of commitment by senior management" (Liker & Franz, 2011, p. 15).

CONTINUOUS IMPROVEMENT AS A CULTURE

Continuous improvement reinforces the intrinsic motivation everybody is born with.

Finally, continuous improvement is a culture. This culture sustains improvements through "a combination of top leadership commitment and a culture of continuous improvement" (Liker & Convis, 2012, p. 4). At the center of this continuous improvement culture is that deep understanding that continuous improvement requires continuous learning.

Continuous improvement reinforces the intrinsic motivation everybody is born with. If a student has 20 percent correct, then 31 percent, then 39 percent, then 47 percent, and then 58 percent, but is rewarded with F, F, F, F, and F, intrinsic motivation is blown asunder. Likewise, suppose an inner-city school is given a federal mandate of 60 percent of the students meeting state standards because only 20 percent are meeting the standards now. The school improves to 31 percent, 39 percent, then 47 percent, and last year 58 percent. The school is rewarded with the "needs improvement" label, then "really needs improvement" followed by "failure school" to "at risk of being closed or turned into a charter" and finally the principal and half of the staff are fired. Do you think any teachers still have intrinsic motivation for their profession? If there is any motivation left, it is spent on applying for a teaching job where there are rich kids.

What should these teachers hear from their local, state, and federal leaders? They need to hear, "Wow, you improved from 20 percent to 58 percent meeting standards. Very impressive! What can we do to support you even more?" Intrinsic motivation can be greatly strengthened by education's leaders.

Figure 1.7 is the first example of the Optimization Fishbone with inserted topics; the additions were introduced in this chapter.

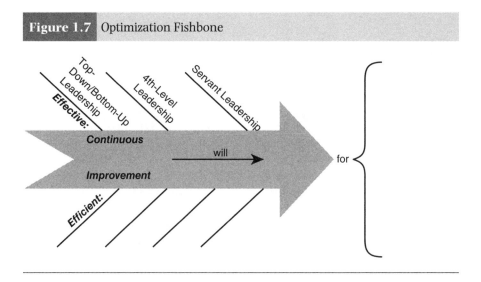

Figure 1.7 Optimization Fishbone

LOOKING AHEAD

The combination of continuous, strategic thinking and improvement is what leaders with a servant mentality must have to carry out their dreams. Servant leaders have the responsibility to solve the root causes of problems. Solving the problem superficially, only to have the same problem tomorrow, is called *firefighting*. Chapter 2 inserts strategic between continuous and improvement, which will guide readers toward **root cause analysis** of problems. *Optimize Your School* is written for school leaders who deeply desire to be a servant leader. If a bully administrator was a bully teacher, I have no illusions about this book being of help. However, for the vast majority of administrators who have a deep desire to be a servant leader, this is their book. They can lead with persuasion, energizing parents, students and staffs, and serving and honoring everybody. This all occurs while meeting accountability requirements.

> *Servant leaders have the responsibility to solve the root causes of problems.*

Reflection

If an administrator who is 100 percent servant is not acceptable and an administrator who is 100 percent leader is not acceptable, what is the proper balance for a servant leader?

2 Adding Strategic to Continuous Improvement

> How we manage our people is the fluid that connects all working parts and brings them the oxygen and nutrients to keep them working as they should.
>
> —Jeffrey Liker and Michael Hoseus, 2008

The practice of submitting five-year plans labeled *strategic planning* has been in education for at least thirty years. Most of these strategic plans were to-do lists such as, "Have 1:1 computers in the middle school by 2016." The items in the plans are there to be checked off as done and reported to the school board as completed.

When *strategic* is added to *continuous improvement,* the term takes on a deeper meaning. All of the adopted strategies are in place in order to bring about even more improvement, not merely a different way to do the job. This does not mean that every chosen strategy *will* bring about improvement, but at the time the strategies were adopted, people believed the strategies had a great chance for documented improvement. Note that the word is strategies, not strategy. "If there were only one ideal position, there would be no need for strategy" (Porter, 2011, p. 16).

> The basis for strategic thinking is base-line data.

The basis for strategic thinking is base-line data. If it is determined that student discipline is an issue and something needs to be done, then the first step is a record of the past. How many referrals to the office for discipline five years ago, four years ago, three years ago, two years ago, last year? Now that we have this data collected, we can analyze not only the trends, but the reasons for the referrals. The last step is to agree upon the strategy to be tested. This strategy is what we believe has the very best chance to reduce future office referrals.

The school does not write in its strategic plan, "We will adopt and implement a purchased discipline program." What they write is the strategy they will implement in order to reduce the problems discovered through analysis. Further, since they have the data from five prior years, they will know if their strategy is successful or not.

RESPECT FOR PEOPLE

The process utilized by top management to establish strategies says everything about their respect, or lack of respect, for their people. The workers all know if the nutrients and oxygen are being drained from them or replenished. The annual strategies tell it all. Teams can be greatly strengthened with agreed upon strategies or they can be destroyed by strategies that only the bosses love. The list of unsuccessful strategies that follow are basically top-down strategies. The somewhat successful strategies show more respect for the people but are not nearly as successful as strategies based upon root cause analysis.

> *The process utilized by top management to establish strategies says everything about their respect, or lack of respect, for their people.*

UNSUCCESSFUL STRATEGIES

- Adding pressure is not a successful strategy.
- Setting numeric goals (quotas) is not a successful strategy.
- Creating a wish list is not a successful strategy.
- Adopting new standards is not a successful strategy.
- Purchasing more technology is not a successful strategy.
- Pouring on more incentives is not a successful strategy.
- Embarrassing staff in the newspaper is not a successful strategy.
- Creating fear in the lives of staff and students is not a successful strategy.

- Creating competition between students is not a successful strategy.
- Creating competition between staff members is not a successful strategy.
- Continually honoring the best students, while the other students watch, is not a successful strategy.

The above list takes schools nowhere and if a school is struggling to survive, it will remain struggling. The items in the list above can all be classified under the heading "Do Not."

SOMEWHAT SUCCESSFUL STRATEGIES

Some struggling schools do institute plans that move them from struggling to getting along. The plans honor the staffs and some improvement does occur. Examples of leadership decisions that can create some improvement are

- Consensus-based decision making
- Improved teacher evaluation
- Development of teacher leaders
- Removal of teachers who are harmful to students
- Removal of administrators who are harmful to staff and students
- Processes for helping first- and second-year teachers be more successful
- Advanced certification for outstanding teachers

Having better and better teachers with poor strategies and processes puts an enormous burden upon talented teachers because they are always responding to the next urgent problem.

I am not negating the list above; my point is that having better and better teachers with poor strategies and processes puts an enormous burden upon talented teachers because they are always responding to the next urgent problem. The first list I wrote does no good as the practices only pressure the people. The second list does some good because it does focus upon helping the people.

EXCELLING SCHOOLS REQUIRES STRATEGIC DECISIONS

The creation of excelling, and then optimized, schools requires strategic thinking for process improvement. Leadership is required at the highest levels. This long-term strategic leadership requires persuasion, energizing others, and honoring and serving the staff.

DEFINE PERFECT IN ORDER TO SEE THE PROBLEM

Defining **perfect** is not the norm in education. However, once everyone understands that no humanly created organization is perfect, then the process of defining perfect is quite valuable. It highlights problems that may be otherwise buried. Some possible perfects and accompanying problems include the following:

1. Perfect is students with either zero or one discipline referral for the school year; the problem is we had forty-five students with two or more office referrals.

2. Perfect is students who attend at least 172 of 180 school days; the problem is we had 135 students who were present fewer than 172 days.

3. Perfect is every high school student earning a 3, 4, or 5 on at least one Advanced Placement exam; the problem is we had 82 percent of students who did not earn a 3, 4, or 5 on an AP exam.

4. Perfect is every high school biology student meeting standards on the state exam; the problem is 13 percent of the biology students did not meet this standard.

5. Perfect is every second grader reading at 100 words per minute and explaining what they just read; the problem is seven students could not meet the fluency requirement, the comprehension requirement, or both.

6. Perfect is every fifth-grade student scoring five points on each of the six writing traits dichotomous rubrics (explained in Chapter 12). The problem is that 15 percent of the Grade 5 students had no fives and 40 percent did not score a five on all of the rubrics.

DETERMINE ROOT CAUSE(S) OF PROBLEMS

Once problems are described, the next step for strategic improvement is root cause analysis (RCA). This simply means digging below the surface to discover the root or roots of the problems. The root cause must be within the power of the staff to fix; the root cause cannot be a blame-somebody-else exercise, better known as "blamestorming" (Maxwell, 2013, p. 61).

> *The root cause must be within the power of the staff to fix; the root cause cannot be a blame-somebody-else exercise.*

Louis M. Savary and Clare Crawford-Mason (2006) recount a root cause story from a hospital. Problems were occurring with the medication cart. The answer to the first "why" for this problem was the computers provided to read the barcodes were going dead. Hospital administrators originally thought it was nurse error with the computer but then found out the batteries in the computers were not charged. They checked out the battery charger and it was working OK. The next discovery was that the outlet where the charger was plugged in was not live. Why? Water was splashing on the outlet from the nearby sink and it tripped the ground fault. Why? The sink had too high a water pressure and once this was resolved, the medication carts worked. Who would think that the water pressure in the sink was a root cause of possible errors administering medication?

Students, parents, and the legislature cannot be a root cause. For example, a school may have a problem with high school graduation rates. This particular state requires that students meet all of the local standards plus pass a state exam in order to graduate. Some students are meeting all local requirements but are not passing the state mathematics exam. Why? It could be that some of the questions on the state exam are from middle school curriculum that students have not studied for four years. They admit that they forgot their middle school math. The root cause of the failure can be solved by local faculty.

COUNTERMEASURES ARE NEXT

My caution here is to not rush to **countermeasures**. Time is necessary to determine these steps: (1) What would perfect be? (2) Where are we now? and (3) What are the root causes of the gap between perfect and where we are now? If these steps are rushed, the countermeasures will be yet another collection of opinions rather than real countermeasures.

A countermeasure is a hypothesis linked to a root cause.

A countermeasure is a hypothesis linked to a root cause. In the high school math example above, this means that the hypothesis the staff agrees to test must have something to do with forgetting the middle school math problem. The hypothesis cannot be test-taking practice after school for three weeks. Thus one countermeasure the staff could agree upon is that *every* high school math assessment includes three middle school problems. This countermeasure is implemented in all math classes and all courses from algebra through calculus. Since the staff knows how many students in their high school are failing the state exam, they can track the results each year to determine if their countermeasure was successful or not.

TEAMWORK

Jeff Burgard, author of *Continuous Improvement in the Science Classroom* (2010), asked his eighth-grade science students what hypothesis they could test to improve their class results on weekly **LtoJ**® quizzes (details explained in Chapter 5). The students stated that if they sat by their friends, the scores would improve. So, Jeff said, "Sit wherever you want for the next three weeks. Let's test out your hypothesis." Jeff wrote, "This was a negotiation I contributed to as well. We also agreed that there could not be an increase in reminders to be quiet when they needed to be. The change needed to have a positive impact on the learning and the culture of the room. (personal communication, February 2015). Three weeks later, the students said, "Mr. Burgard, put us wherever you want; that didn't work."

Jeff could have told the students at the outset that moving seats will not help them learn more. He had the power to say this. However, the negative would have had long-term consequences as the oxygen and nutrients would have been sucked right out of his students. They would have thought, "OK, Mr. Burgard, you are the boss. Have it your way." Bosses must have the courage to allow their teams to test hypotheses that they believe will not work. Often the bosses are right, but on other occasions, the bosses are really surprised. You see, the students in Mr. Burgard's class could have been correct, and many other times they were correct. In a **top-down/bottom-up** organization staff members must have the autonomy to test the countermeasures they believe will solve the root of some agreed upon problem.

I realize that in the example above, the hypothesis is not connected to a root cause. However, I chose to include the story as it exemplifies the dilemma of leaders. Leaders must not determine the countermeasures to be tested or we are back to top-down, do-it-my-way administration.

TOP-DOWN/BOTTOM-UP

The top-down aspect of the strategic placed into continuous improvement is providing time and direction for staffs to follow the steps outlined above. Staffs *must* determine what would be perfect, gather data from past years, write down the gap between perfect and current reality (the problem), brainstorm root cause(s), and agree upon countermeasures to test during the upcoming year. This is top-down.

The bottom-up aspect of the strategic placed into continuous improvement occurs when staffs are allowed to determine the countermeasure to test. Bosses don't get to do this. As soon as the boss determines the countermeasure, the teamwork is lost and the staffs think, "OK, Boss, have it your way. We will look for oxygen and nutrients for our souls outside of work."

Reflection

What percentage of prior school decisions were top-down? Bottom-up? Top-down/bottom-up?

CONTINUOUS STRATEGIC IMPROVEMENT

Continuous, strategic, and improvement are welded together into one process that will be utilized throughout the rest of this book. Figure 2.1 is the Optimization Fishbone with the welding accomplished.

Two divisions of continuous strategic improvement are subtraction and addition; the practices that need to be subtracted (efficiency) from schools and the practices that need to be added (effectiveness). The next chapter is subtraction, which is labeled with a more harsh term: *removing waste.*

Figure 2.1 Optimization Fishbone

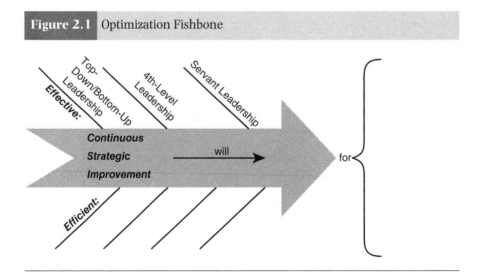

Efficiency

Removing Waste

3

Eliminating waste is done by *people, not* to *people.*

—Jeffrey Liker and Michael Hoseus, 2008

Toyota uses the word **waste** to describe the space between perfect and current reality. This may seem like a harsh word to educators, but their focus is clearly worth considering. "'Muda' or 'waste'" is "Toyota's term for anything that takes time, but does not add value for your customer" (Liker, 2004, p. 10). It is worth considering that "some companies are able to get more out of their inputs than others because they eliminate wasted effort" (Porter, 2011, pp. 2–3). A key responsibility of leaders is guiding their organization toward becoming more and more efficient, which is simply removing waste.

THREE CATEGORIES OF EDUCATION WASTE

Education has three categories of waste: time, money, and student enthusiasm. In this chapter, I explain strategies for reducing time wasters and enthusiasm wasters. In Chapter 14, the system for reducing money wasters is described.

> *Education has three categories of waste: time, money, and student enthusiasm.*

Perfect would be 100 percent of our time in education utilized to help students learn. Clearly education is not there. Secondly, perfect would be 100 percent of the students maintaining their kindergarten level of enthusiasm for learning over thirteen years. Not there either (see Resource A). It will help readers to realize that only nature is perfect with no waste. If people established something, there is waste. Always. No human organization was ever perfect, meaning no waste. "A. V. Feigenbaum estimated that from 15 to 40 percent of the manufacturer's costs of almost any American product that you buy is for waste embedded in it" (Orsini, 2013, p. 19). Business is not there either. Our purpose in this chapter is to strategize ways to move closer to perfect year after year.

> *No human organization was ever perfect, meaning no waste.*

TIME WASTERS

Step 1 in reducing time wasters is to calculate the number of minutes of instructional time in a school year and also the number of minutes available for work during noninstructional time.

Step 2 is to list all of the school requirements that do not add to student learning: taking attendance, school photographs, lunch counts, and the list goes on and on. Come to a consensus on how much time is wasted for each of these activities. "So if we sincerely desire to make college an option for record numbers of students, our task is simple: We need to reclaim the hundreds of hours each year that are now spent on nonacademic tasks" (Schmoker, 2011, p. 28).

Step 3 is to list time wasters caused by students, such as waiting for their attention, discipline issues, and unprepared students.

Step 4 is to list time wasters that are traditional expectations but do not seem to be assisting with student learning. Schmoker (2011) writes, "always with an eye to reducing time spent taking home or grading papers" (p. 79).

Step 5 is to conduct a root cause analysis of time wasters. Why are certain activities conducted during learning times and not before or after school? Why are certain requirements placed on teachers to perform after school is over? Is the new technology saving or wasting instructional time?

Step 6 is to select one or more of the time wasters and come to a consensus regarding a countermeasure to test. It may be that a faculty will not all test the same countermeasures. There may be six to ten different groups, each testing a different countermeasure and reporting back to the faculty as a whole.

Step 7 is to collect the data and determine if the countermeasure was successful. If yes, the strategy did save time, then cement the new process into "the way we do things around here."

Step 8 is to start over saving even more time, remembering, "No one ever heard of a report being abolished" (Orsini, 2013, p. 52). You can start the report elimination national movement.

Administrators who take seriously their responsibility to subtract, as well as to add, will be admired by their staffs. I placed the chapter on subtraction prior to the chapter on addition. Why? Faculties will be much more willing to test countermeasures that add to their work if they know their leaders are equally concerned about subtraction. The following quote from Toyota should be placed on the walls of every administrator's office: "It saved the team members and the company a very valuable couple of seconds per car" (Liker & Hoseus, 2008, p. 80). If everybody looked at time like this, it would be amazing what could be accomplished. (Go ahead and figure this out: If we saved one minute per period for 180 school days times thirteen years, how many additional school days would we have?)

> *Faculties will be much more willing to test countermeasures that add to their work if they know their leaders are equally concerned about subtraction.*

ENTHUSIASM WASTERS

I asked over 3000 teachers in various US and Canadian seminars what grade level they teach (or taught formerly, if now an administrator) and what percentage of the students love school at their grade level. Kindergarten was an average of 95 percent and each subsequent grade level had a decrease in enthusiasm until a low of 37 percent in Grade 9. Grades 10, 11, and 12 were slightly higher than Grade 9. There are a number of reasons for the Grades 10 to 12 increase, one being that the percentages do not include high school dropouts.

W. Edwards Deming (1992) stated that the aim of education should be to "increase the positives and decrease the negatives so that all students keep their yearning for learning." Ponder what school would be like if the students still had their kindergarten enthusiasm for learning in high school. Resource A is the graph from a 3000 teacher survey.

Schools can have a great impact on student attitudes in school. The tools for having this

> *Schools can have a great impact on student attitudes in school. The tools for having this impact are located on the side of our heads; they are called ears.*

impact are located on the side of our heads; they are called *ears*. When a school wishes to reduce the waste of student enthusiasm, they must employ formal listening, the same advice given to businesses: "Maintain the emotional connection with consumers, and the mojo that comes with it" (Burlingham, 2005, p. 75). The formal listening steps for reducing enthusiasm waste follow.

Step 1 is to administer a happy face survey to students. A sample is in Resource B. Students are asked to check a happy face, straight face, or sad face for each subject. A fourth column is labeled NA for students who are not enrolled in a particular course or subject. The average percentage of happy faces for each grade level is calculated. Hopefully this survey is conducted electronically with a minimum of staff time devoted to calculation. The happy face survey for the whole school is an annual event. It provides the baseline data so everyone can determine if their efforts at reducing enthusiasm waste are working.

Step 2 is to tell the students that you have two big goals for the year: (1) that students learn a lot and (2) that students love learning the content. If you have a great time here but learn nothing, I have not been successful. If you learn a lot but never, ever want to study this subject again, I have failed. You are a person, not a robot. This means I must care about your brain and your attitude. Thus, I will need your help monitoring both learning (explained in Chapter 5) and in monitoring attitude. Please take both seriously, because I do.

> *You are a person, not a robot. This means I must care about your brain and your attitude.*

Step 3 is to ask students to complete a monthly enthusiasm graph for each teacher. The sample graph is located at Resource C. Each month students record how they feel about their courses. The data is not collected centrally; it is for the teachers' feedback so they can make adjustments as necessary (thanks to Jeff Burgard for this graph).

Step 4 is to supply each month a plus/delta (+/Δ; see Resource D) for each student. On the plus/delta, students write under the + what went well in class this month, and under the Δ what could be done to make next month better. It is *most* important for teachers to say, "There's a bunch of you and one of me. I can only make one change a month, based upon what you students suggest. I promise you that I'll do my best to make this one change and will let you know which one I am making. So, take the plus/ delta seriously because I do." Here's the secret—people like bosses better that listen to them. This "like" translates into a maintaining of enthusiasm. "Good leaders motivate others by their listening skills" (Maxwell, 2002, p. 1544).

An addition that can be made to the traditional plus/delta is a statement by the student with a suggestion regarding what students could do, rather than what the teacher can do. In this way, many more suggestions can be implemented. On Resource D, I have added this statement.

Ask students, either orally or as a written assignment, to describe why they or a friend lost enthusiasm for learning a particular school subject. The advice is to "patiently read through these stories to see what they were telling me. I put my trust in the stories, not the theories. The result was a discovery of a different model of decision making" (Klein, 2013, p. 99).

Step 5 is to monitor the monthly enthusiasm graph for trends. Ask questions, inquire whether the plus/delta or other suggestions improved attitudes.

Step 6 is to study annual results from happy face surveys to determine if attitudes in school are improving. Add annual happy survey results to the radar chart (see Chapter 8).

In addition to these more formal steps, watch reactions—always. Kids "watch when they understand and look away when they are confused" (Gladwell, 2000, p. 102).

As I write these steps, I can hear teachers saying, "Who has time for monitoring all of this; I have a lot to teach." My response is, "If we never take time to reduce the time and energy wasted because of a lack of enthusiasm, we are doomed to the same problems forever. With positive student attitudes, we can teach far more than we can with poor student attitudes."

> If we never take time to reduce the time and energy wasted because of a lack of enthusiasm, we are doomed to the same problems forever.

Darron Arlt, principal of Central City (NE) Middle School conducted a happy face survey with his students with the astonishing results of 93, 98, 82 and 84 percent happy faces in Grades 5 to 8. Results like this are not an accident; it takes leadership with talented teachers. If this practice were the norm in the United States, it would be amazing how much more students would learn. We must optimize our time and our students' enthusiasm.

Everything I just wrote about teachers and their students can be duplicated for administrators and their staffs. Remember people like bosses better who listen than bosses who think they have no need to listen.

Some bosses have an open-door policy, which places the burden for listening upon the staff members. Reducing the waste of enthusiasm will not occur by passive open doors; it will only come about by aggressively tackling the waste. Waste management is much more than a fancy name for a garbage truck.

Reflection

Is it possible for a servant leader to be a poor listener?

If nothing new was added to education and the responsibilities of educators other than to reduce the waste of time and the waste of enthusiasm, increases in student learning would be guaranteed. Figure 3.1, The Optimization Fishbone, is inserted here again with the addition of removing waste at the bottom left.

Figure 3.1 Optimization Fishbone

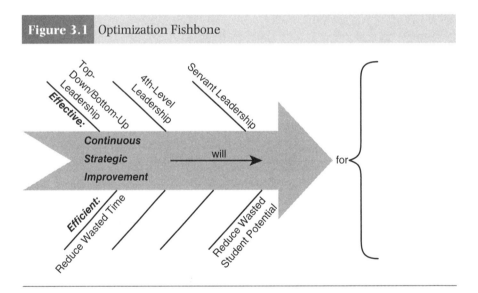

LOOKING AHEAD

The partner chapter for this subtraction, efficiency chapter, is the addition, effective chapter. What countermeasures can we test to make learning better? We are going to attempt something we have not done before.

Effectiveness

4

Testing Countermeasures

Anything out of standard is subject to problem solving, not finding someone to blame.

—Jeffrey Liker and Michael Hoseus, 2008

The truth is that schools, like every other organization, will never be perfect. The purpose of the strategic plan is to write a collection of countermeasures that have the real possibility of moving a school or school district toward perfection. Countermeasure and hypothesis are synonyms, but they have a subtle difference. A countermeasure is a hypothesis designed to solve the root cause of a problem. A hypothesis can be written without root cause analysis. It might improve the organization, but without root cause analysis, the hypothesis may be far off the target. It is the job of leaders to create effective organizations through year after year of small gains through testing countermeasures.

ROOT CAUSES EXAMPLE

After defining perfect and listing problems, the next step is determining root causes of problems. Skill is necessary. Root causes are not a blame statement. The root causes cannot blame students, parents, the school board, or the legislature. The

It is the job of leaders to create effective organizations through year after year of small gains through testing countermeasures.

root causes must be aspects of schooling that the school controls or can greatly influence. Far too often educators want to blame "negligent parents, social ills, or out-of-touch government expectations . . . Whatever the problem, [educators thought it was] largely outside their control" (Ripley, 2013, p. 36). John Maxwell (2013) wrote, "If you can find the right balance where you take responsibility for the things you can control and let go of the things you cannot, you will accelerate your learning process" (p. 66). For example, a New Mexico high school created the **Pareto chart** in Figure 4.1. The data shows the number of errors its students made in each mathematics strand, based on results from their state high school math exam. The columns are raw numbers of errors and the sloping line is the cumulative percentage of errors gradually rising until 100 percent of the errors are recorded. The data necessary to create the Pareto Chart is available in most states.

Just like business, however, the numbers are all over the place, and not very helpful or clear. Kurt Eichenwald (2005) writes about Enron,

Figure 4.1   High School Math Pareto Chart

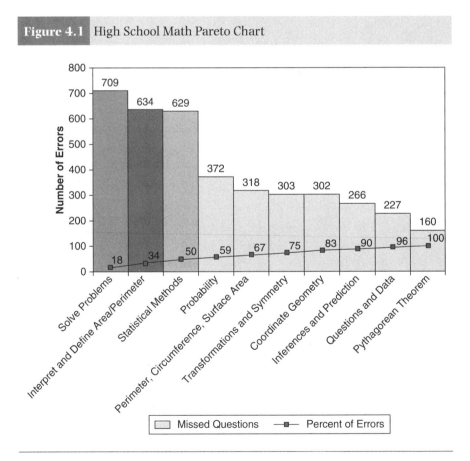

"Numbers floating all over with no explanation where they came from. Page after page of gobbledygook" (p. 99). It seems the contractors for state assessment results must be paid by the spreadsheet. Why else would there be so much gobbledygook? Simple charts like the Pareto Chart must be provided by the state assessment contractors. Educators need to see the Pareto Chart for their students, for the school as a whole, the district as a whole, and the state. Directions for creating a Pareto Chart are included in Resource Y.

THE FIVE WHYS

Root cause analysis is often called the Five Whys. The reason is that organizations usually need to ask why at least five times to find the true root causes. In the New Mexico math example, however, they only had to ask why three times. Here is a summary of questioning:

Question 1: Why did 43 percent of high school students not meet state math standards?

Answer: One root cause is that 25 percent of the errors came from statistical methods and probability.

Question 2: Why so many errors in statistical methods and probability?

Answer: Statistical methods and probability were not taught.

Question 3: Why weren't statistical methods and probability taught? They are in the state standards.

Answer: These topics are not in the Algebra 1 or geometry textbooks.

  Countermeasure: Divide up the state math statistical and probability standards among Algebra I and geometry teachers.

WHY THIS COUNTERMEASURE?

With 34 percent of the errors coming from problem solving and area/perimeter, it would be easy to be critical of the school's countermeasure. More errors were in problem solving and area/perimeter than in statistical methods and probability. Why only a countermeasure for statistical methods and probability? Educators are often implored to be more businesslike, but learning from business includes what not to do as well as what could be done. Jim Collins (2009) wrote, "Having studied both sides of the coin, how companies become great and how companies fail, I've concluded that there are many more ways to fail than to become great" (p. 19). One of the failure methods we can ascertain from business is taking on too many initiatives at once. Remember Rubbermaid? "As Rubbermaid realized too late, innovation can fuel growth, but frenetic innovation—growth that erodes consistent tactical excellence—can just as easily send a company cascading through the stages of decline" (Collins, 2009, p. 49). One successful countermeasure per department or grade level per year will add up to amazing results, far more than five major initiatives mandated by the combined "efforts" of the federal legislators, state legislators, school boards, and superintendents. "We will never implement what is most important for kids if we continue to pursue multiple new initiatives before we implement our highest-priority strategies and structures" (Schmoker, 2011, p. 15).

THE MAJOR ROOT CAUSES OF EDUCATIONAL PROBLEMS

My 2013 book *Permission to Forget: And Nine Other Root Causes of America's Frustration with Education* describes in detail root causes that are present in US school systems. The title, *Permission to Forget*, comes from the spelling process established in first grade with new content for each week, an exam on Friday, forgetting on Saturday, and a new set of words the next week. This failed process continues on with chapter tests for at least eleven more years. While in my book I attempt to outline the most pervasive, common problems in schools (that schools can solve—not problems caused by society, families or poor legislation), I cannot list all root causes. The New Mexico root cause analysis is an example outside of what is included in the book. However, the process I used in writing the book—asking why, over and over—is the exact process schools must use to be strategic in their planning. Countermeasures, designed to attack root causes of problems, are much more effective than random hypotheses or new programs.

> *Asking why, over and over, is the exact process schools must use to be strategic in their planning.*

TWO TYPES OF PROBLEMS

There are two types of problems that organizations face: common and special. Common problems are built into the organization and experienced by all, whereas special problems may come from the outside for a period of time. W. Edwards Deming stated, "Common causes (of problems) are more difficult to identify than special causes are. Moreover, the removal of common causes calls for action by administration at a high level" (Killian, 1992, p. 46). The math story from New Mexico is an example of a common problem—only state standards included in the textbooks were being taught. It will take action at a high level in the administration to eliminate this problem throughout the school district.

CONTINUOUS STRATEGIC PLANNING

Strategic planning is continuous because schools will never be perfect. A gap between perfect and current status will always be present. Creative people who can design brilliant countermeasures to bring the organization closer to perfect are in every school system. Perfect is 100 percent of students meeting standards. State boards of education set standards for some subjects and grade levels. Local agencies set the standards for behavior, attendance, participation in extracurricular activities, physics, kindergarten through Grade 2 reading, college readiness, career readiness, attitude toward school, and all other aspects of schooling where no state standard exists.

STEPS FOR CREATING COUNTERMEASURES

The steps are (1) describe perfect, (2) list problems (which are the gaps between current reality and perfect), (3) conduct root cause analysis of problem(s), (4) agree upon a countermeasure to test, (5) gather data after testing countermeasure to determine if closer to perfect or not, (6) solidify process into organization if improvement occurred, and (7) start over.

Reflection

How can we change the conversations from blamestorming to countermeasures?

BACK TO SERVANT LEADERSHIP

I have yet to observe a bully using force, intimidation, exchange, and manipulation who is successful in root cause analysis or any other aspect of strategic thinking described in *Optimize Your School*. It is only servant leadership that eliminates worry from staffs allowing their best thinking and countermeasure testing because "anything out of standard is subject to problem solving, not finding someone to blame" (Liker & Hoseus, 2008, p. 319).

> *It is only servant leadership that eliminates worry from staffs allowing their best thinking and countermeasure testing.*

LOOKING AHEAD

The remainder of this book will build upon the continuous strategic improvement principles outlined in the first four chapters. The purpose is to optimize every aspect of schooling. The journey will travel from classrooms to the major departments within the central offices.

PART II

The Classroom
First and Foremost

5 Continuous Strategic Improvement

Classroom

The true measure of a leader is getting people to work hard together.

—John Maxwell, 2007

Two first-grade teachers approached me after a seminar asking if I had any ideas for graphing homework completion. After inquiry, I found out that the homework assignment was to read at home twenty minutes a night with parents signing a form, assuring the teachers that the reading had actually occurred. The teachers said the homework process was a failure. I asked why and they informed me that the students were not reading twenty minutes each evening, even though some parents lied and said they were.

My response was to try intrinsic motivation instead of the current extrinsic motivation of a parent signature. The suggestion was to provide students a Grade 1 story on Monday and on Friday each student would read the story to the teacher for one minute and graph how many words they read. Further, the class would add up how many words were read in a minute by the whole classroom. (The two graphs the teachers used are located at http://LtoJConsulting.com/free-ltoj-support/blank-graphs/.)

The teachers were awed by how much the students read at home. Students practiced and practiced in order to see their personal graph and the classroom graph go up. They were not given any trinkets; the reward was internal, knowing that they had improved and helped the classroom improve. "The highest reward for our toil is not what we get for it, but what we become by it" (Maxwell, 2013, p. 78).

> *They were not given any trinkets; the reward was internal, knowing that they had improved and helped the classroom improve.*

In the simplest of terms, this chapter is about the power of a dot. Yes, dots; dots on graphs.

CONTINUOUS IMPROVEMENT HELP FROM ALL SOURCES

I have read seven of Jeff Liker's Toyota books on continuous improvement. It's not cars that interest me, but the details of continuous improvement in a corporation with a long history using continuous improvement as the driving force of the company. One cannot read much about Toyota without realizing that continuous improvement is deeply imbedded in engineering, personnel, finance, and sales. However, the focal point of all their effort is the factory floor. If continuous improvement is not on the factory floor, all the other efforts are of little use.

THE CLASSROOM: FRONT AND CENTER

Likewise, if continuous improvement is in all aspects of a school district except for the classrooms, the work is for naught. The classroom is front, center, and first. Thus, the details on continuous strategic improvement in school systems must begin with the classroom. Administrators must be able to implement continuous strategic improvement in every operation of a school district, including classrooms. Chapter 16 is specifically written for principals as they implement continuous improvement in their schools. A deep understanding of the content in Chapter 5 will make Chapter 16 suggestions understandable.

Before I delve into the details of continuous strategic improvement in the classroom, I will distinguish between **optimization** and **sub-optimization**. Sub-optimization means that a portion win at the expense of the whole. Most classrooms are sub-optimized; some kids win and some are continual losers. It's not because teachers have this desire, but it is a result of the classroom strategies they inherited. Further, some school subjects in at the expense of other subjects, often resulting in a very **depleted curriculum**.

The classroom is front, center, and first.

If classrooms are not optimized, then the rest of this book is of limited value. As you read on in this chapter, you will see that it is possible for every student to be a winner. It is not that every student wins every week, but every student experiences winning and has hope for future winning. In an optimized classroom, winning is outperforming your prior best; it is not outperforming anybody else. Further, winning is being a part of a team that outperforms its prior best.

Critics say that children need to learn to lose; it is a part of life. These critics are partially correct. Children do need to learn how to lose in athletics and games. Likewise, they also need to learn how to be a gracious winner in athletics and games. Education is more important than athletics and games so it is a poor place to learn how to lose. That said, with the process you are about to read, students do lose often. "Lose" means that they did not have their all-time-best; it does not mean they are a loser kid incapable of ever having another all-time-best. Because readers of this book are educators or at the minimum understand classrooms, Chapter 5 is the very best place to understand what optimization means for schools.

THE POWER OF THE SUM

If you ask a kid on a sports team, "How is it going?" two answers are automatically reported. One is how the team is doing and the other is how the kid is doing as an individual. If you ask the very same kid, "How is school going?" you receive one answer, which is how she is doing as an individual. There are no teams in classrooms. "The true measure of a leader is getting people to work hard together" (Maxwell, 2007, p. 261). This insight provided for leaders of adults is equally as important as leaders (teachers) of young people. Even in classrooms where the teachers are masters at getting the kids to work together, the results of working together are seldom visible, except in the arts and athletics. Nobody even thinks the team total is missing. Interesting, because if the team total was missing at a sporting event everybody would notice, and yet the missing team totals in classrooms are never mentioned. The scoreboard at athletic events is simple addition, the sum of all team members' contributions; the same scoreboard is essential for education's future. The sum!

TEAMWORK IN THE CLASSROOM

For years, educators have known that industry values employees who are great team members, but the how of creating teams at school has been difficult to create. Creating teams in schools is a part of creating healthy individuals. "People who are the healthiest focus on developing satisfying personal relationships, growing as individuals, and contributing to their community" (Deci, 1995, p. 129). I wish all readers could visit a classroom of students where the practices described in this chapter are fully implemented. Ideally you will be there the moment the students learn the class, as a whole team, outperformed their prior best record. Watch the joy on the students' faces, especially the countenance of a student who struggles with school learning. Dennis Bakke (2005) captured well the feelings when he wrote, "I think this little guy with a crooked smile and troubled past was saying, 'I want to contribute. I can make a difference. I want to be a part of the team. I'm somebody'" (pp. 19–20).

Basic leadership for continuous strategic improvement requires two classroom learning measurements. The first is how each student is achieving and the second is how the classroom is progressing. The leader of the team is the teacher. Many of America's teachers are also athletic coaches and many, many more of America's teachers were members of athletic teams or music groups during their childhood. They know how coaches and directors create teamwork on the athletic field and stage; with continuous strategic improvement, they can use this knowledge for classroom learning.

> *The leader of the team is the teacher.*

STUDENT FRIENDLY TERM—LTOJ®

Since 2003, I have called the process that I'll describe in this chapter *LtoJ*®. At first people think this is about my initials; they are wrong. The **L** represents the shape of the histogram at the beginning of a course, the bell curve is for the middle of the year, and the **J** is the desired shape of the curve at the end of the course. If I knew how to create perfect schools, this process would be called *LtoI* but since the goal is only to move closer to perfection, I have settled for *LtoJ*®. Figures 5.1 through 5.3 show three histograms moving from the *L* to the bell to the *J*. The *L* histogram is from the first week of school, the bell is from the middle of the school year, and the *J* is from the last week of the year. A formal definition of a *histogram* is "a plot of the data which has possible values on one axis and frequencies for those values on the other axis. The frequency is traditionally placed on the vertical axis, so that the observations accumulate in a pile at each value" (Wheeler & Chambers, 1992, p. 27).

The three graphs show how the observations pile up over each value. Kids love observing the *J* gradually appear because "not knowing the results of their work is not only demoralizing, it also reduces productivity

Figure 5.1 L Curve

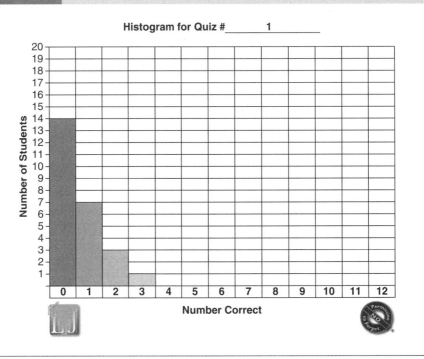

Source: © From LtoJ® Consulting Group, Inc.

and increases the potential for errors" (Ha, 2002, p. 14). The histogram answers the question, "Are we meeting standards?" The J curve, at year's end, documents that most students learned what was communicated at the very beginning of the course.

On the website, www.LtoJConsulting.com, under "Free LtoJ Support," are many sample graphs from classrooms to supplement the few included in this chapter. Review these and you will see the results of a multitude of personalities involved—both teachers and students. Unlike programs teachers are asked to implement with fidelity, continuous strategic improvement in the classroom is a process that requires teacher leadership and unique teacher/student personalities.

THIS YEAR'S LEARNING EXPECTATIONS

Step 1 for classroom continuous strategic improvement is informing students precisely what they will learn. Lists of content, for background knowledge, and dichotomous rubrics for performance are provided to students at the beginning of the school year. Chapter 10 describes how

Figure 5.2 Bell Curve

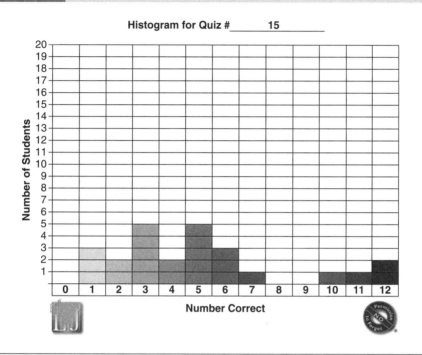

Source: © From LtoJ® Consulting Group, Inc.

these lists and rubrics are aligned. Chapter 12 is devoted entirely to the dichotomous rubric: explanations and examples. Once copies of the expectations are printed for teachers, students, and support staff, the continuous strategic improvement process is ready to begin. In 1992, when Damon Cropsey, fifth-grade teacher in Enterprise District (Redding, California), first experimented for me, he stated, "Lee, you know that the hardest part of this is determining exactly what you want the students to know at the end of the year" (Jenkins, 2003, pp. 37–40). In over twenty years, this has not changed; the hardest part of classroom continuous strategic improvement is describing in student-friendly terms precisely what students are to know by the end of the year (or course). Educators with any experience at all know that there are dusty standards on the shelves of American classrooms. The way to take the dust off is twofold: (1) Write the standards in student friendly terms, and (2) give copies to the students for them to check off as they learn them. What educators probably do not know is that this process of collecting dusty standards is not unique to education. "Standards abound in medical labs. We had notebooks full of standards. Unfortunately, that was as far

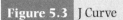

Figure 5.3 J Curve

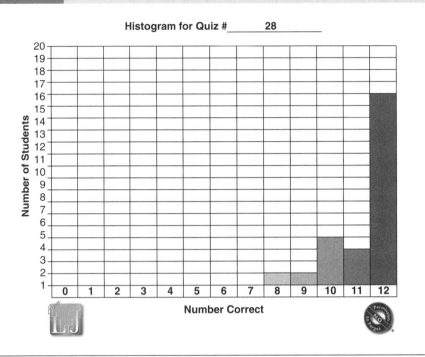

Source: © From LtoJ® Consulting Group, Inc.

> *Lists of content, for background knowledge, and dichotomous rubrics for performance are provided to students at the beginning of the school year.*

as the standards got—onto pages in notebooks" (Liker & Franz, 2011, p. 231). Resource E lists the mathematics key concepts that are new for Grade 5. A complete set of key concepts for mathematics and many other examples of key concepts created by teachers are posted at http://LtoJConsulting.com/free-ltoj-support/key-concepts/. Resource F is an excerpt from a high school Spanish vocabulary list and Resource G is the **key concept list** for the US Constitution.

NON-GRADED QUIZ

Step 2 is a non-graded assessment of student knowledge. The process is simple—randomly sample content from the whole year and quiz students on this content. The only procedural issue is how many questions to ask. The answer is the square root of total content for the year. For example, if a modern language teacher expects students to know 400 vocabulary words at the end of the year, then students are quizzed on twenty randomly selected vocabulary words each assessment. If the seventh-grade math teacher has fifty math concepts, then the quiz is seven items. If the first-grade teacher wants students to know the 220 Dolch sight words, then students are quizzed at each assessment on sixteen randomly selected words. The synonym for the LtoJ® process is review-preview as students are always asked questions from prior taught curriculum and asked questions about upcoming curriculum, as a preview. The review aspect is vital as educators have been fooled far too often by students' chapter test results, only to learn three weeks later they do not really know the content. "Information must make it to permanent memory to become part of our background knowledge . . . Effective processing of information in working memory depends on certain critical activities: the information is processed multiple times, detail is added, and associations are made with other information" (Marzano, 2004, p. 24). It is the multiple times on LtoJ® quizzes along with little details and associations that put key concepts into students' long-term memory. On the LtoJ® website (www.LtoJConsulting .com) under "Free LtoJ Support" are free PowerPoint hyperlinked quizzes for classroom implementation. One is the US Constitution set of questions written by Dan McCaulley, author of *Continuous Improvement in the Social Studies Classroom* (2010). Because there are one hundred concepts, teachers will ask ten randomly selected questions per quiz. Dan has written different questions for various concepts. His key concept list that matches the PowerPoint for quizzes is located in Resource G. I stated earlier that teachers provide key concepts for the entire year and the US Constitution will be a unit of study, not a year's content. However, I recommend that this LtoJ® quiz be given over a whole year with some quizzes prior to the unit and some after the unit of study. Teachers who accept this advice will be amazed at how much their students remember about the US Constitution even years after the course is over. I would also tell students that 25 percent of their final exam at the end of the year will be Constitution questions. The twenty-eight non-graded Constitution quizzes are given to assure learning and success on the final.

Resource H is a sample math quiz written to match the Grade 5 math concepts described earlier. The quiz contains seven Grade 5 questions, plus two Grade 4 questions and one Grade 3 question. All ten questions are randomly selected from their respective grade-level key concept lists.

SEVEN TIMES A QUARTER

I learned from Nebraska school superintendent, Julie Otero, that the ideal number of non-graded assessments is twenty-eight per year. Seven times a quarter provides ample feedback for students and their teachers, but it does not set up an unrealistic expectation of quizzing every week, or thirty-six times. "The purpose is to have a short time frame for comparing what actually happens with what we had planned (the standard), so that people can tell how they are doing in real time" (Liker & Franz, 2011, p. 92).

Seven times a quarter provides ample feedback for students and their teachers.

"[A] loop that takes months is too big to grasp, and feedback is too slow" (Liker & Franz, 2011, p. 71). When teachers first hear this it sounds overwhelming. However, assessing first graders on sixteen randomly selected Dolch sight words twenty-eight times a year is far easier than assessing each first grader on all 220 words four times a year. Random selection of a sample is simpler than large scale assessments. On the website, www.LtoJConsulting.com, are blank graphs for 5, 6, 7, 8, 10, 12, 16, 20, and 24 items. Each of the blank graphs is for twenty-eight weeks. Obviously, teachers with courses other than year-long ones will need to adapt to block schedules, semester, quarter, trimester, and other structures. Teachers who meet their students for art, music, physical education, and technology once or twice a week find that six assessments per year is reasonable.

YOU HAVE GOT TO BE KIDDING—ASK QUESTIONS ON CONTENT NOT YET TAUGHT?

The very first objection to what I have just written is assessing students on content not yet taught. How is this fair? Remember, these assessments are *not* graded. The first week of school, about all the teacher can say is, "Thank you for creating the *L* curve and it is guaranteed your graph will go up."

Liliana Velasco, a Columbus, Nebraska, high school Spanish teacher wrote,

> I have implemented LtoJ in my classroom for the past 5 years; I have also assisted teachers as they start using LtoJ. One of the most common questions I get is the relevance of previewing information. As teachers, we have been trained to ask our students questions about what we have taught them . . . so why would I ask them questions about what I have not taught them? Well . . . for me, the answer is simple—previous knowledge. As teachers, we understand that tapping into our student's previous knowledge about a concept is key for retention and meaningful

comprehension. We know that if there are any previous experiences that can be tied to what we are teaching, these experiences will allow our students to connect, understand, and remember better what we hope they learn.

Previewing information in LtoJ gives me the opportunity to provide my students with previous knowledge, so when I am actually teaching a concept, I can connect them to their previous experience.

One of the most important principles of LtoJ is to keep explanations of concepts being previewed quick and simple. This is key!!! In my class, I prepare these quick explanations ahead of time. I prepare them as I plan my essential elements.

I present my students with what is more relevant in a concise way. For example, it is during my previewing of information that I present them with endings for specific verbs, with mnemonic devices to remember irregular verbs, or with examples of how it is applied. In other words, I do not inundate them with details or lengthy examples. In my opinion, an essential aspect about previewing is to present this short explanation in the same way every time, even using the same vocabulary.

One other practice that has helped me is to ask my students to write the correct answer for the concepts being previewed using a different color on their LtoJ quiz. I believe it is through writing the correct answer, even if they still don't understand it, that learning begins to take place.

STUDENTS COMPLETE THEIR PERSONAL STUDENT RUN CHART

The third step is graphing progress. The students graph their progress on the **student run chart**. In each student's data folder are two documents: the key concepts to be learned and the student run chart. Students check off the concepts they answered correctly as shown on Figure 5.4. Then they graph their individual progress. Figure 5.5 is a student run chart from a high school physiology course and Figure 5.6 is a student run chart from an elementary classroom. It doesn't matter whether students create a column graph or a line chart—either will work for the LtoJ® student run chart. The student run chart answers the student question, "Am I getting smarter?"

Figure 5.4 Individual Item Analysis

Geometry Key Math Concepts

Congruence

1. Know precise definitions of angle, circle, perpendicular line, parallel line, and line segment, based on the undefined notions of point, line, distance along a line, and distance around a circular arc.

2. Represent transformations in the plane using, for example, transparencies and geometry software; describe transformations as functions that take points in the plane as inputs and give other points as outputs. Compare transformations that preserve distance and angle to those that do not (e.g., translation versus horizontal stretch).

3. Given a rectangle, parallelogram, trapezoid, or regular polygon, describe the rotations and reflections that carry it onto itself.

4. Develop definitions of rotations, reflections, and translations in terms of angles, circles, perpendicular lines, parallel lines, and line segments.

5. Given a geometric figure and a rotation, reflection, or translation, draw the transformed figure using, for example, graph paper, tracing paper, or geometry software. Specify a sequence of transformations that will carry a given figure onto another.

6. Use geometric descriptions of rigid motions to transform figures and to predict the effect of a given rigid motion on a given figure; given two figures, use the definition of congruence in terms of rigid motions to decide if they are congruent.

7. Use the definition of congruence in terms of rigid motions to show that two triangles are congruent if and only if corresponding pairs of sides and corresponding pairs of angles are congruent.

8. Explain how the criteria for triangle congruence (ASA, SAS, and SSS) follow from the definition of congruence in terms of rigid motions.

9. Prove theorems about lines and angles. *Theorems include the following: Vertical angles are congruent; when a transversal crosses parallel lines, alternate interior angles are congruent and corresponding angles are congruent; points on a perpendicular bisector of a line segment are exactly those equidistant from the segment's endpoints.*

10. Prove theorems about triangles. *Theorems include the following: Measures of interior angles of a triangle sum to 180°; base angles of isosceles triangles are congruent; the segment joining midpoints of two sides of a triangle is parallel to the third side and half the length; the medians of a triangle meet at a point.*

11. Prove theorems about parallelograms. *Theorems include the following: Opposite sides are congruent; opposite angles are congruent; the diagonals of a parallelogram bisect each other; and conversely, rectangles are parallelograms with congruent diagonals.*

Geometric Measurement and Dimension

12. Give an informal argument for the formulas for the circumference of a circle, area of a circle, volume of a cylinder, pyramid, and cone. *Use dissection arguments, Cavalieri's principle, and informal limit arguments.*

13. Use volume formulas for cylinders, pyramids, cones, and spheres to solve problems. ★

14. Identify the shapes of two-dimensional cross-sections of three-dimensional objects, and identify three-dimensional objects generated by rotations of two-dimensional objects.

Figure 5.5   High School Student Run Chart

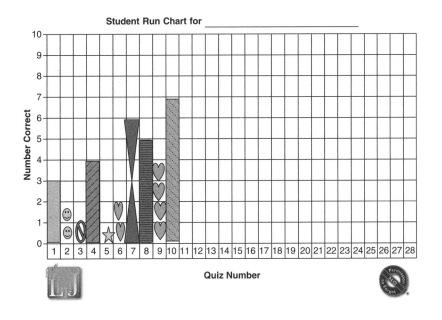

Source: © From LtoJ® Consulting Group, Inc.

Figure 5.6 Elementary Student Run Chart

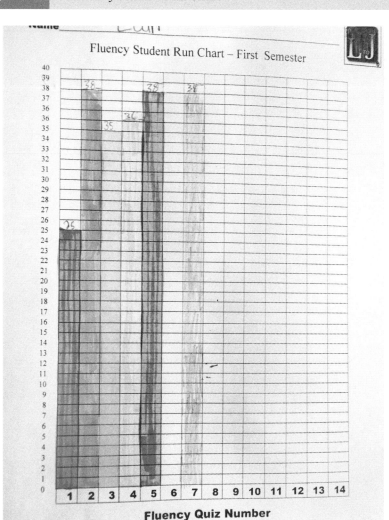

GRAPHING THE CLASS TOTAL—THE WOW FACTOR!

Students in most classrooms don't know how the class, as a team, is performing. The solution is to add up the contribution of each member of the classroom. Addition is as powerful a motivator as ranking is a demotivator. Grading on the curve, and other ranking devices, creates the doldrums for the majority of students. ***This lack of student engagement can be reversed by addition! Everybody's work counts!*** "Peer pressure is much more powerful than a concept of a boss. Many, many times more powerful. People want to live up to what is expected of them" (Gladwell, 2000, p. 186).

To create blank **class run charts** determine which blank run chart to download from http://LtoJConsulting.com/free-ltoj-support/blank-graphs/. The y-axis along the left side must rise to what perfect would be. Remember, perfect is not the

Addition is as powerful a motivator as ranking is a demotivator.

goal; the goal is to improve and come as close to perfect as you can. So, if the Spanish class has twenty-five students and they are quizzed on twenty random vocabulary words (out of the year's total of 400) on each LtoJ® quiz, then perfect is 500 vocabulary words correct for the class as a whole. The y-axis needs to rise to 500 and stop there (25 students × 20 words = 500 possible correct answers). If the y-axis goes to 800, for example, it is discouraging as students cannot ever reach that high with the twenty-five students and twenty words.

Figure 5.7 is a class run chart as a line graph and Figure 5.8 is a class run chart as a column graph. "While the histogram collapses all the data, showing its overall shape, the running record stretches out the data, showing the sequential information that is obscured by the histogram" (Wheeler & Chambers, 1992, p. 33). The class run chart answers the question, "Is our team improving?"

"The charts and graphs look great in the conference-room presentations, but the reality of the shop floor is far from the TPS (Toyota Production System) ideal" (Liker & Hoseus, 2008, p. 4). This business quote applies equally well to

---

Figure 5.7   Class Run Chart (Line)

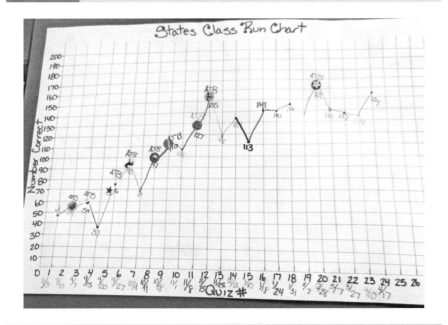

> The charts and graphs belong on the classroom walls and in the school hallways every day; that is our ideal.

education. We could write it, "The charts and graphs look great in the board presentations, but the reality of the classroom is far from ideal." The charts and graphs belong on the classroom walls and in the school hallways every day; that is our ideal.

Figure 5.8 Class Run Chart (Column)

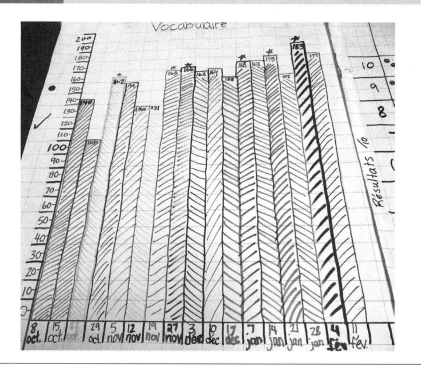

THE SKEPTICS

"Leaders have to help people taste success that they never have experienced before" (Fullan, 2011, p. 7). Figure 5.9 is from the third week of the 2014–2015 school year for Mark Twain Elementary School in Colorado Springs, Colorado. Yes, it sounds crazy to start off the year quizzing students on fluency that is expected at the end of the year, but it is the results that help people understand. Teachers care deeply about their students' success and when the success is posted in the hallway for all to see, they are happy. So, skeptics are natural when an initiative depends upon intrinsic motivation, but most are convinced of the process when they observe weekly the totals for the whole student body, their classroom, and their students. The advice in "Let's Fix Math Fluency," located

Figure 5.9 Grade-Level Math Fluency Charts

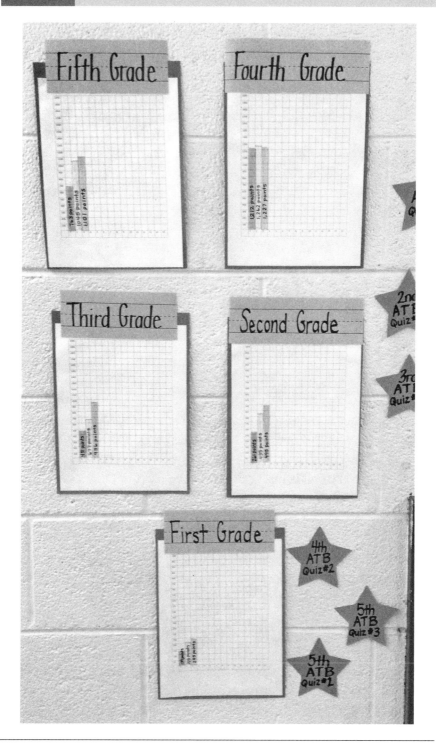

Source: Photo by Melinda McConnaughey.

at www.LtoJConsulting.com, is written so kids can experience success in a way they never have before. Figure 5.10 is from Wilson Elementary School in Norman, Oklahoma. It also displays the total correct math fluency questions for the whole school.

| Figure 5.10 | Schoolwide Math Fluency Chart |

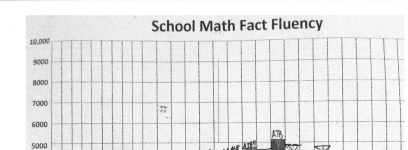

Source: Courtesy of Chris Crelia.

Further, every child can take pride in the graphs. Contrast this to the bulletin board of a football field with a paper helmet for each child. Some children have their helmet at the 0 yard line and some at the 100 yard line, with the remaining helmets sprinkled in between. Every day when some kids arrive at school they have "in their face" the fact that they are a loser. Again, "Leaders have to help people taste success they have never experienced before!" (Fullan, 2011, p. 7).

PREVIEW MINI-LESSON

When **preview questions** are randomly chosen, the most common practice of teachers is to give a thirty-second mini-lesson on the concept and then estimate when it will be taught in depth. However, there are times when students beg for more knowledge *right now* and teachers have to determine whether to teach now or later. Sometimes now is the teachable moment.

CELEBRATIONS—NOT REWARDS

At athletic events when the scores go up, the team and the spectators shout and clap for joy. Nobody stops the game to give the players stickers or cupcakes. Likewise, with continuous strategic improvement, teachers do not bribe the students to work hard and then give them food or other stuff. The term **celebration**, instead of reward, is used for all-time-bests (ATB). An ATB is the best total so far this school year; it is not merely better than last week. Figure 5.11 shows a class run chart with eleven ATBs over the course of most of a school year.

W. Edwards Deming (1994) wrote, "Rewards motivate people to work for rewards" (p. 13). The distinction is significant. A reward is like a bribe; a celebra-

A reward is like a bribe; a celebration is a "thank you."

tion builds upon intrinsic motivation as "any motivation or incentive other than self-motivation is likely to lead to problems and limitations" (Liker & Meier, 2007, p. 213). There are numerous ways that teachers say thank you to students for their hard work. They include a short dance, putting the classroom hamster ball in the center of the room

| Figure 5.11 | Class Run Chart With 11 ATBs |

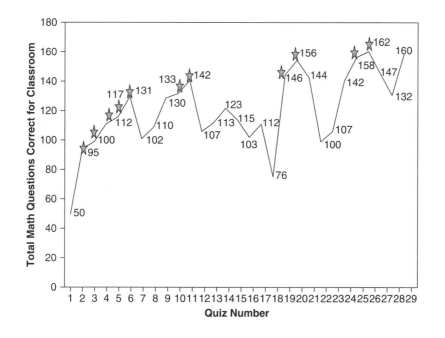

and watching where it goes, the teacher doing cartwheels, singing a song with rounds (a new round added for each ATB) with options going on and on. Some classrooms have six to ten different celebrations and roll a die to see how they will celebrate. The kids call this fun, which is "defined to mean rewarding, exciting, creative, and successful" (Bakke, 2005, p. 24).

GRADED VERSUS NON-GRADED QUIZZES

We have known since the 1970s from the book *Wad Ja Get?* that grades motivate about half of the students (Kirschenbaum, Napier, & Simon, 1971). I often ask the teachers what percentage of their students are motivated by grades. Figure 5.12 is the result from approximately 3000 teachers attending my seminars.

This is counterintuitive; students are more motivated by non-graded quizzes than graded quizzes?!

Nothing has changed in over forty years. Grades motivate about half of the students according to two-thirds of the respondents. Teachers with several years' experience utilizing the LtoJ® process state that approximately 90 percent of students are motivated by LtoJ®. This is counterintuitive; students are more motivated by non-graded quizzes than graded quizzes?! Why the higher motivation rate? I believe it is for two reasons: (1) People love seeing evidence of their improvement, and (2) contributing to the team's success brings great joy. It is the "power of collective capacity" (Fullan, 2011, p. 9) that brings such amazing results. Both of these factors are much more powerful than motivation by grades. Research has added to

| Figure 5.12 | Grades Motivate What Percentage of Students? |

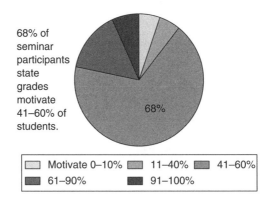

68% of seminar participants state grades motivate 41–60% of students.

68%

☐ Motivate 0–10% ☐ 11–40% ☐ 41–60%
☐ 61–90% ☐ 91–100%

our knowledge of these facts. "Kage found that the use of evaluative quizzes to motivate learning led to lowered intrinsic motivation and to poorer performance on the final examination than did the self-monitored, non-evaluative quizzes" (Deci, 1995, p. 49). Joe Montalone wrote, "One would assume that giving students an assignment where there was no reward of a grade would be met on deaf ears. Actually, it was quite the contrary! Students were motivated to learn skills that were initially 'above their pay grade,' this seemed to lure them into the fascination of touching knowledge" (personal communication, September 15, 2014).

THE SECONDARY PROMISE

For middle and high school students there is another factor. When the teacher provides the key concept lists and dichotomous rubrics for the whole course, there is a promise that the graded assessments will come from the same key concept list or rubrics as the non-graded quizzes. Students understand that if they are answering half of the non-graded questions correctly half-way through the course, they are on target and will do well on graded assessments and the final. They know they do not need to study (cram) for the exams, as they already have the content in their long-term memory. Students are not provided ahead of time the precise questions; they are given the key concepts and performance expectations from which questions will be derived.

ADDING STRATEGIC TO CONTINUOUS IMPROVEMENT

The strategic aspect of classroom continuous improvement is the same for increasing background knowledge and performance expectations. The class run chart will have three distinct phases—inclines, plateaus, and valleys. When the graphs show an incline, rejoice and celebrate. When the valleys occur, ask why. The reasons can be identified as absences, bad luck (too many preview questions), homecoming week, state assessment week drained our brains, or an emotional event such as a weather alert. When plateaus occur, nobody knows why. Thus hypotheses are established to test so that an incline can return. Even with very young children, involve them in the hypothesis setting. Sometimes the teacher says, "I think this will help us, so for the next three weeks we are going to add this practice to our regular procedures." Sometimes, the students create the hypothesis and are able to test out their idea.

The students will be very creative "producing decisions that are not expected" (Ackoff, 1994, p. 28). Either way it is strategic, not mere hope.

When plateaus occur, nobody knows why.

CONTINUOUS IMPROVEMENT IN THE CLASSROOM IS A FEEDBACK SYSTEM

Feedback and **evaluation** are not the same. For teachers, what the principal says about them is evaluation and what the students say is feedback. The LtoJ® process is feedback that allows the teacher, as leader of the classroom, to adjust strategies and pacing before it is too late. Seth Godin (2010) wrote, "The most generous thing you can do is to open yourself to the feedback that improves your art and helps it spread" (p. 209). John Hattie (2009) described the power of feedback this way. He wrote, "The remarkable feature of the evidence is that the biggest effects on student learning occur when teachers become learners of their own teaching" (p. 22).

> *For teachers, what the principal says about them is evaluation and what the students say is feedback.*

THE BIGGIE: TIME

Who has time to create all these graphs? For the classroom, the answer is easy; the students have the time. My suggestion is that teachers select students who will create the graphs after every quiz. Use the same students each time. The reason is to be efficient first and fair second. When teachers focus on the fairness first, they sometimes become discouraged with the time it takes to teach graphs. When the process is moving along quite smoothly, then switch to fairness and gradually share the graphing responsibility with other students. What is the alternative to graphs? The alternative is pages and pages of computer spread sheets or walls covered with data. Neither are as effective as graphs because only graphs can display so much information on a single sheet of paper.

> *Who has time to create all these graphs? For the classroom, the answer is easy; the students have the time.*

MORE LATER

My purposes in placing the classroom early in this book has been stated: If continuous strategic improvement touches all aspects of a school system except the classroom, what real value has been added to the system? This chapter includes the basics of classroom continuous improvement, Chapter 15 describes advanced implementation.

THE PURPOSE OF DATA

Data is a key aspect of continuous strategic improvement at the classroom, school and district level. How else will people know when improvement occurs? Data, however, does not provide answers to problems. Please remember "the purpose of analysis is insight rather than the numbers" (Wheeler & Chambers, 1992, p. 81). This insight is gained from testing hypotheses. We can add to our clichés, "A trial is worth a thousand opinions" (Liker & Franz, 2013, p. 203).

HYPOTHESIS OR COUNTERMEASURE?

A countermeasure is a hypothesis that is designed to help with the root cause of a problem. My recommendation is that adults generally use the term *countermeasure* in their work because the adults can conduct root cause analysis with their problems. So, in the chapters that are outside the classroom, I use the term *countermeasure*. However, in this chapter, I have stuck with hypothesis. I am not suggesting that students embark on root cause analysis. That said, when I listen to history teachers discuss the War Between the States they are deeply involved in root cause analysis. All students, beginning in kindergarten can understand hypothesis and the *J* curve. Therefore, I chose to use hypothesis for the classroom vocabulary.

The Optimization Fishbone and the Optimization Matrix are both inserted as Figures 5.13 and 5.14. The purpose is to bring the fishbone up to date and to start a similar process with the matrix.

Reflection

What school practices, implemented with the best of intentions, created student losers? Can these practices be replaced with the processes explained in this chapter?

LOOKING AHEAD

It would be great if graphing of continuous improvement and testing hypotheses, by themselves, would create all excelling schools; they will not. Excelling schools require great instruction and high standards. Chapter 6 is about high standards and Chapter 7 is about exciting teaching practices.

I stated earlier that the most difficult aspect of continuous strategic improvement in the classroom is determining the end of the year expectations in student-friendly terms. Chapters 6 and 7 are written to ease this process. We want to be very sure that all of this working hard together is worth doing.

Figure 5.13 Optimization Fishbone

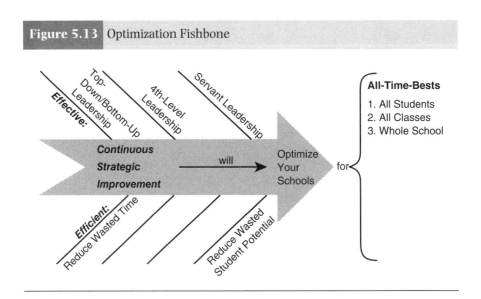

Figure 5.14 Optimization Matrix

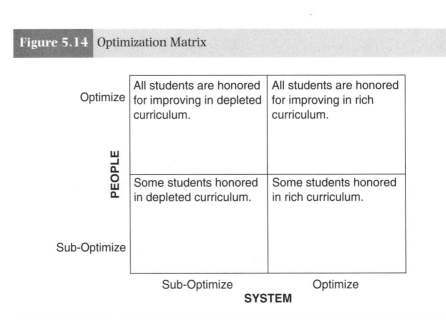

Student Experts 6

The Standards

There are no problems without standards.

—Jeffrey Liker and Gary Convis, 2012

Recently I had the privilege of listening to Ron Rutowski of Arizona State University give a presentation on the eyesight of butterflies. He clearly reinforced my understanding of what it takes to be an expert. Rutowski knows a lot about butterflies and also knows how to research to find out more about butterflies. In the simplest of terms, experts know a lot and can do a lot.

I learned that there are more than 20,000 different species of butterflies and that each butterfly eye has thousands of lenses, each pointing in a slightly different direction. In the horizontal plane, the span of the human visual field is about 190°, while in butterflies it is about 344°, making it very difficult to sneak up on a butterfly. Further he described research he conducted to determine how close a female butterfly of a medium-size species has to fly to a male butterfly in order for the male to see the female. They found it was typically one to two meters. However, larger butterflies can see further away.

Regarding color vision, butterflies probably have better color discrimination than humans. Humans have three cones or photoreceptor types for seeing color—red, green, and blue. In contrast, butterflies can have as many as five photoreceptor types including ultraviolet. The human eye cannot always determine the difference between the male and female butterfly, but humans with an ultraviolet camera lens can often see what the butterfly sees.

Experts know a lot and can figure out how to do a lot to increase their knowledge.

HOW DO I KNOW IF STANDARDS ARE WORTH MEETING?

Look at the standards for one subject from kindergarten through the last course in high school. When students have the background knowledge in their long-term memory and they have met the performance standards, would they be considered an expert in this subject? If not, the standards are incomplete. Standards worth meeting will create student experts. There will be no evidence of a pendulum swing either favoring background knowledge or performance expectations.

In this chapter, I will combine the principles of Common Core State Standards and continuous strategic improvement regarding experts in order to help educators have standards that are truly worth meeting. These standards will need to be written in student-friendly language (Chapters 5 and 15), and be aligned with each other (Chapter 10).

> *Standards worth meeting will create student experts.*

EXPERTS

Expert students know a lot and can do a lot. The current term for "know a lot" is *background knowledge* and "can do a lot" is *performance*. Both are essential to become an expert and schools that swing the pendulum between students learning background knowledge to performance and back to background knowledge are greatly reducing the number of experts created in schools.

Educators often state that their purpose is to create lifelong learners. While this aim is admirable, educators have no way of knowing if they have been successful with this purpose statement. The simple reason is that the educators are older than their K–12 students and thus will most likely not outlive their students. Today's educators will not live long enough to know if their current students are lifelong learners.

AIM FOR EDUCATORS

So, what is a reasonable aim for educators? As stated above, I am proposing that a major purpose of educators is to create as many student experts as possible. Our students can graduate from high school as experts. Educators will know when their graduates are experts when their students have a great deal of background knowledge stored in their long-term memory and have the skill to solve real problems using their background knowledge in creative ways. The senior project required in many high schools can be one way for students to demonstrate their expertise. The concept can be expanded to have public demonstrations at the end of Grades 5 and 8 also (Schmoker, 2011, p. 37).

Expert students remember the whole year's curriculum and prior years' curriculum. They do not cram for exams and then promptly forget. Thus, under the continuous strategic improvement umbrella is the process to eliminate permission to forget. We must remember that students do not know about cramming until they enter Grade 1; it is taught to them through the weekly spelling list and test. It is up to administrators to set up the processes that eliminate this educational blind spot. Directions for elementary educators for eliminating the spelling cram/forget cycle are included in the e-booklet "Let's Fix Spelling," located at www.LtoJConsulting.com.

> Expert students remember the whole year's curriculum and prior years' curriculum. They do not cram for exams and then promptly forget.

Continuous strategic improvement is one aspect of education that is essential for creating expert students. Continuous improvement, by itself, however, is not enough. Think about it—continuous strategic improvement in learning nonsense does not create an expert. Students who cannot make sense of the lessons cannot become experts. Schools that are disconnected from grade level to grade level have a much more difficult time creating experts because they are teaching the same content over and over. Students who are victims of ill-conceived data procedures, such as grading on the curve, are far less likely to become an expert. Students who are continually bribed with stickers, food, and parties will be far less likely to become experts at anything beyond playing the game to get stuff.

Recently, I observed a TED video by Dr. Stefan Larsson, http://www.ted .com/talks/stefan_larsson_what_doctors_can_learn_from_each_other .html. Readers will want to watch the whole YouTube clip, but the essence is that improving medical care will be much more difficult without standards. The example is hip replacement. What is a quality hip replacement? After two years of debate, it was agreed that a quality hip replacement lasts at least seven years and preferably never has to be revisited. Once agreement is reached on the definition of quality, then people can work together to improve the quality.

Whether readers are in a US state with Common Core State Standards adoption, another state, a Canadian province or another country, standards are the essential starting place. Continuous improvement comes second. Without standards, how would anybody know if improvement occurred? We track progress of individual students, classes, grade levels, schools, departments, and whole school systems to see if progress is on track. We measure progress toward perfect, which would be 100 percent of the students meeting 100 percent of the standards. Since perfection is not going to occur, strategies will be selected to bring about even more improvement. I am going to rely on John Hattie's research for the strategies in Chapter 11. Hattie's research is the springboard for my advice on establishing countermeasures for creating more and more student experts.

AN AIM FOR EACH ACADEMIC SUBJECT

With teachers, administrators, parents, school board members, and some adult experts, school systems need to agree upon an aim for each academic discipline. The only synonym I know for aim is *purpose*. In other words, before we write standards in student-friendly terms, we must write the aim for each subject. The aim will not change; standards may be tweaked and the focus from year to year may slightly change, but the aim will not change. The aim will communicate to everyone the purpose for meeting the standards in each academic discipline. Further, the aim does not change by grade level; it works for everyone K–12.

Before we write standards in student-friendly terms, we must write the aim for each subject.

Below are ideas for the aims for each subject. They are not the final word but are written to be a spring board for local educators to create their aim. I found in my years as a school administrator that bringing a blank sheet of paper to groups of people for brainstorming did not always give us the desired results. However, when I put my thoughts on paper, the group was able to create the correct thoughts because they could easily see how to improve, trash, revamp, or resequence my thoughts. So, with that in mind, here are five aims to help local educators generate the aim for each subject.

Mathematics: The aim of mathematics instruction is to use patterns to solve problems. Students who are the most successful in school mathematics see the patterns and the students who are least successful do not see the patterns. It is incumbent upon educators to start the teaching of every new mathematics concept with lessons that create patterns in mathematics. From these patterns, formulas are created. When instructional materials skip the patterns and jump directly into the formulas, many students are lost.

Reading: The aim of reading instruction is to gain meaning from print. Any time the brain looks at print that makes no sense, it is naturally disinterested. Since educators desire for students to learn to read well, and also to have a desire to read, it is crucial that the making sense aim be foremost in the mind of educators every day.

> *The aim of mathematics instruction is to use patterns to solve problems.*

Writing: The aim of writing instruction is twofold: learning and communicating. Thoughts come to mind through the discipline of writing that would probably never be considered without putting thoughts in print. The secondary aim of writing is to clearly communicate to others. As I write this book, I know for sure that the first aim is true and with editing assistance I can become better with the second aim.

Science: The aim of science instruction is "to develop students' positive attitudes about science through activities that relate to the natural world and their applications to daily life" (Burgard, 2010, p. 28).

Social Studies: The aim of social studies instruction is "to equip students to act justly and to participate in a changing world as informed, confident, and responsible citizens" (McCaulley, 2010, p. 14).

Do not skip this step; the creation of an aim for each subject is one of the most powerful staff development activities possible. Overall, the aim of education is to create student experts, with extensive background knowledge and the skill to research problems. Underneath the overall aim are aims for each academic subject. OK, you're not convinced that the time necessary to agree upon an aim is important. Give me one more shot at this. In my seminars, I asked 3000 teachers to rank the ten root causes of educational frustration described in *Permission to Forget: And Nine Other Root Causes of America's Frustration with Education* (2013). "No Clear Aim" is almost always the number one frustration with teachers; they do not know where they are supposed to go. They have federal, state, local, and school requirements and desperately want clear aims to help them organize where they are heading.

SPECIFIC GRADE-LEVEL EXPECTATIONS

Once the aims are agreed upon, bring teachers and administrators together to create learning expectations for each grade level and each subject. These must be written in student-friendly language and given to students, parents, media specialists, support staff, and anybody else who interacts with the students. The Common Core State Standards can be of significant help in this process because these standards increase performance expectations. As local educators write their student-friendly standards, however, they must always balance them between background knowledge and performance expectations. In order to have enough instructional time to meet all of the increased performance standards, it is essential that the background knowledge lists remove trivia. Trivia, of course, is taught to make the classroom a more interesting experience. Students, however, must be held accountable for only what is essential to place in long-term memory.

> *Students, however, must be held accountable for only what is essential to place in long-term memory.*

MATHEMATICS

In mathematics, performance is usually called *problem solving* or *word problems*. A good word problem has easy to understand language and difficult math. A poor word problem has difficult to understand language and easy math. An example of a good math problem to solve is, "What is the volume of our classroom?" Sample problems for both PISA (Program for International Student Assessment) and NAEP (National Assessment of Educational Progress) are posted on their respective websites. Let's follow their examples and post or print sample math problems for each grade level and course. The standard for problem solving can be widely communicated to students and beyond.

Typically, math problem solving is evaluated with rubrics or merely the correct answer. When more is evaluated than the answer, educators rely upon rubrics. Resource I is a dichotomous rubric for mathematics problem solving. The first question is, "Could the process (selected by the student) have led to a correct answer?" If yes, the student will score a 3 or 4 on the rubric. The next question, "Is it the correct answer?" determines if the score is a 3 or a 4. If the student has the correct process, but makes a computational error, then the rubric score is a 3. When a student has both a correct process and a correct answer, the rubric score is a 4. Some students select a method for solving the problem that will not lead to a correct answer. In those cases, the rubric score will be a 1 or a 2 depending upon whether or not there is some correct computation.

READING

From pre-Kindergarten on to Grade 12, what are the expectations in reading? How can we make this as clear as possible? My suggestion is that we use both audio and video recording, plus print, to communicate expectations as clearly as possible. Post on the school's website students demonstrating end-of-the-year expectations.

For every grade level, post precisely what is to be accomplished by the end of the year.

For pre-kindergarten, expectations will be items such as knowing print moves from left to right and holding the book upright, starting at the beginning of the book and so on.

For kindergarten, the list will include letters, sounds, and sight words.

From Grade 1 on to Grade 12, I suggest that schools post an example of a fiction and a nonfiction story students should be able to read by the end of the year. Accompanying the story will be example questions and expected fluency rate. Why not post a video or audio recording of a student reading the grade-level stories? Select an average boy and an average girl reader to be the example. In first grade, the selected students should be ones who entered first grade meeting kindergarten standards, but were nowhere close to reading the expected sixty or seventy words per minute. Record these students at the end of the year so that future students can hear what they aspire to accomplish by the end of the year.

ALIGNMENT

The most important advice I have on writing student-friendly expectations for each course for every year is in Chapter 10, Alignment and Stabilization. I am not referring to **alignment** with Common Core State Standards, but aligning grade levels and courses with each other. When an expectation is written down for a grade level, it must not be written down again. When the same standard is written down in multiple grade levels, nobody sees themselves as responsible. It's the same as when the school board requires five signatures on a purchase order; nobody thinks themselves as the one with the responsibility.

> *When the same standard is written down in multiple grade levels, nobody sees themselves as the one with the responsibility.*

STANDARDS FOR STUDENTS ARE VERY SPECIFIC

These student expectations are very specific. A general standard might be, "Know major geographic locations in North America in Grades 3–6." This is not acceptable for students; the educators must agree upon the precise locations students are expected to know and locate on a blank map. Further, the student-friendly documents must list locations for Grade 3, then Grade 4, then Grade 5, and finally Grade 6 with no duplicates at any grade level.

When I write this, I can hear people say, "Yeah, but . . ." because students forget prior years' knowledge. Thus, a system must be in all classrooms to assure that students retain prior knowledge. **Permission to Forget**® is alive and well in private, charter, and public schools. The continuous strategic improvement process described in Chapter 5 is designed to remove Permission to Forget®. Experts retain knowledge; they do not cram, get a grade, and forget. This process of cram/get-a-grade/forget, that starts in Grade 1 spelling and continues on through college and must be eliminated if we have any hope of creating student experts.

Once standards are in place, students, teachers, parents, and administrators must know if students are on target to meet the standards by the end of the year. My whole career we have had two assessments that fail to tell us if we are on target. We have chapter tests which measure short-term memory and thus inform nobody whether or not students are placing the required knowledge in their long-term memory. Secondly, we have standardized exams that do measure long-term memory. The problem with these exams is the results are returned after the students have left for the year. The results arrive too late to be of any help for the teachers. Chapter 5 described the LtoJ® process to continually measure long-term student learning so that there is ample time to improve the success rate.

THE SEQUENCE THUS FAR

1. Agree upon an aim for education. I suggested, "The aim of education is to create student experts with extensive background knowledge and the skill to research problems."

2. Agree upon an aim for every subject. Do not leave anybody out—include the arts, the career-tech opportunities, and health and physical education.

3. Write in student-friendly language aligned learning expectations for every grade level, every subject. Include both background knowledge and performance expectations. Distribute these widely.

Reflection

Are the suggestions in Chapter 3 necessary in order to implement the processes described in Chapters 5 and 6? If so, how do we proceed?

Our Optimization Fishbone is inserted here again, in Figure 6.1. The language at the very bottom on creating student experts is now included.

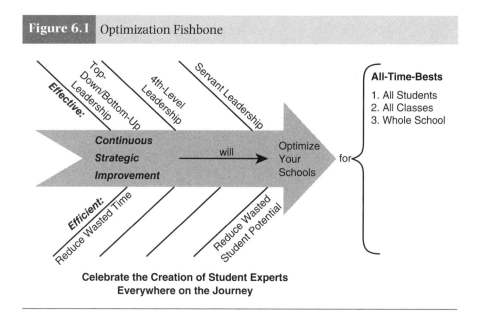

Figure 6.1   Optimization Fishbone

LOOKING AHEAD

In Chapter 7, we will look more closely at the instructional practices that can be of the most help in meeting the aims and standards we have written.

7 *Practices That Support Powerful Standards*

Problems are the gaps between the standards and the actual.

—Jeffrey Liker and Gary Convis, 2012

Once the three steps in Chapter 6 are completed, school systems can move onto the practices that have the most potential for creating student experts. My intention in writing the suggestions is to provide advice that teachers and administrators can carry in their heads on a daily basis. Nobody will need a check sheet to implement these practices; they can become second nature.

RIGOR

First of all, rigor doesn't mean pile on the homework. Rigor has to do with the difficulty of the work, not the quantity. One math problem such as "What percent of the cafeteria is covered by tables?" is much more valuable than problem after problem of homework.

> Rigor has to do with the difficulty of the work, not the quantity.

In order for leaders to lead their schools with rigorous curriculum, they must understand that for years influential people have been removing the rigor with readability formulas. Educators were told that words like *coyote* with three syllables were inappropriate for Grade 1 reading, while *fox* was appropriate because it had one syllable.

Remove all the multisyllable words from students' lists and the rigor is destroyed.

Nonsense. The children entering school want rigor. Resource J lists the words requested by four first-grade children learning to read in Marion Nordberg's Fullerton, California, classroom. The question she asked was simply, "What word would you like to read today?" The practice spread from her classroom to five other first grades. I gathered up all the words from these six classrooms (average of sixty words each for 180 children) and classified them. The largest student interest was science with over 40 percent of the words. Remove all the multisyllable words from students' lists and the rigor is destroyed.

Working with a New Mexico agriculture teacher, I learned more about rigor. First, the ag teacher taught the students the welds he wanted them to be able to perform. Once competence had been demonstrated, the students had to perform all the same welds again, but this time they couldn't look at their actual work; they had to complete all the welds looking in a mirror. Rigor was added to the basic requirement. It seems that rigor is the last step in teaching sequence. Students must build upon a pattern of success in order to have the confidence to attack the rigor.

Schools can become much more rigorous when we remove curriculum that demeans learning and always conclude units of study with the rigor. Kids start out in school asking for rigor and the United States has a history of rigor. Read the selection in Resource O from *Studies in Reading, Grade 8,* by James W. Searson and George E. Martin published in 1910. If kids ask for rigor and it was present in 1910, we can reverse the misleading notions that have damaged rigor in US schools.

CREATIVITY

As a child, I thought I was not a creative person because I was not talented in music or art. I learned that creative people were good in music or art and I wasn't among them. I can remember when I began to think of myself as creative. It was when Peggy McLean and I wrote a book titled *It's a Tangram World* (1971). We combined geometry, fractions, geography, and tangrams in the mathematics curriculum.

Later, I learned a definition of creativity that stuck. Creativity is combining two or more known elements in a new way. What Peggy and

Creativity is combining two or more known elements in a new way.

I did was combine the 2000-year-old tangram puzzle with geometry, fractions, and geography. What we did matched this definition of creativity and I changed my mind about myself. So, my advice for educators in regard to creativity is to be on the alert for creativity in children and the genuine compliment is, "Wow! That was really creative for you to put together _____ and _____. How clever. You are a creative person."

I do like constraints to foster creativity. That is why I like ABC Books as a class or individual assignment. The teacher has just finished reading *Charlotte's Web* and now the next day the class is writing the "ABC Book of Charlotte's Web." Each student writes a page that either begins with the letter or for harder letters, such as *J, Q, X*, the word only needs to have the letter in the word. The constraint of having to connect a particular letter of the alphabet to an occurrence from the book sparks creativity. A kindergarten class, at the conclusion of the unit on occupations, wrote the "ABC Book of Occupations." One student wrote, "Y was for yo-yo-maker." Without the constraint of the ABC Book, yo-yo maker probably would never have made the list of occupations.

In order to model this constraint and encourage reflection time, I have included Chapter 17 as my "ABC Book."

When the elementary teachers remove the purchased pictures adjacent to each letter of the alphabet above the whiteboards and replace them with words and pictures done by students, the same creativity occurs.

I know that there are resources to assist educators as they work to develop more creativity in children. I am not discounting them. However, we can develop a lot of creativity in students by nurturing the creativity we see every day. Tell the students this definition of creativity and then honor their creativity. When a visitor enters the classroom, be sure to point out to the visitor some of the creative thinking that is currently present in the classroom.

COLLABORATION

In Chapter 5, I described what I call the LtoJ® process. When the total is added up for the classroom, grade level and school, collaboration happens. Students naturally want to help each other when they realize that everybody's success contributes to the team total. Students, even in the youngest grade levels, understand the power of a team of students working together.

Another collaboration idea takes place at the end of an assignment. When the students have completed the work, the teacher gathers up the papers and corrects them right then in the classroom. While the teacher is correcting, the students are put into groups of three or four to complete the assignment again, as a group. The students collaborate on the answers. It takes about the same time for the teacher to score all the classroom papers as it does for the students to collaborate on the worksheet. Resource K is a page from *It's a Tangram World* that has enough rigor for teachers to be fairly certain that collaboration will be necessary for students to agree on all of the answers.

It can always be an option for students to collaborate at their initiative. Give an assignment of say ten problems or questions. Tell the students that they can work together on the assignment if they wish. If they want to work with somebody, go ahead. But now they have twenty problems to complete. If three want to collaborate, that is fine. The thirty problems are here. Another example of this is giving students the assignment to write a ten-page dictionary. Each student writes a dictionary based upon an interest. One student's dictionary might be titled "My Dictionary of Baseball Words." Each word is on one page and has the word, definition, phonetic pronunciation, antonyms, synonyms, a sentence with the word, and an illustration. When each word is on a single page, it becomes very easy to alphabetize the dictionary at the end of the project. The work cannot be copied out of a dictionary but must be with the students' own vocabulary. Thus it is important for the topic to be a subject the student knows a lot about. The collaboration aspect is, "If you want to work with a friend that is OK. However, the dictionary is now twenty words long." Many students will accept the collaboration challenge.

PROBLEM SOLVING

I do not know how many problems are solved in only one day, but it has to be very, very few. We all know this. Therefore, let's conduct problem solving in schools with this knowledge. When it comes to problem solving, replace "teacher" with "patience." Do not be tempted to "teach" the answer but let the student have the time to problem solve.

One of my most enjoyable experiences with patience was working with a middle school math teacher. We provided four students with a sheet of paper with twelve miniature geoboards (Resource L), geoboards, and rubber bands. The assignment was to divide the geoboard in one-half, twelve different ways. Immediately, the students came back with the geoboard divided into half four ways: a horizontal line, a vertical

I do not know how many problems are solved in only one day, but it has to be very, very few.

When it comes to problem solving, replace "teacher" with "patience."

line and two different diagonal lines. They said four is all that's possible. Here is where the temptation to be teacher comes in to play. Instead the teacher and I utilized patience. The students were told to think about it, but while they were thinking, here is another math assignment for you to complete. The next morning, the students came in and said they were sure—only four ways existed. They worked on other math during the math period. The third day, they said there were five ways, but that was ALL. They worked on other math at school. The fourth day, they came in with twelve completed halves. They said that the geoboard had sixteen small squares and if you put eight squares inside the rubber bands and left eight squares outside the rubber bands, the geoboard would be divided into half no matter at what angles the rubber bands were placed. In fact, the next step was to realize that the geoboard could be divided up into triangles and half would be 50 percent of triangles inside the rubber bands.

It will serve readers well to reflect upon where they solve some of their most perplexing problems: in the shower, in the car, on a bike, or waking up in the middle of the night. Kids are no different; let them problem solve normally.

CRITICAL THINKING

Let's look for ways to require thinking. As school superintendent, I was observing classrooms. The second graders had a typical worksheet of addition and subtraction problems. A student had answered $7 + 7 = 14$ and two rows later answered $8 + 6 = 14$. I asked him, "How can you do two different problems and get the same answer?" He immediately erased the answers and twenty minutes later the students at his table were still debating how you could do two different problems and get the same answer. I call this critical thinking and it is almost always fostered by teacher questions.

A man and his wife decided to go on a picnic. They looked on the map, picked out a lake, and took off. About eight kilometers off the highway, they looked where the lake should be, but no lake. Perplexed they drove back two kilometers to a country store and asked the owner about the lake. He said, "I've lived here eighty years and there has never been a lake there. Your map has a mistake." So, to be nice, the couple wrote the map publisher to tell them of their mistake and the reply was, "We know; we put the mistake there on purpose." The critical thinking question is,

"Why would map makers do this?" You relate the story to the students but do not tell them the correct answer until the last day of the school year. Even if they are correct, do not let them know. If you want to know the correct answer, go to http://resources.corwin.com/jenkinsoptimize for the map answer.

An archeology critical-thinking activity is to ask eight friends to empty their work wastepaper basket into a grocery bag at the end of a day. Divide the classroom up into seven groups, each with a sack. The students' job is to determine the occupation of the person who emptied the trash. When the first group finishes, trade sacks with them using the one left over. When every group has analyzed all eight sacks, then discuss the thinking process for each sack. They can be told the correct answer when all are done.

A student was given the problem $25 \times 20 = ?$ to solve with base ten blocks. He made 25 piles of 20, regrouped, and wrote down the answer. Next he was given $20 \times 25 = ?$ He made 20 piles of 25, regrouped, and wrote down the answer. When he discovered both problems had the same answer, he exclaimed, "You tricked me; but you won't trick me again." Six months later, he was learning to add, subtract, multiply and divide fractions with *Fraction Tiles*. He was overheard saying, "There's a trick here somewhere. If we can figure it out, we don't need these tiles." Is looking for the "trick" an aspect of critical thinking?

> Critical thinking comes about by asking questions that might even be considered trick questions.

Critical thinking comes about by asking questions that might even be considered trick questions. The only criterion is that students have to think about what is happening and not rely upon a teacher to provide the answer. The teacher can verify the answer, but if critical thinking is the goal, the teacher does not provide the answer.

With the PISA (Program for International Student Assessment) example questions, at http://pisa-sq.acer.edu.au/, give students a question and a reasonable amount of time to solve. Then pair off the students and ask them to agree on the answer. The next step is to place the students into groups of four, then eight, and finally the class as a whole. The class has to agree on the answer. This process of arguing, disagreeing, listening, and looking over the problem again is a part of critical thinking. It is very hard to teach critical thinking. However, it is not all that difficult to set up procedures that require the students to think critically. Having a "critical thinking" classroom can be as simple as this practice: "I noticed that you three answered the same question, but you have three different answers. Can you three work together and let me know when you have the real answer."

INFORMATIONAL TEXTS

Students want to learn about our world. I mentioned earlier that over 40 percent of the words first graders asked for were science words. The second category was social studies, which we defined as holiday and vacation words plus names of friends. This was 22 percent. Fantasy was only 12 percent of the words. Our students start out elementary school desiring informational texts. We can provide them. The concept of dividing literature 50/50 between fiction and nonfiction deserves serious consideration at all grade levels.

Students can write their own informational texts. One example is writing the classroom encyclopedia. All that is needed is a binder with alphabetical dividers. Every classroom has students who are experts in something. Should a student be an expert in bees because a parent is a beekeeper, have the student write the encyclopedia entry for bees. Type it up and print two copies; one is to take home and one is to be three-hole punched and placed in the classroom encyclopedia. The encyclopedia grows from year to year. This same idea can be implemented at any grade level, any course. The binder is now labeled "How to . . . ." Students who have mastered a particular skill in a course are given the assignment to write up the steps exactly as they would explain them to a friend. One copy is placed in the binder and one goes home.

Every school has employees and parents who are experts with some hobby or interest. Ask them to write about their expertise, have the high school English students edit the article, send the editing back to the author, and have the author give the final approval. Place the name of the adult on the document as the author and then this writing can be used for informational text. What if the author was a cafeteria worker? Think about the conversations that could occur between students and the cafeteria worker.

ACADEMIC VOCABULARY

A major aspect of creating student experts is having students who comprehend the vocabulary for various academic disciplines.

There is much to be said for having a district strategy for learning academic vocabulary. I am not one that has much confidence in learning glossary definitions, but the vocabulary is important to know and internalize. A major aspect of creating student experts is having students who comprehend the vocabulary for various academic disciplines. We cannot discount the power of understanding both the text and the teacher.

My suggestion is that districts utilize staff development days for teachers to write the essential vocabulary for each academic subject from kindergarten through Grade 12. No word can be duplicated; once it is placed in a grade level, it is not to be repeated. The process utilized in Chapter 5 is then used to help students remember the vocabulary from both current and former grade levels.

Once the words are determined, then student-friendly definitions must be written and distributed both in print and on the district's website. Adding computer games that utilize the vocabulary is clearly helpful, especially when posted on the district website.

I realize that not all parents are helpful in their children's education. However, many more can and will help when they know what is expected. Placing the academic vocabulary on the web enables more parents to help, even in the summer preparing for the next grade level.

WHAT NOT TO DO WITH ACADEMIC VOCABULARY

An administrator goes to a conference, hears research about the value of academic vocabulary, returns to work and pressures the teachers to pay more attention to academic vocabulary. Then force is used to ensure that there is evidence of vocabulary instruction in lesson plans and bulletin boards for academic vocabulary are displayed. The administrator announces, "I will be looking for word walls." Please look back at Maxwell's four "do nots" and three "dos."

DIGITAL LITERACY

It seems there are two steps for assuring student digital literacy. The first is standards by grade level. What digital literacy is expected at each grade level and how will we know if the accepted level of literacy has been accomplished?

The second step is creating flexibility with assignments so that students can always utilize their digital knowledge. The process is simple:

1. The learning expectations are always clear. Teachers refer to the annual list of expectations and which content is being addressed today.

2. When giving assignments, students are provided three to six options as ways to prove their knowledge. A couple of these options must always require digital expertise.

3. The most creative direction is to state to students, "If you have another idea, beyond the six ideas I provided, come talk to me about your plan. I hope it works out for me to give you permission to pursue your idea."

4. Lastly, tell students if they have an idea regarding how they can meet the requirements of two teachers at once, come ask for permission so a three-way conversation can take place between the two teachers and the student. Encourage the meeting of one of the digital literacy standards through the project.

PREVIEW FUTURE LEARNING

When student learning expectations are aligned for every grade level and course, teachers will need to be most familiar with their current grade level; but they also need to know what was expected the past two years and what is expected the next two years. In Chapter 5, I wrote a formative process for placing standards in students' long-term memory, always asking questions from the prior two years or more. Next is the responsibility to introduce the content coming up in the next two years. Time allocation must be studied in order to have time to introduce future years' content. Removing Permission to Forget® is the major way this is accomplished. In my surveys of over 3000 teachers, the average teacher reports using one-third of the school year teaching content students should already know. There is a better use for these sixty days.

The very worst picture of the future that teachers can give their students is fear of the future. We've all heard, "You better shape up; next year in ___ grade they will not allow you to act like that!" Instead of telling students how bad the future is going to be, set aside time to prepare for a better future. "You are so lucky that you are going to attend ___ middle school next year. One of my jobs is to introduce you to some of the ideas they will teach you. It's sort of like seeing a preview of a television program, just a little bit about what is coming to create interest."

> *Time allocation must be studied in order to have time to introduce future years' content.*

Schools can establish a pattern of time for introduction of future curriculum. This could be every Friday or every short week, every minimum day, or some other structure. The ideas below are not exhaustive; they should provide readers with direction for previewing future years' content.

MATHEMATICS PREVIEW

I wrote earlier about the responsibility of teachers to review at least two grade levels. In addition to making sure the current year's content is solidly in place, there is the responsibility to introduce the next two years' mathematics. The introduction is with manipulatives. Teachers do not have the responsibility to teach any formulas for future grade levels but should let students use manipulatives to begin the learning. A simple example is multiplication in Grades 1 and 2 in preparation for more formal teaching of multiplication in Grade 3. The process is simple. Provide students with cubes or squares and ask them to arrange the cubes or squares into squares or rectangles. Suppose a student creates the rectangle below:

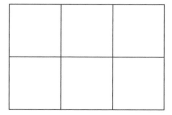

Ask the student to count how many squares going up and write down that number. Then count how many squares go across and write down that number. Explain that multiplication uses an × to mean *by*. This is a 2 by 3 rectangle, which is written $2 \times 3 = ?$ Now count the squares

The power is not only in content learned but the positive attitude toward what is coming.

and write the answer. The student will write $2 \times 3 = 6$. After this is done, the student makes another rectangle or square and records the multiplication sentence. Students who have this assignment a couple of times in Grade 1 and another couple of times in Grade 2 are more ready for Grade 3 lessons on multiplication than students who have never previewed multiplication. The power is not only in content learned but the positive attitude toward what is coming.

One more example of introduction is mathematics race games in the primary grades. The games are played with three players—the banker and two competitors. There are multiple race games for every aspect of primary mathematics, but I'll explain one, Race for A Week. The necessary materials are chips of some type labeled *hours*. Ten chips can be glued together and labeled *ten hours*. Next, prepare two strips of tagboard for each day of the week. Label them *Sunday, Monday, Tuesday*, and so on.

A sheet of tagboard labeled *one week* is created that is exactly the same size as the seven days. The last item is a blank die labeled *5 hours*, *½ day*, *8 hours*, *10 hours*, *12 hours*, and *20 hours*. The banker has all of the chips, days, the week, and the blank die. Players take turns throwing the die and the banker provides the corresponding hours. When players have twenty-four hours, they trade for Sunday, and when twenty-four more, they trade for Monday. The first player to accumulate seven days, trades for the week and is now the banker for the next game.

The race games are almost endless: Race for a Day, Race for 1000 (with base ten blocks), Race for 5 gallons, Race for a Meter, Race for Waffles or Pancakes (a fraction game). The point is that race games introduce students to content that will be studied formally at future grade levels.

SOCIAL STUDIES PREVIEW

One summer my wife, Sandy, and I flew from California to the East Coast to visit historical sites. Of course at the end of every location, there was a gift shop and we always walked out with a 32-page picture book. Upon our return home, we organized the books into chronological order and my wife read one of the books to her third graders each week. The students' assignment was to illustrate and write about the book. Some of the students' writing is posted on my website at http://LtoJconsulting.com/free-ltoj-support/social-studies/. The Grade 5 history was not taught in the same detail that was taught two years later, but the introduction to the curriculum paved the way for future anticipation and success.

From that experience, it occurred to me that all students should have an introduction to future history. It really does help students organize their understanding at a later time when the curriculum is taught in much more detail. It is very common for teachers to read novels to their class. So, why not read a historical fiction novel to students about future history curriculum? "Kids, next year you will study about ancient Romans. You will really enjoy learning about all they accomplished and how their decisions impact your life today. To help you prepare for next year, the next novel I read to you will be _____."

Once the curriculum is aligned for history and it is determined which segments of history are taught at each grade level, a timeline should be placed above the whiteboard in each classroom where history is taught. For example, if a timeline is created for US history, the portion for elementary US history is posted on the north wall. The portion of US history taught in middle school is posted on the east wall and the segment of US history taught in high school is posted on the south wall.

This same timeline is posted in all elementary, middle, and high school classrooms where US history is taught. This way, teachers can more easily review and preview content from prior and future years.

> *We can create student experts in every school. It will require standards worth meeting and daily practices that keep students engaged.*

We can create student experts in every school. It will require standards worth meeting and daily practices that keep students engaged. The suggestions for both standards (Chapter 6) and instructional practices (Chapter 7) were written for just this purpose: helping educators everywhere create more and more student experts.

Reflection

What could a servant leader do to assist all teachers in implementing the Chapter 7 educational practices?

LOOKING AHEAD

Chapters 8 and 9 outline a formal strategic planning process that requires everybody's brains. What has the best chance of helping more and more students become experts? Instead of a selected group of employees meeting to update the five-year strategic plan, the process that will be explained requires everybody to establish countermeasures to solve the problems they face.

PART III

Continuous Strategic Improvement for Instructional Leadership

8

Optimization With the Radar Chart

What's in greatest demand today isn't analysis, but synthesis—seeing the big picture.

—Daniel Pink, 2006

The National Council of Teachers of Mathematics (NCTM) is dedicated to the improvement of mathematics in the United States; it is their passion, responsibility, and their job. The National Science Teachers Association (NSTA) has the same responsibility for science. These two organizations and their counterparts, for each academic discipline, need not study the whole of education; their responsibility is very focused.

RESPONSIBLE FOR THE WHOLE OF EDUCATION

Optimize Your School, however, is written for people who are responsible for the whole of education. These leaders need a clear picture of their school system's progress in instruction, personnel, and business. "Enterprises are not currently organized to facilitate managers focusing on interactions, only on the actions of parts taken separately" (Ackoff, 1994, p. 34). In this chapter, we will look at the whole school district which is "a network of interdependent components that work together to try to accomplish the aim of the system . . . The secret is cooperation between the components toward the aim of the organization" (Deming, 1994, p. 50). Regarding seeing the whole system, Daniel Pink (2006) wrote, "What's in greatest demand today isn't analysis, but synthesis—seeing the big picture, crossing boundaries, and being able to combine disparate pieces into an arresting new whole" (p. 66). The **radar chart** is synthesis' best friend.

The radar chart is synthesis' best friend.

Continuous strategic improvement provides school executives and legislators tools to see and understand how every aspect of schooling is connected to every other aspect of education. "People who hope to thrive in the Conceptual Age must understand the connection between diverse, and seemingly separate disciplines. They must know how to link apparently unconnected elements to create something new" (Pink, 2006, p. 134). Mihaly Csikszentmihalyi wrote, "Creativity generally involves crossing the boundaries of domains" (quoted in Pink, 2006, p. 135). Creativity lives at the heart of this ability because "boundary crossers reject either/or choices and seek multiple options and blended solutions" (p. 136). "Sometimes the most powerful ideas come from simply combining two existing ideas nobody else ever thought to unite" (p. 137).

On a recent trip to Greer, Arizona, I observed five children playing on playground equipment designed like an airplane. There was a seat in the front for the pilot and two seats behind for the passengers. The wings were turned into a teeter-totter with a child on the end of each wing. I listened intently as the pilot announced that bad weather was coming and at this cue, the two sitting on the wings started the violent motion of the teeter-totter and rocked the whole plane. A few minutes later the pilot announced that smooth weather was ahead and the teeter-totter kids brought the plane to a standstill. My whole life I've seen teeter-totters and airplanes, but never have I seen the simple combining of these two common objects. This is what the radar chart will do for executives; it will destroy the power of the silo.

YOU ALREADY OWN THE RADAR CHART

Lynn Kelley (2011) could have described the purpose of the radar chart with this language: "The goal was to view the organization as an integrated system rather than a series of silos that operated independently and often suboptomized one another, especially when single areas of focus were being evaluated and scored" (p. 21).

Data are locked in spreadsheets. When the data are rescued from these spreadsheets, which graph will best communicate "Where are we now?"

The beauty of the radar chart is that it allows leaders to study trend data, instead of only two data points, and at the very same time, visualize possible connections among all aspects of the school system.

Surprise—it is the radar chart, which comes with Excel. You already own it. "You'd have to be the federal government to prefer the complicated, expensive measures over the simple, inexpensive ones" (Gilbert, 2012, p. 86). The radar chart is not complicated or expensive. The radar chart displays all key data on one graph. Writing about another chart, Dan Roam (2010) wrote, "This single image summarized everything in the hundreds of pages of data we'd been given" (p. 18). He could have written the same about the radar chart! Further, the radar chart can show the data from five or more previous years and clearly designate where the school or school system achieved its all-time-best (ATB) results. The radar chart is one powerful single page!

The beauty of the radar chart is that it allows leaders to study trend data, instead of only two data points, and at the very same time, visualize possible connections among all aspects of the school system. "We have to change the culture from one in which people simply do their own job in their own function to make their numbers look good (a vertical focus) to one in which people are focused horizontally on the customer and on improving value streams that deliver value across functions" (Liker & Convis, 2012, p. 4). Each **vector** on the radar chart can be a vertical, silo focus. However, when all the vectors are put on one piece of paper, it is much easier to see how to deliver value across functions. *Flow* is the term used by Jeffrey Liker (2004) for this value across functions. He wrote, "Creating flow means linking together operations that otherwise are disjointed" (p. 101). We are looking for "an increase in value (that) can occur only if the parts can do something together that they cannot do alone" (Ackoff, 1994, p. 24). Superintendents and their key staff members must always have documents before them, such as the radar chart, that allow them to see the interconnecting aspects of their districts.

Not many of us would have come up with the word *flow* for this coming together, even though, when we see somebody else's use of the word it makes complete sense. What we would have most likely written, "There was a lot of great information and insight there; it was just buried so deeply and spread so widely that nobody could find it" (Roam, 2010, p. 17). When I have assisted school administrators in creating their radar charts, they have literally found the custodian's hand truck and come into the meeting room with five boxes of spreadsheets. I recognize that in 2015, school systems might not have five boxes; they might have electronic gobbledygook. "Data when it is packed away in individual files and records, it's impossible to look at the big picture—but getting everything out in the open makes otherwise invisible connections visible" (Roam, 2010, p. 56). The radar chart creates flow by making invisible connections visible.

READING THE RADAR CHART

A little work is necessary to make the radar chart legible when multiple years' data are displayed. Figure 8.1 is a district radar chart with alterations to make it more readable. When the radar chart is first created in Excel, there are far too many lines. Eliminate all the lines except the most recent year.

Resource N is a set of directions for creating the radar chart in Excel. The steps describe how to create the radar chart, eliminate most of the lines, highlight the most recent year, and point out all-time-bests.

Even with this reformatting, the first look at the radar chart is a little daunting. Color is essential for reading the radar chart, so readers may want to go to http://resources.corwin.com/jenkinsoptimize and download and print Figure 8.1 in color. I do suggest that readers become very comfortable with the radar chart before continuing. To assist in understanding the radar chart, note some of the details that can be gleaned from Figure 8.1.

1. Reading results, in Grades 1, 4, 5, and 8, were at an all-time high, designated by the double asterisks.

2. Math, in Grades 1, 2, 4, 7, 8, and Algebra I, were at an all-time high.

3. Geometry tied its all-time-best, designated by the single asterisk.

4. More students scored a 3, 4, or 5 on AP exams than ever before.

5. Art has slipped but music is improving.

6. More students are participating in extracurricular activities than ever before.

7. Attendance and student discipline are tied for best year ever.

8. Attitude toward school (happy face survey) is better than ever before.

Figure 8.1 Radar Chart

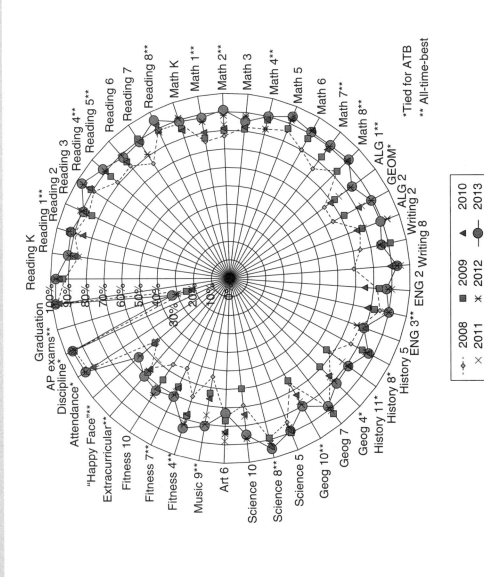

EVERYBODY FINDS THEMSELVES ON THE RADAR CHART

All employees, involved in instruction, need to be able to find themselves on the radar chart. That said, too many vectors can be placed on the chart. "If we can't identify a decision that could be affected by a proposed measurement and how it could change those

> *All employees, involved in instruction, need to be able to find themselves on the radar chart.*

decisions, then the measurement simply has no value" (Hubbard, 2010, p. 47). "The variables that clients used to spend the most time measuring were those with a very (even zero) information value" (p. 111). Everybody finding themselves at least once is the key to how many vectors are on the radar chart.

"The real obstacles to measurement . . .are mostly conceptual, not the lack of understanding of dozens of more complicated methods" (p. 119). The more complicated statistical tools are best suited for analysis and not for the synthesis required to manage the whole school district. Readers of this book often have earned their doctorate but probably have not been taught synthesis statistical tools.

One way to assist people in seeing the power of the radar chart is to compare it to the normal way of communicating **results data**. Each of the vectors on the radar chart could be replaced by a line or bar chart. For example, I created two run charts: one with a line (Figure 8.2) and one with columns (Figure 8.3). These graphs are clear and easily understood.

Figure 8.2   One Vector of Radar Chart as Line Graph

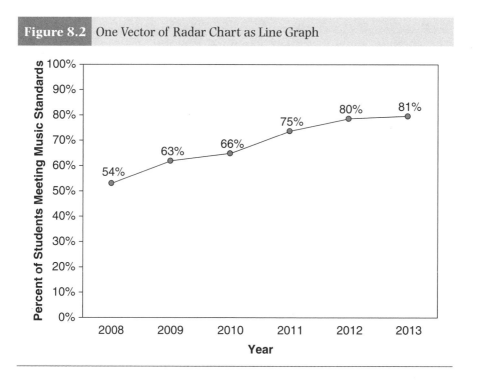

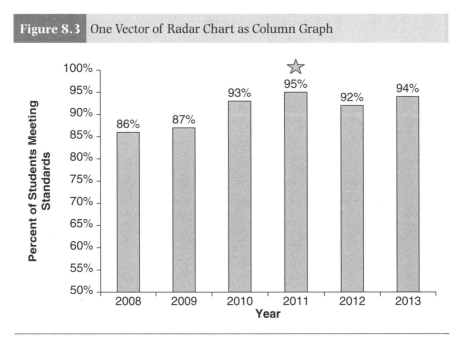

Figure 8.3   One Vector of Radar Chart as Column Graph

The problem comes when people are presented with forty-five of these, each shown on a separate PowerPoint slide. The mind is overwhelmed with all of these charts displayed one by one. So, the radar chart is actually quite refreshing, as people can study one sheet of paper and have a very complete picture of their school or school system. "Measurements that are useful are often much simpler than people first suspect" (Hubbard, 2010, p. 7).

STORIES AND POWER PLAYS VERSUS THE CHART

"The difference between using anecdotes to prove a point and using science to prove a point is that in science you can't just cherry-pick the story that suits you best" (Gilbert, 2012, p. 87). We all know that leaders, far too often, make decisions based upon stories or pressure applied to them. The radar chart is a key tool for leaders because it can be used to require the story teller and power broker to look at the radar chart together while dispensing their story or power. The leader can continually refocus the conversation upon the whole organization and not the sub-optimized story.

The more complicated statistical tools are best suited for analysis and not for the synthesis required to manage the whole school district.

INTRODUCING THE RADAR CHART

I have two recommendations for sharing school progress using radar charts. First, explain the radar chart to school board members prior to the public meeting so members can spend time discussing the data rather than trying to figure out how to read the chart. "Think about how much time could have been saved by simply laying out the big issues side by side on the table and letting everybody just take a look" (Roam, 2010, p. 57). Board members will really appreciate not having to look at fifty or more data slides at the annual accountability board meeting. Second, print the radar chart on 11×17 paper when possible and always print in color. "Leaders must first understand the current situation in detail and the gaps between it and the ideal solution" (Liker & Convis, 2012, p. 76). The radar chart is all about gaps! The radar chart lets leaders celebrate successes and study gaps at the exact same time.

SUB-OPTIMIZATION

Sub-optimization is the enemy of schooling; it occurs when one aspect of the organization wins at the expense of the whole organization. Suppose a car has the best engine ever manufactured, but the car is always in the repair shop because the steering, brakes, suspension, or transmission is faulty. The car manufacturer was sub-optimized by the engine division. Sub-optimization can occur in any organization. The radar chart, with the whole district's data on one sheet of paper, assists leaders in the optimization of the school district.

> *Sub-optimization is the enemy of schooling; it occurs when one aspect of the organization wins at the expense of the whole organization.*

The federal government has sub-optimized education in many ways. The Individuals with Disabilities Act (IDEA) gave rights to disabled students, but Congress refused to keep its promise to fund it. The federal government currently provides about one-third of the funds for special education that it committed to in the original legislation (Education Commission of the States Newsletter, March 5, 2015). Therefore, school systems must subtract from the total education of the system to fund federal mandates. Even though the mandates are generally good, just like a top-notch engine is good, the overall damage is significant.

Next, the federal government passed No Child Left Behind (NCLB) putting intense pressure on schools for reading and mathematics test scores. When the legislation is successful, the schools have great engines (reading) and transmissions (math), but the rest of the car is a junk heap. All over the United States, elementary schools have virtually eliminated

Since social studies was left out, I see a dismal future for history and geography—classic sub-optimization.

science, history, and geography; only reading and math are taught. Science is beginning to be tested, so it is making somewhat of a comeback. Since social studies was left out, I see a dismal future for history and geography—classic sub-optimization.

An Australian mining company was not obtaining the results they wanted. Management was the problem. Management finally realized they "preach 'tons, tons, and tons' every day to every crew, and now we're surprised that's what they're doing" (Liker & Franz, 2011, p. 212). Does this remind you of the politician who preaches NCLB accountability day in and day out and then is surprised that students don't know much about US history?

TAKE CONTROL OF THE DATA

Back to the radar chart; it is the leader's greatest tool for avoiding the evils of sub-optimization. In front of everybody is the whole picture. Of course, the data points required by state agencies are on the radar chart, but the school system is not limited to these subjects. The district leaders are free to add what is important to them so that all employees can find their contributions on the radar chart.

Additions on Figure 8.1, beyond state mandates, are writing in Grades 2, 7, and 12; science in Grades 5, 8, and 10; extracurricular participation; reading and math in kindergarten, Grades 1 and 2; history in Grades 5, 8, and 11; geography in Grades 4, 7, and 10; art in Grade 6; music in Grade 9; physical fitness in Grades 4, 7, and 10; "happy face" results; attendance; discipline; Advanced Placement exams; and graduation rate. State boards of education determine what is successful for state-mandated exams, but for the additional measures, districts make the determinations. For example, if schools expect second graders to read at 100 words per minute and be able to explain what they read, then what percentage of students met this standard? If successful behavior is determined to be either one or zero discipline referrals for the year, then what percentage of students met this criterion? Local agencies can take control of the data by including everybody.

AVERAGES DO NOT BELONG ON THE RADAR CHART

The number entered into the radar spreadsheet is *never* an average. For example, it is not the average attendance rate. It is what percentage of students met the standard for successful attendance. If a system determines that 172 days of attendance out of 180 days (95%) is success, then what percentage of students met this criterion? Further, for the students who enrolled after the beginning of the school year, what percentage of students were present 95 percent of the possible days? I have given three examples of possible standards—

The number entered into the radar spreadsheet is never an average.

Grade 2 reading, school behavior, and attendance; educators must come to agreement on all standards to be included on the radar chart. "There are no problems without standards. Problems are the gaps between the standards and the actual" (Liker & Convis, 2012, p. 115). The standard setting process of describing "perfect" is so crucial in building a culture of continuous improvement. Perfect is displayed on the outer edge of the radar chart and when the school system has a record of continuous improvement from year to year, the data is visible for all to see.

The power of the radar chart will be completely lost if a school chooses to use it for averages. The servant leader wants to know what percentage of students did not meet standards, not the average correct for the student body. What does the servant leader do with the data that first-grade students read, on the average, forty words per minute? Not much. However, the servant leader can go to work when the radar chart shows that 12 percent of the first-grade students did not meet the standard of sixty words per minute.

TRIANGULATION

One of the contributors to sub-optimization is the requirement for triangulation. This means that the district must have three test scores for every student in reading and mathematics. The logic is that one cannot put too much weight on one exam, but if all three show the same results, then the tests must be accurate. The educators responsible for improving reading and math are doing their best for reading and mathematics. However, these educators are not responsible for the whole of education; they are

One of the contributors to sub-optimization is the requirement for triangulation.

thinking analysis and not helping the people responsible for synthesis. At the local level, educators naturally respond with the complaint, "Who has time to test reading and math three times and then think about science, history, geography, art, music, and physical education?"

Much better than triangulation is some data in each aspect of schooling. When the need arises to ascertain if an assessment is correct for an individual student, there are ample assessments that can be given to these individuals without wasting everybody's time.

A–F GRADES FOR SCHOOLS

People in schools really do want to improve and the greatest motivation for improvement is evidence that past efforts worked.

"Where are we now?" is a much more complex question than giving the school a grade of A–F. The theory behind the A–F designation is classic extrinsic, carrot-and-stick, motivation. The radar chart, on the other hand, is based upon intrinsic motivation. People in schools really do want to improve and the greatest motivation for improvement is evidence that past efforts worked. We have known since the 1970s that grades motivate half of the students and we'll soon learn that grades motivate half of the schools. However, with the radar chart and intrinsic motivation, we can expect to see a much higher percentage of schools improving. "People are asking for better schools, with no clear idea of how to improve education nor even how to define improvement of education" (Deming, 1994, p. 8). The radar chart goes a long ways toward defining improvement in education.

Reflection

What questions do you anticipate school board members might ask when studying the radar chart, Figure 8.1?

The second iteration of the Optimization Matrix is shown in Figure 8.4. It combines the optimization of student success (Chapter 5) with the optimization of all academic subjects.

LOOKING AHEAD

The next continuous strategic improvement step is to use the radar chart for a second purpose, improvement of education. The radar chart not only gives an accurate picture of "where we are now" but is used as the cover and table of contents for the strategic, improvement plan. "We know that people are happiest when they're appropriately challenged—when they're trying to achieve goals that are difficult but not out of reach. Challenge and threat are not the same thing. People blossom when challenged and whither when threatened" (Gilbert, 2012, p. 87). The next chapter organizes systemic challenges for everybody.

Figure 8.4   Optimization Matrix

	Sub-Optimize	Optimize
Optimize	All students are honored for improving in depleted curriculum. Some subjects rob time from other subjects.	All students are honored for improving in rich curriculum. No subjects can rob time from other school subjects.
Sub-Optimize	Some students honored in depleted curriculum. Some employees know their contribution to success of system. Some subjects rob time from other subjects.	No subject can rob time from other school subjects. Some students honored in rich curriculum. Some employees know their contribution to success of system.

PEOPLE

SYSTEM

9 *The Strategic Plan*

We know that people are happiest when they're appropriately challenged.

—Daniel Gilbert, 2012

The numerals in parenthesis on every vector of Figure 9.1 are the only change made to the Figure 8.1, the radar chart. The two figures are identical twins. These numerals are page numbers, as the radar chart, is now the table of contents for the strategic plan. Figure 9.1 is also located at http://resources.corwin.com/jenkinsoptimize.

The data are now linked to the planning. If an aspect of the district is important enough to have its own history, on its own vector, then it is important enough to improve. The idea for improvement is written on one page and the numerals in parentheses tell readers on which page to look for any particular strategic plan.

THE TWO UNDERSTANDINGS

The radar chart displayed as Figure 8.1 clearly displays the gaps between perfect and current results. The radar chart moves the leader from spreadsheet to graph. The next transition is from radar chart to strategic planning; two understandings are essential for this move. The first is "the idea that the goal is perfection, and therefore that every process can be improved" (Liker & Ogden, 2011, p. 13) and the second "is the truth that nothing is perfect and everything can be improved" (p. 14).

> *If an aspect of the district is important enough to have its own history, on its own vector, then it is important enough to improve.*

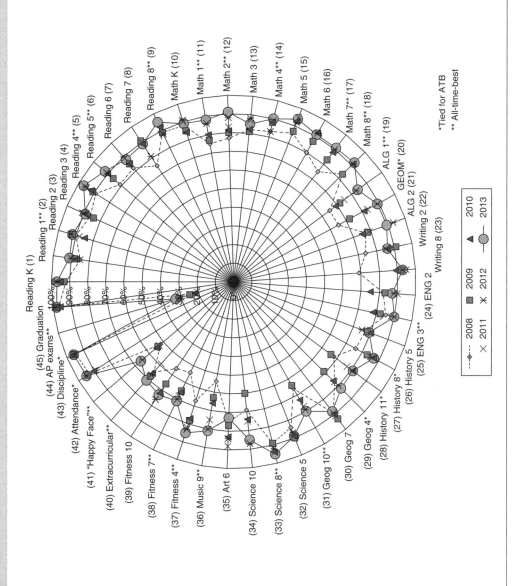

Figure 9.1 Radar Chart as TOC for Strategic Plan

99

Continuous strategic improvement rests on a deep, unwavering adherence to these two understandings.

THE STRATEGIC PLAN OUTLINE

The current concept of a strategic plan is a glorified to-do list approved by the school board. It is basically a top-down document prepared by the administrators. I estimate that 99.9 percent of the teachers and support staff have no interest in the success of the plan. Further, they do not know which items are checked off or when this occurs.

The strategic plan with continuous strategic improvement is a top-down/bottom-up document. The top-down aspects are

1. Creation of the radar chart

2. Communicating that the gaps (waste) on the radar chart are problems to be addressed in the strategic plan

3. The required outline for each page of the strategic plan which is

   a. The problem

   b. Root cause(s)

   c. Countermeasure

4. Root cause analysis (RCA) staff development

5. Deadline for submitting pages for the school or district strategic plan

The bottom-up aspect of the strategic plan is staff members write the plan. It includes

1. Writing down the problem shown on the radar chart

2. The root causes of the problem

3. The selected countermeasure to be tested in the upcoming year

Leaders have every opportunity to practice servant leadership in this process. First of all, leadership is present; the leadership in "servant leadership" is not on vacation. Secondly, the leader should do everything possible to help staff members be successful with their countermeasures.

One of the major advantages of this process is that teams of people are agreeing upon one countermeasure to test for the school year. We have amazingly creative people in America's classrooms, but we have a problem. "If a person creatively improves the work but it does not become a standard, then the work is only improved while that particular person is doing it. And nobody else will build upon that improvement" (Liker & Meier, 2006, p. 112). When a group of people test one person's creative idea, the success can become a part of the culture, instead of one teacher's idea that dies when he retires.

All employees will know some of the results for the strategic plan because they wrote the countermeasures and conducted the experiment. The strategic plan is a living document, updated and owned by everyone.

TOO MUCH!

School leaders initially respond that there are too many vectors and thus too much planning; after all, forty-five (more or less) plans is a great deal of planning. This is correct in a top-down organization where the administrators and board write the strategic plan. Deming (1994) wrote, "This book is for people who are living under the tyranny of the prevailing style of management" (p. xv). By that he meant everything was top-down with all intrinsic motivation smashed to smithereens. There is a top-down component to continuous strategic improvement: the creation of the radar chart, the distribution of the radar chart, the requirement that there be an annual countermeasure (hypothesis) written for each indicator on the radar chart, and then staff development. Continuous strategic improvement, however, is both top-down and bottom-up. District leaders are not writing the hypotheses but are mandating that those closest to the students write them. This is the bottom-up aspect of continuous strategic improvement. Research in psychology supports this process. "The most effective, autonomy-supportive managers and teachers allow their workers or students (whether individually or as a group) to play a role in decision making" (Deci, 1995, p. 145).

THE OUTLINE FOR PLANNING

The outline for each page of the strategic plan is (1) the problem, (2) the root cause(s), and (3) one countermeasure written as a hypothesis. Closing the gap between the outer circle of the radar chart and current results is the purpose of the countermeasure. In a single page, "a 'problem-solving story' that summarizes the problem, its root cause, and the countermeasures taken to solve the problem" is written (Liker & Convis, 2011, p. 95).

Closing the gap between the outer circle of the radar chart and current results is the purpose of the countermeasure.

Educators have been convinced that strategic plans are to be written for five years. Clearly one can write a five-year to-do list, but this is far too long for a strategic plan where educators are checking results against the plan. "It is rarely possible—or even particularly fruitful—to look too far ahead. A plan can usually cover no more than 18 months and still be reasonably clear and specific. So the question in most cases should be, Where and how can I achieve the results that will make a difference within the next year and a half?" (Drucker, 2009, p. 39). For education, the countermeasures will be for the next year only. If success is achieved with a certain countermeasure, there is no reason to drop this plan and change direction; stay with the success for as long as possible.

BURDEN, THEN VISION

The easiest step with the continuous strategic improvement is naming the problem; it is actually self-evident from the radar chart. For example, 10 percent of Grade 4 students did not meet the district's math standard on Figure 9.1. "Burden always comes first, then vision" (Maxwell, 2002, p. 1189). The gap between perfect and where we are now is the *burden*, a synonym for the problem. Next is determining root causes. The root causes cannot be a blame game; it must be an aspect of education that educators control. Blaming kids, parents, poverty, board members, or the legislature is not determining a root cause. In most organizations, people skip the root cause step either by blaming others or by jumping straight to solutions without identifying the problem to be solved. "As often happens, the team members skipped over the understanding of the problem and started firing off ideas about how they could start fixing things" (Liker & Franz, 2011, p. 193). One Arizona school district, with disappointing results on the state reading test, was prepared to purchase a new phonics program. They saw the problem—poor reading scores—skipped root cause analysis and jumped to a solution. However, when we completed a Pareto Chart on reading errors, it was discovered that the biggest reading problem in the school district was knowledge of literature, not phonics. At other times, the team members reject the root cause. "When root causes were uncovered, they were dismissed because they ran counter to tribal knowledge or 'years of experience'" (Liker & Franz, 2011, p. 219). In my book, *Permission to Forget: And Nine Other Root Causes of America's Frustration with Education*, I argue that one of our biggest root causes of educational problems is teachers are spending too much time grading papers and thus not nearly enough time thinking and planning. This root cause is almost always immediately rejected because it is counter to years of experience and thinking about the wrong teacher responsibilities.

In most organizations people skip the root cause step either by blaming others or by jumping straight to solutions without identifying the problem to be solved.

DIFFICULT, YET ESSENTIAL AND VITAL

What is being described is difficult, essential, vital work. "You can't get by just slapping Band-Aids on problems or even with 'good enough' solutions to a problem. The rest of the production line [future grade levels, for education] depends on problems being solved at the root cause so that they do not return" (Liker & Ogden, 2011, p. 16). Some readers will be repulsed by the fact that there are Toyota quotes sprinkled throughout this book. From my perspective, I did not research Toyota books because of a love of cars or even their cars; it was because of their decades of experience with continuous improvement. And since education does not have even one decade of experience with continuous improvement, here goes again. "The Toyota Way demands that any problem be thoroughly investigated before any conclusions are reached. It demands that problem solvers 'go and see' the problem firsthand and not rely on abstract, thirdhand reports. It demands thoughtful and critical reflection to find root causes and develop effective solutions. Most of all, it demands that every team member openly bring problems to the surface and work to continuously improve what is within their control" (Liker & Ogden, 2011, p. xv). Compare this with what Edward Deci (1995) says normally occurs in organizations: "By failing to deal effectively with the stresses and pressures in their own lives, individuals add stresses and pressures to the lives of others" (p. 1). Determining what to do from spreadsheets adds stress and pressure, while "go and see" provides help and hope.

DIGGING DEEPER

One of the first root cause questions that could be asked by fourth-grade teachers is, "In what mathematics strand did the Grade 4 students make the most errors?" Figure 9.2 is a Pareto Chart from Grade 4; it displays the mathematics errors from most to fewest. All the information necessary to create a Pareto Chart is almost always included in state test reports, but it must be mined (see Resource Y for directions to create Pareto Charts). The report tells educators what percentage of students answered questions correctly in each strand. In the example provided, 630 students were administered the exam with errors in rank order.

Figure 9.2   Elementary Mathematics Pareto Chart

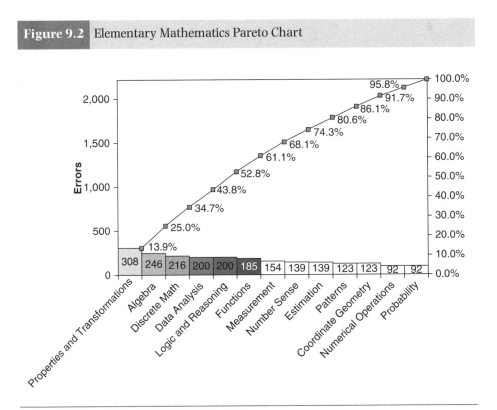

MORE QUESTIONS EQUALS MORE ERRORS?

It is often true that more questions equals more errors, it is not always true. There were seven questions in data analysis and only four in discrete math for the data utilized to create Figure 9.2. Further, there were nine questions in properties and transformations and ten questions in algebra. There is not a perfect correlation between number of questions and number of errors. For the data to be helpful, educators need to know the ranking of the error count with minimal regard to the number of questions. Often, the test contractors inform districts how their students compared strand by strand with other school systems. This information is useless in creating a working counter-measure to bring the district closer to perfect. In this example, the hypothesis for strategic planning must be a countermeasure to reduce errors.

Toyota does not believe that a "countermeasure is *the* solution; rather, it is the measure that is currently being tested" (Liker & Franz, 2011,

p. 30). This is quite different from most organizations, including educational ones where "planning for an experiment, checking, and adjusting based on the outcomes of a particular action are nonexistent" (Liker & Franz, 2011, p. 37). Continuous strategic improvement requires "continuous innovators everywhere all the time" (p. 21).

Returning to Figure 9.2, fourth-grade teachers may decide to establish their annual countermeasure to reduce errors in numerical operations. They could, however, after studying the Pareto Chart realize that geometric properties was not taught at all. Their countermeasure could be written to allocate ten days in their pacing guide for instruction in geometric properties.

Another possible countermeasure is to look at the first three strands that together are approximately 50 percent of errors. Their countermeasure could be to attach these three as a unit. It must not be lost that the countermeasures are quite different from what normally occurs when problems surface. Typically, there's no root cause analysis and people run head first into solutions such as new textbooks, a computer for every student, revised homework policy, and daily pacing guides mandated from the top down. The "solution" has nothing to do with the problem and often costs a lot of money. I have used both the plural root causes and the singular root cause in this chapter. When educators sit down to determine what is causing their problem, there will almost always be multiple root causes. However, on the strategic plan, my advice is to work on one and only one root cause. "Attempting everything, like attempting nothing, will suck the life out of you. It will sap you of energy and new opportunities. And whatever momentum you have going for you will be diminished" (Maxwell, 2007, p. 41). One countermeasure per vector on the radar chart is plenty.

NO PERFECT SOLUTION

I have focused upon mathematics strands for root cause analysis and the establishment of the annual countermeasures written as hypotheses. However, the gap between 100 percent and current results might be decreased by focusing upon a subset of students. Maybe there are students who did not receive the necessary instruction because of a glitch in scheduling. Educators are admonished to look at all aspects of schooling, prior to agreement on the plan that has the most promise for closing the achievement gap. "The philosophy of continuous improvement begins with the assumption that there is no perfect solution, nor is it desirable to spend excessive time trying to find one" (Liker & Meier, 2007, p. 132). Peter

Drucker (2009) stated the same advice in a more direct way: "To aim at results that cannot be achieved—or that can be only under the most unlikely circumstances—is not being ambitious; it is being foolish" (p. 39).

NO QUOTA

The educators must not write a numerical goal as a part of their strategic planning. This is foolishness.

The educators must not write a numerical goal as a part of their strategic planning. This is foolishness. The plan is a hypothesis written to counter one of the root causes of an identified problem and success will be moving closer to perfection. Success is not meeting a quota; it is merely getting better. An industry admonition that applies equally well to education is, "If you can't ask an operator to make exactly 15% bad parts every day, how can you ask him or her to make exactly 0% or even 1%?" (Ha, 2002, p. 64).

OPTIMIZATION FOR EVERYBODY

Since continuous strategic improvement is a top-down/bottom-up process, everybody involved in instruction must participate. "The Toyota Way means more dependence upon people, not less. . . You depend upon the workers" (Liker, 2004, p. 36). It will occur that something or somebody is left off the radar chart and thus some teachers might think they do not need to contribute to the collection of countermeasures. Wrong. The solution is to add vectors to the radar chart so that all employees are enriched. "The opportunity to make even these small choices had made a difference in their experience and had strengthened their intrinsic motivation . . . People who were asked to do a particular task but allowed the freedom of having some say in how to do it were more fully engaged by the activity—they enjoyed it more—than people who were not treated as unique individuals" (Deci, 1995, pp. 33–34). "When everyone has a part in the change, fear of change will vanish" (Orsini, 2013, p. 41). If sub-optimization is to be avoided, then everybody is included. For example, twelfth-grade government is not on the radar chart included in Chapters 8 and 9. The problem is corrected by adding government and establishing a standard for success. The government teachers will then add their countermeasure as a hypothesis to close the achievement gap along with everybody else.

When adding electives for high school, leaders will need to decide what is100 percent. Is 100 percent all of the students in the school or is it

100 percent of the students in the classes? Advanced Placement (AP) can be used as an example of the thinking necessary for this determination. If the goal of a high school is to have every student score a 3, 4, or 5 on an AP exam, then 100 percent is the enrollment in the junior and senior classes. If there is not a goal of every student meeting this standard, then 100 percent is the AP enrollment.

If a school is located in a ranching or farming community and there is the desire that all students enroll in agriculture courses, then 100 percent is all students. On the other hand, if ag is a relatively small program, then 100 percent is the students enrolled in agriculture.

Another possibility is a district requirement that every student complete at least one vocational course. Then the radar chart could display the percent of students meeting standards in their particular course.

ROLE OF SENIOR LEADERS

The beauty of continuous strategic improvement is everybody has a countermeasure to diminish the negatives of a root cause. "The role of the senior leaders is not to judge the solution of those close to the problem as much as it is to judge the problem-solving process used to arrive at the proposed solution" (Liker & Ogden, 2011, p. 15). In business, "innovation is killed with the two deadliest words . . . Prove it" (Martin & Riel, 2010, p. 72). In education, we say the same thing with other words—Where is your research? Further, senior leaders must communicate often that "people are responsible for innovation—it does not come from computers" (Liker & Franz, 2011, p. 52). Administrators can have constructive conversations with teachers regarding their countermeasure for problem solving and how the testing of their hypothesis is going. Further, there are results at the end of the year. From the perspective of the superintendent (or director in Canada), this amount of strategic planning seems overwhelming. Remember, each staff member is involved in very few, or even one, of the countermeasures. Compare this to staff members implementing three to five new programs every year and you will find an increase in morale. Jeffrey Liker and James Franz (2011) wrote, "The effort that was being put forth in the attempt to identify root causes of long-standing issues and in trying countermeasures to deal with them was definitely a morale booster" (p. 218). "As we try ideas, some will fail, but we still learn something important from each thing we try" (p. 71). Educators also model for students that failure is a part of achieving success because "success is falling down and getting up one more time without end" (Collins, 2009, p. 123).

A school or school system cannot be optimized without everybody's contribution. Everybody means everybody: teachers, administrators, support staff, and the leaders of all district office functions. We even need contributions from students, as outlined in Chapter 5.

The Optimization Matrix (Figure 9.3) now includes the statement that all employees involved with student learning can see the result of their work. The next year's radar chart records results after a year of testing the countermeasures. If an employee cannot find the result of their work on the radar chart, there were not enough vectors. Somebody was missed in the planning process.

Reflection

If every employee is testing a countermeasure and each student testing a hypothesis, how will conversations change?

Figure 9.3   Optimization Matrix

	Sub-Optimize	Optimize
Optimize	All students are honored for improving in depleted curriculum. All employees know how they contributed to success of system. Some subjects rob time from other subjects.	All students are honored for improving in rich curriculum. All employees know how they contributed to success of system. No subject can rob time from other school subjects.
Sub-Optimize	Some students honored in depleted curriculum. Some employees know their contribution to success of system. Some subjects rob time from other subjects.	No subject can rob time from other school subjects. Some students honored in rich curriculum. Some employees know their contribution to success of system.

PEOPLE (vertical axis label)

SYSTEM

More has been added to the Optimization Fishbone (Figure 9.4). Sub-optimization has been added as a subtraction and there are more all-time-bests to celebrate at the far right.

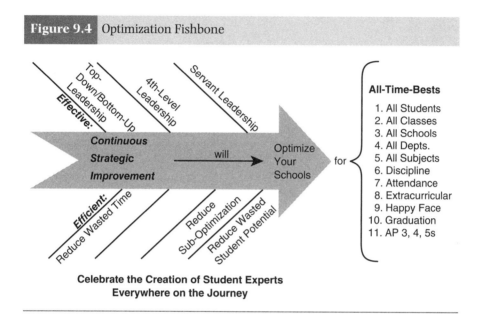

Figure 9.4   Optimization Fishbone

**Celebrate the Creation of Student Experts
Everywhere on the Journey**

LOOKING AHEAD

When readers look at the radar charts, the subjects are lined up: K math, 1 math, 2 math, and so forth. However in reality, curriculum is not aligned. The same content is taught over and over and over. Alignment, with "each other" is essential for continuous strategic improvement to have the highest probability of overall success. Alignment and stabilization are next in Chapter 10.

10 *Alignment and Stabilization*

The unparalleled vagueness of our curricular guides makes our system the most chaotic and unfair in the world.

—Don Hirsch, 2006

The **alignment** of key concepts and performance expectations from grade level to grade level and course to course is absolutely essential. The aligned documents are written in student-friendly language and posted on the school's website. In addition, printed copies are given to students, parents, instructional assistants, librarians, and special education staff. It takes at least a day, and probably more, for teachers to align and stabilize the content for one subject, K–12. Alignment is skipped in most school districts and **stabilization** is not even considered. The result is like being on a rocking horse, going nowhere fast. The proper place to spend time and money to go nowhere fast is a carnival.

> The alignment of key concepts and performance expectations from grade level to grade level and course to course is absolutely essential.

WHY ARE ALIGNMENT AND STABILIZATION SO IMPORTANT?

Why does this responsibility rise to the top of the to-do list? E. D. Hirsch (2006) explains it best. He writes, "The vagueness of the local guidelines produces an educational experience that is sparse, repetitive, incoherent, and fragmented. For teachers, the incoherence produces an intensely unsatisfactory professional experience, which induces a large percentage of them to leave the profession each year" (p. 117). "The unparalleled vagueness of our curricular guides makes our system the most chaotic and unfair in the world" (p. 119). E. D. Hirsch did not say we had the most chaotic and unfair teachers in the world, he did not say we had the most chaotic and unfair administrators in the world and he did not make the comments about our school boards. He did not blame people but clearly stated that our system is a mess. And since it is not our people that are a mess, the current legislative habit of more and more teacher evaluation, implementation of merit pay, and ranking of teachers by test scores does not address this chaotic and unfair system. It is the lack of alignment and stabilization that makes the system so chaotic.

"Lastly, and in some ways most importantly," writes Marc Tucker (2012), "the various pieces of the policies and practices in the top-performing countries were developed to work smoothly together. The ministries of education are deeply committed to the effectiveness and efficiency of the system as a whole. In the United States, we keep adding more programs, more initiatives, more laws, more regulations, all piled on what went before. There is no system" (p. 26).

> Teachers going into their classrooms and doing their best in a chaotic system does not educate children well.

"Much is left to individuals to figure out, and people make gallant efforts to produce good results" (Liker & Meier, 2007, p. 112) but, "No amount of care or skill in workmanship can overcome fundamental faults of the system" (Deming, 1994, p. 33). Teachers going into their classrooms and doing their best in a chaotic system does not educate children well.

ALIGN TO WHAT?

Educators naturally think of alignment as matching local expectations with state or Common Core State Standards. Alignment with state responsibilities is only one step. The more important component is alignment with *each other*, grade by grade, kindergarten through Grade 12. Everything needs to be aligned including spelling words, geography locations and vocabulary, Latin and Greek prefixes, suffixes and root words, mathematics concepts, literary terms, and so on. The textbooks cannot be depended upon to align content. Some publishers focus upon elementary grades, some on high school, and almost nobody is publishing K–12. Alignment of curriculum seems to not even be a consideration.

Central to Deming's approach was a radical expansion of the definition of *customer*. Historically, customers were considered to be the end users of a product. In education, we would say the students are the end users of our efforts. "Deming taught that 'the customer' is also the next stage of a process" (Liker & Ogden, 2011, p. 7). The middle school teachers are the customers of the elementary teachers, for example. Elementary teachers must know what the middle school teachers expect. It is the alignment of the key concepts and performance expectations that makes this possible. The elementary teachers know what students will be learning in the middle school and how their work makes the middle school's success possible. "Stevenson and Stigler found that teachers have much greater job satisfaction when they can depend on one another in a supportive chain over the grade levels" (Hirsch, 2006, p. 118).

STUDENT FRIENDLY

These aligned key concepts, principles, vocabulary, and performance expectations are to be written in student-friendly language. The documents by course and grade level are posted on the school system's website and provided in print to students, parents, and support staff. Instead of wasting time creating pyramids of who reports to whom, let's diagram the learning expectations. "A diagram, as an organizational chart, is far more meaningful than the usual pyramid . . . A pyramid does not describe the system of production. It does not tell anybody how his work fits into the work of other people in the company" (Deming, 1994, p. 60).

> Instead of wasting time creating pyramids of who reports to whom, let's diagram the learning expectations.

It is common for educators to provide students with sentences or paragraphs with errors. The students are to find the errors. This editing practice (often called *daily oral language*) is positive; we do want students to become good editors. The problem is there is no editing system in US schools. What errors do we expect students to find in Grade 1? Grade 2? Grade 3? Editing practice occurs in many locales all the way to Grade 12, but nobody knows what editing skills are expected at each grade level. So, the student-friendly documents provided to students and posted on the district website, merely state, at each grade level, the expected editing skills. Think how much time this would save teachers as they prepare editing documents; they know what is expected instead of a random selection of errors day after day. It will take representatives from each elementary grade plus the secondary English teachers a full day to align and stabilize the editing system for a school district.

ONLY THE ADMINISTRATORS . . .

Standards are not repeated. When Grade 1 writes down key concepts, no other grade level can have those concepts. They are taken—written only one time. Teachers will naturally reject this notion because they know full well that not all students have learned the content of prior grade levels. Teachers will need copies of learning expectations from prior grade levels for review purposes. However, a review topic is taught differently than a completely new standard. How do teachers generally align now? The teachers ask the students, "Now, you were taught this last year, right?" And the students, on cue, respond, "No, we never saw this before." The adults must be in charge of alignment, not the students. This lack of alignment is not the fault of teachers as they cannot call substitutes for themselves or arrange a summer workday to align curriculum. It is only the administrators who can fund the process of bringing teachers together to align.

> *Teachers will need copies of learning expectations from prior grade levels for review purposes.*

PACING VERSUS ALIGNMENT

The use of pacing guides has spread all across US education in recent years. Pacing guides basically tell teachers what page they are to be teaching on each day of the year, or what objectives are to be taught each day. Some pacing guides are more flexible with required content by the week, month, or even the quarter. Much money has been spent inspecting teachers to be sure they are at the required spot in the curriculum at the right time. I am sure there are teachers who appreciate top-down pacing guides, but I have not met any yet. The teacher I've quoted next uses the term *scope and sequence* instead of alignment. Regardless of terminology, what the teachers are asking for is simple: What is to be taught in my grade level or course, what was taught in prior years, and what is taught next? An elementary teacher wrote, "*We (my partners and I) are completely frustrated with our district and the lack of definitive scope and sequence. I have been teaching for 10 years and we have harped and harped on this at every grade level or district meeting. It is so frustrating!*" (personal communication, 2009). Teachers really do appreciate paid time to collaborate with colleagues to create aligned documents from Grades K–12. When I have had the opportunity to work with teachers to align spelling, it takes much of a day of hard, productive work. Figure 10.1 displays the number of spelling words by grade level and also the number of spelling words in each week's spelling test from current

It is only the administrators who can fund the process of bringing teachers together to align.

and prior grade levels in the Egyptian, IL Elementary School. The document displays both their alignment and stabilization (explained later). I wish readers could listen to teacher conversations with me as the alignment documents are being written. They will hear teachers say, "I didn't know you taught that; I've been teaching it also and never knew," "We just teach the same stuff over and over year after year," and "I've been in this district for 20 years and this is the first time the middle school and high school teachers talked about what each other are teaching." In industry these aligned documents might be labeled standard operating procedures. The purpose of them "is to nip common problems in the bud so that staff can focus on solving uncommon problems that come their way" (Liker & Meier, 2007, p. 115). The common problem is that nobody knows what was taught before and what is taught later. Any administrator who provides time for teachers to align their K–12 curriculum and then provides guidance plus secretarial assistance will be practicing servant leadership in a magnificent way!

Figure 10.1   Alignment and Stabilization

Grade Level	Total New Words for the Year	Words per LtoJ® Quiz	Number of Words From Current Grade	Review Words From Previous Grades
1st	150	12	12	0
2nd	200	16	12	4–1st
3rd	250	20	15	4–2nd 1–1st
4th	300	24	18	4–3rd 2–2nd
5th	400	24	18	4–4th 2–3rd

YEAH, BUT . . .

When I wrote the statement "making sure standards are not repeated," I heard a lot of loud "yeah, buts." I tried to alleviate the concern earlier, but because this is a big issue, here are more details. The solution is to provide the students the key concept list for this year and necessary prior years. For example, it would be wise for the Algebra II teacher to provide, at a minimum, the key concept lists for both Algebra II and Algebra I. Teachers then say, "We are going to start on Algebra II today, the first day of class. If there's anything you do not remember from the Algebra I list, let me know and I'll reteach it to you. Further, every graded exam and every non-graded quiz will have 30 percent of the questions from Algebra I and middle school. This will help you remember and give you a head start on earning a good grade in here. Understand that if I follow the book, which has a huge amount of Algebra I review, you will be bored and we'll not have time to explore the very interesting mathematics at the end of this book."

> *The common problem is that nobody knows what was taught before and what is taught later.*

WHAT ABOUT READING TESTS?

Because of legislative fear attached to reading test scores, we have a generation of students well versed in reading skills but ignorant about the rest of the curriculum. We have been duped into thinking if the car has a great engine (reading), the quality in the rest of the car does not matter. So, when I advocate aligning curriculum for all academic subjects, some will believe their reading test scores will plummet if all subjects are taught. Just the opposite is true, as students will be able to comprehend much more content because they have background knowledge all across the spectrum. Hirsch (2010–2011) writes, "The practical problem of helping all students achieve adequate reading comprehension depends on our schools being able to narrow down what seems at first glance to be vast amounts of heterogeneous information into a teachable repertory that will enable students to understand the diverse texts addressed to the average citizen" (p. 32).

Another "yeah, but" is, "I only introduce some topics; I don't expect mastery of these items." For decades, educators have written curriculum documents with three categories: introduce, master, and reinforce. Introduce is written for two years, master for one year, and reinforce for two years. Thus each concept is written five times. These documents were written for teachers instead of students and probably ended up gathering dust. This process probably met some compliance requirements. I am recommending that the alignment documents include only what students are to place in their long-term memory. *Master* is probably the wrong word for long-term memory but certainly not a harmful word. Of course, teachers can introduce a concept two years early and

Writing everything five times is unproductive. reinforce two years later, but writing everything five times is unproductive. Write curriculum one time and distribute multiple grade-level documents to teachers as needed. The wide distribution of multiple grade levels allows teachers to be in charge of alignment plus know how their work fits into the total system of learning.

Latin and Greek root words, suffixes, and prefixes can be used as an example. My suggestion is that Grade 5 teachers be handed five sheets of paper—one each for Grades 3–7. Thus, teachers know what they are to assure students learn in Grade 5, what is to be reinforced from Grades 3 and 4, and what could be introduced in preparation for Grades 6 and 7. Compare this to typical documents. The teacher is given a list for Grade 5 only. The list includes new items plus selected Grade 3 and 4 items that are considered, by somebody, really important and are to be reinforced. The Grade 3 and 4 items are not italicized, or in some way designated as review. The teacher teaches all on the list as if they were new content, which wastes time and communicates to students that schools are not very well organized. Further, they introduce items, but the teachers really do not know if Grades 6 and 7 and actually going to expect "mastery" of these terms. Let's make this simple: Write key concepts and performance expectations once for one grade level only and distribute as necessary.

STAFF DEVELOPMENT

For readers responsible for staff development, I suggest this activity. Assign groups of two to five people a grade level from kindergarten to Grade 12. Do not assign by room arrangement as you do not want any grade level to be able to hear the conversation of adjacent grade levels. The task is for each group to write down five locations on a globe or map that students should learn at their grade level. Don't take too much time before you bring together the kindergarten and first-grade groups. They are to align, which means that any locations on the first-grade list that are already taken by kindergarten must be erased and replaced with new locations. I have found the participants having fun making harsh buzzer-type sounds when they hear a duplicate location. The next step is to have the kindergarten and first-grade group form a U-shape and invite the second-grade group. They read their list and respond to the *nyet* sounds by replacing their duplicates. This continues all the way up to Grade 12. When the activity is over you have a list of sixty-five locations with no duplicates. This exercise is particularly helpful for administrators who hold the responsibility of bringing together the teachers to make these determinations in their schools. When a group of administrators experience this activity, they return to their respective jobs knowing how unaligned schools are now, how important it is, and know how to guide teachers as they align their actual curriculum. To shorten the time allocation, I have had two groups working at the same time; one is K–5 and the other is 6–12. Then when both groups are done, the overall alignment is completed as a whole group.

Another "yeah, but" is now coming from readers who say, "This geography example sounds like facts and we have computers now. What about 21st century skills?" With computers, students must comprehend what they are reading on the screen. "Comprehension skill cannot be automatically transferred from one text to another because the skill of comprehension is basically the skill of filling in enough of what has been left unsaid—that is, filling in enough of the blanks—to make sense of the text. The ability to fill in these blanks depends entirely on whether children know what is to be filled in" (Hirsch, 2006, p. 37). Students cannot expect to comprehend text if they have no background knowledge. "A content-neutral, skills-oriented concept of education has the unintended effect of depressing reading scores and diminishing the shared content we need for communication and solidarity within the nation as a whole" (p. 107). Of course we want what is referred to as higher-order thinking skills, but higher order built upon nothing equals nothing. "Reading and critical thinking are always based on concrete, relevant knowledge and cannot be exercised apart from what psychologists call 'domain-specific' knowledge" (Hirsch, 2010–2011, p. 31). Television reporters and writers should expect that when news comes out of Morocco they do not need to take time to explain where Morocco is located. Because of computers and smartphones, educators must determine what student experts should be expected to know and what can be looked up on a search engine.

Of course we want what is referred to as higher-order thinking skills, but higher order built upon nothing equals nothing.

In the workshop example, I started with kindergarten and worked up to Grade 12. Often alignment experts advise starting with Grade 12 and working backward. Which is preferred? Actually, both have value. An example of working backward is to download the list of Latin and Greek suffixes, prefixes, and root words necessary to comprehend the vocabulary in high school biology. Then work backward—which of these syllables can be taught in Grade 8, which in Grade 7, and so on. The process of preparing these students for high school biology success can begin in Grade 1. Further, this preparation will involve many different subjects creating a real team effort for future success. I actually prefer aligning both directions: K to 12 and 12 to K. Why? Usually Grade 1 and 2 teachers are not thinking about preparing for high school biology success and so backward planning is perfect. On other occasions, high school teachers do not understand how much six-year-olds can actually learn, so starting with elementary school and moving upward raises the expectations for high school.

POSTING ALIGNED CURRICULUM TWO WAYS

In addition to providing students paper copies of the key concept lists, students can be given the lists electronically and posted on the school's website. I suggest that the aligned lists be posted both vertically and horizontally. The horizontal listing is all the content for a particular grade level or course. The vertical takes one subject, from kindergarten through Grade 12 and posts it.

STOP THE PENDULUM

The third chapter in my 2013 book, *Permission to Forget*, advocates removing the pendulum from education. We have the reading pendulum that moves every twenty years or so from teaching beginning reading with sounds to words to sentences. Some labels readers may recognize are *phonics* (for sound), *Dick and Jane* (for word approach) and whole language or literature-based (for sentence approach). The major pendulum swing, however, is between background knowledge (called *basics* by its advocates) and performance (called *higher-order* or *21st Century skills*). I do not want to be on either side of this argument and want to advocate for a balanced curriculum between background knowledge and performance expectations. So while I have described the alignment process for background knowledge and pointed out how this will help reading comprehension, not harm it, I want to be as passionate about aligning performance expectations. The process is to align the dichotomous rubrics and other performance expectations in every grade and every course. I would align performance second, after the alignment of background knowledge is aligned, however. Why? It is because once background knowledge is aligned and the expectations are communicated on student-friendly documents, background knowledge is learned more quickly, providing more classroom time for performance expectations.

> We have the reading pendulum which moves every twenty years or so from teaching beginning reading with sounds to words to sentences.

WE CAN NEVER LEARN ALL OF THIS

The first time students and parents are provided the complete learning expectations for the whole school year or course, they think, "We'll never learn all of this." However, the shock soon wears off and confidence appears; "Of course, I can learn this in a year." Quickly, the expectation of the families changes also. They want to know ahead of time what is to be learned every year. It pains me to know that education has spent billions of dollars on school reform and the United States still does not have the first step in place: Tell the students what you want them to know and be able to do by the end of the year or course.

"Quality can be broken down into three areas of concern to the customer: (1) design quality, (2) manufacturing quality, and (3) performance quality or reliability" (Ha, 2002, p. 6). For education the terms are (1) *Aligned, stabilized, powerful curriculum* that will produce student experts, (2) *continuous strategic improvement*, and (3) *optimized results*. "The most complex activity in an automobile assembly plant is not making the cars—it is getting all the parts and components into the right place as the production lines move inexorably on" (Liker & Convis, 2012, p. 126). It seems to me that the most complicated part of the administrator's job may be having everything in place. I am not willing to state this is more complicated than the teacher's job, but it is more complicated than all or almost all of the other administrator responsibilities. Logistics is not a part of the everyday vocabulary of administrators, and yet all of this alignment work is logistics over a thirteen-year period. Let's not skip alignment and stabilization in our rush to improve other aspects of education. Remember, "It is only when the process is stable that you can begin the creative progression of continuous improvement" (Liker & Meier, 2006, p. 112).

> *Quickly, the expectation of the families changes also. They want to know ahead of time what is to be learned every year.*

STABILIZATION

Once alignment is completed, the next responsibility is stabilization. Essentially, these decisions make it much more certain that students will become student experts as they retain the content in their long-term memory. Let's take middle school science as an example. The teachers have completed writing the key concepts and performance standards for Grades 6–8 science. There are no duplicates; every concept is new for the grade level as well as every new performance standard. Now comes stabilization.

The Grade 7 science staff wants the students to remember the Grade 6 science. They neither want to reteach Grade 6 nor do they want to communicate that Grade 6 is over; forget it. Stabilization is deciding what percentage of each graded exam and each non-graded quiz will be from Grade 6 curriculum. A typical answer is 30 percent. Now Grade 8 curriculum is added to the mix; what is the percentage of Grade 6 and Grade 7 questions on Grade 8 assessments? The staff could select 20 percent from Grade 6, 20 percent from Grade 7 and then 60 percent from Grade 8. Or the staff could say they want 10 percent Grade 6, 20 percent Grade 7, and 70 percent Grade 8. The top-down direction is to stabilize the curriculum; the bottom-up is the formula.

Stabilization is essential for creating student experts. We can no longer allow students to forget prior years' content! Further, we cannot have student experts if we spend weeks reviewing the prior years' content in the fall. We must start each new year with new content in order to have enough time to teach all of our content. It is the stabilization process that keeps prior years' content in students' long-term memory and, at the same time, provides time for the current year's responsibilities.

The top-down direction is to stabilize the curriculum; the bottom-up is the formula.

The primary reason for stabilization is experts have a great deal of knowledge in their long-term memory. However, a secondary reason is that the authors of major exams expect students to remember content from multiple grade levels. University faculties expect students to actually remember their high school curriculum. We have often wondered how a student with a great grade point average in high school could be assigned to remedial college classes. One of the major reasons is that students in high school could receive all As by cramming for the current course while forgetting the prior grade-level content.

When I have worked with high school teachers to stabilize their curriculum, they often ask questions from as far back as Grade 6 in classes for juniors and seniors. For example, high school math teachers decided to organize the ten-question, non-graded LtoJ® quiz with this structure: one Grade 6 question, one pre-algebra question, one algebra question, two geometry questions, and then five Algebra II questions. Resource M is an example of stabilization for middle and high school science from Massac County, Illinois.

In the Introduction of this book, I described Level 4 leadership. Nowhere is Level 4 leadership more obvious than when administrators work with teachers to align and stabilize the curriculum.

LOOKING AHEAD

A school district could set aside a year to align and stabilize their curriculum. When they study the radar chart, there will be gaps everywhere. I suspect that no vector on the radar chart will have a dot at 100 percent. As written in Chapter 9, the staff members are now given the responsibility to describe the gap, conduct a root cause analysis, and establish countermeasures that people believe will bring the dots closer to perfect. It is here that research from other locales can be of help. I have chosen to reflect upon the meta-analysis of John Hattie as a way of giving readers ideas for countermeasures. Hattie's research is the focus of the next chapter.

11

Strategies Worth Testing

Anecdotal evidence suggests that Americans waste an extraordinary amount of tax money on high-tech toys for teachers and students, most of which have no proven learning value whatsoever.

—Amanda Ripley, 2013

John Hattie's research on "Effect Sizes of Various Influences on Achievement" is the outline I am using for describing aspects of great instruction. Once educators have the aligned and stabilized standards, continuous strategic improvement in place in classrooms and schools, and the establishment of countermeasures is the norm for strategic planning, then they are ready to fully implement what Hattie has found to be more successful. Few, if any, systems can tackle all of the successful strategies Hattie lists, so careful consideration must be undertaken. Further, each initiative chosen for improvement must be considered a countermeasure to a root cause and not a guaranteed improvement. Also, note there is a lot of overlap between what I have written thus far and Hattie's research, so following the sequence I just listed is not entirely possible. This chapter is placed here because the closer any vector gets to 100 percent success on the radar chart, the harder it is to agree on the countermeasures to improve learning. The easy answers have already been utilized and now come the really tough cases. Thus, this chapter of Hattie reflections is written to assist educators in establishing the necessary countermeasures. Of the 138 influences upon student achievement, I have selected thirteen from the top sixteen to elaborate. As you read these thirteen student-achievement influences keep in mind the aim of creating student experts.

SELF-REPORTED GRADES

All over the United States, teachers are recording data on students in a computer database. The former practice of the teacher recording data with a pen or pencil in a grade book has been replaced by the teacher recording the same data in a computer. The result is the same: unengaged students. Engagement is greatly increased when students do almost all of the recording of data.

Let's take reading fluency, for example. Students are assessed on words per minute (WPM) in most primary classrooms. Who records the WPM? The teacher does the recording. Where is it recorded? WPM are recorded in a computer. Far better is for students to graph their own words per minute. Resource P provides a graph for students to record their words read per minute. This graph is to be accompanied with a graph displaying the total words per minute for the whole classroom. I have selected Grade 2, which typically has an expectation of 100 words per minute with both fiction and nonfiction text. Who adds up the total correct for the whole classroom? Designated students have this responsibility, which is best accomplished by using base ten blocks (The selected students do not have WPM by student name, but they do have the numerals in order to calculate the total for the classroom). My opinion is that once students reach 100 WPM with both fiction and nonfiction, I would allow those students to finish their graph for the year and each month give the class credit for these students' 100 WPM; but I wouldn't assess fluency again for these students. Yes, I'd accelerate the curriculum but wouldn't really care if some students read 135 WPM or 162 WPM. The time is better spent helping the student reading 50 WPM. Students are self-reporting their own reading progress and every student in the classroom can explain the graph on the wall with the total WPM for the class as a whole. Even further, in the hallway, outside the second-grade classrooms is a student-created graph of all second-grade students together.

TIME?

Who has time for all this graphing? Students have the time. Remember, Hattie's meta-analysis results indicate that self-reported grades is our number one strategy for improving student learning.

If the standards are written in student-friendly language, the non-graded quizzes twenty-eight times a year are based upon these standards, and if the graded exams are based upon the same standards, then students will be able to predict their grades with great accuracy. If at 40 percent through the year, students can answer 40 percent of the questions about the year's curriculum, then they will know their grade will be an A because they are meeting the standards. There will be no surprise and no need to be involved in last minute cramming.

Who has time for all this graphing? Students have the time.

Students are recording their own results on each of the twenty-eight LtoJ® non-graded quizzes, they are creating the class totals as graphed on class run charts, and they are creating all of the analytical graphs. Therefore, the students are self-reporting as outlined in Hattie's research.

The dichotomous rubric is the most accurate way for students to record, with understanding, their progress on performance assignments and thus their grades. Resource Q is a dichotomous rubric written by Traci Wierman. She is a Curriculum Implementation Network Director for the Lawrence Hall of Science at the University of California, Berkeley. Her work is located at www.scienceandliteracy.org. This rubric utilizes a 1–6 scale making it very clear what is most important to the instructor and what aspect of the work is the "final touch."

After Jeff Burgard, author of *Continuous Improvement in the Science Classroom* (2010), and I developed the dichotomous rubric, Jeff estimated that his students were 85 percent accurate in predicting their rubric score. When they handed in their science paper, they had to estimate their rubric score. Jeff wrote "that the conversation about students over estimating or underestimating their scores is also really valuable. Over confident students are humbled and under confident kids are surprised and impressed with themselves (personal communication, February, 2015). Students can easily follow the dichotomous rubrics and completely understand their scores. Prior to the dichotomous rubric, Jeff said students thought their rubric score depended upon whether or not the teacher liked them. Estimating a rubric score at the completion of an assignment is a form of self-reporting. Resource R includes a graph for recording progress on performance-based assignments evaluated with the dichotomous rubric. It is set for a 1–6 scale to match Wierman's work noted above. Teachers might consider having students record their estimated rubric score on the graph when the work is turned in and then in a different color of pen record the teacher's evaluation. Obviously, the ideal is when the teacher and the student land on the same exact score.

The dichotomous rubric is so important to success with the higher standards being implemented in the United States that Chapter 12 is devoted to this measurement tool. For now, I only want to note that self-reported grades (and I would add self-reported progress) is entirely possible.

John Maxwell (2013) wrote, "I only want to be superior to my former self" (p. 85). This should be true for students, teachers, principals, and school system leaders at local, regional, and state levels. The term for doing better is *all-time-best*—ATB. When students report their own progress, there should be a symbol for ATB or the mere writing on the graph the 3 letters *ATB*.

Another way for students to show progress is to have ATBs on quarterly exams. Many teachers in middle and high school have adopted the process of giving the end-of-the-year final four times during the year. Some teachers make slight changes each quarter and some leave the final exactly the same. The change is not the exam, per se, but the grading scale. Arnie Cerny, biology teacher in Beatrice, Nebraska, has a final of 176 questions. At nine weeks, 44 correct is considered a perfect paper, at semester it is 88, and at third quarter, 132 is perfect. The grading scale is built for each quarter, just as it will be at the end of the year when 176 is perfect. Students record their grades, can visualize their improvement and know what is expected the next time around. No surprises.

> Estimating a rubric score at the completion of an assignment is a form of self-reporting.

Every student can improve and should be thanked for this improvement. Please note that I did not say students should be given stuff for their improvement; I wrote, "thanked."

PIAGETIAN PROGRAMS

In 1978, I concluded a dissertation research study (Jenkins, 1978) utilizing Piagetian research as the foundation. Thus, when I read Hattie's ranking of Piagetian Programs as second most successful strategies, I had the normal, "I told you so" attitude. If we consider the fact that children, at the time they are learning to read are prelogical (*operational* was Piaget's term), then much of our national frustration with reading comes from using methods that do not mesh with the children's logical development. Below is a quick summary of the research.

Forty-six children, ages six to nine, in Marysville, California, were categorized into three cognitive levels on the basis of their responses to five Piagetian tasks—conservation of number, matter, area, volume, and displacement. Thirteen children did not answer any of the questions logically

There were no Piagetian conservers with high reading errors.

and were classified as non-conservers. Twelve children conserved on four or five of the tasks and were classified as conservers. The remaining twenty-one were classified as transitional. An analysis of variance was performed to see if the mean ages of the three cognitive groups differed at the 0.01 level. The age differences were not significant.

Each of the children was administered three language development tests and four reading tests. There were no children in this study who were classified as non-conserver with a high language development score and no children classified as conserver with a low language score. One of the four reading tests was the reading of a 100-word passage. The non-conservers had an average of 46 errors, the transitional conservers had an average of 11 errors, and the conservers an average of 0.3 errors. There were no Piagetian conservers with high reading errors, but there were three non-conservers with few reading errors. However, the three non-conservers who did well on reading the prose test did less well than their conserving peers on the comprehension reading test. Figure 11.1 displays the results.

Figure 11.1 Table of Piagetian Research: Prose Reading Errors From 100-Word Passage

	0–10	11–39	40–85
Non-Conserver	3	2	8
Transitional Conserver	12	8	1
Conserver	12	0	0

IMPLICATIONS FOR EDUCATORS FROM PIAGETIAN RESEARCH

1. Society expects all children to read print at a time when not all of the children are cognitively ready to use rule-based methods to learn how to read print.

2. At the same time we are assisting children with reading print, educators must have means of increasing cognitive development. "Piaget has shown that cognitive development occurs by action upon objects rather than by looking at pictures of objects or hearing about objects" (Jenkins, 1978, p. 130).

3. Beginning reading instruction needs to match the logic of the normal five- or six-year-old child. Reading instruction, which requires memorization and application of rules, may not be successful for the prelogical child.

4. Children who are prelogical in their thought at five and six will not be prelogical their whole life. Therefore, it is crucial to not damage these children's self-concept about being smart enough to read so that when they are more logical they will not be handicapped by a terrible learning-to-read experience.

5. When children think in an illogical manner, educators can help them think more logically. This is not accomplished by telling them the correct answer, but by further questioning. When prelogical children are told correct answers, they make up fantasy to explain why something happened. For example, Evelyn Neufeld placed a nickel in a small nesting plastic egg container. Then, with the child watching, she placed the small container into a medium container. She asked if the nickel was inside the medium container. Children at Piaget's prelogical level said, "No, the nickel is inside the small container." So she asked, "Is the small container inside the medium container?" "Yes," the child answered. So then the question is repeated, but the prelogical child cannot understand that the nickel is inside the small container, and the small container is inside the medium container, and therefore the nickel is inside the medium container. One of these prelogical children overheard another student answer the question correctly, so Evelyn called back the first child. She asked, "Why do you think he thinks the nickel is inside the medium container?" The prelogical child answered, "I think he thinks the nickel crawled out of the small container into the medium container." So, we cannot teach logic, but we can continue to ask thought provoking questions to help children become more logical. Educators can look for every opportunity to ask questions such as, "Are you in the classroom? Are you in the school?" If the student answers yes to both questions, ask, "How can you be in two places at once?" No matter what the child says, do not respond with correct or incorrect. The kids go home and think and think. The questions really do create brain motion.

> *Children who are prelogical in their thought at five and six will not be prelogical their whole life.*

6. Special education teachers, reading specialists, and primary grade teachers need to know how to teach reading without a major focus on teaching rules. Some children in every classroom desperately need this help. Asking children what word they want to learn to read, is but one example of non-rule-based reading instruction. Of course, letter/sound relationships are pointed out as well as syllables, but the prelogical child does not need these rules to remember the word.

> *Counting is one of the very best ways for students to make sense of fractions.*

Mathematics instruction is a prime place to contrast rule-based teaching with making-sense instruction. High school teachers lament that their students have such a poor understanding of fractions and are tempted to blame elementary and middle teachers. Actually the culprit is the inability of students to remember and apply so many rules.

Counting is one of the very best ways for students to make sense of fractions. Provide students with pattern blocks and label the hexagon as 1, the trapezoid as $\frac{1}{2}$, and the 60° rhombus as $\frac{1}{3}$. The assignment is for students to count by fractions to 10. For example, when students are counting by $\frac{1}{3}$'s they place a rhombus adjacent to them and write $\frac{1}{3}$. Then they pick up a second rhombus and write $\frac{2}{3}$. Examples from the sequence of their writing, all the way to 10 follow:

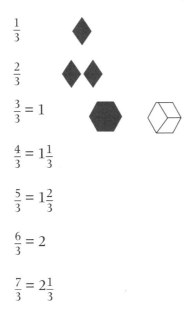

$\frac{1}{3}$

$\frac{2}{3}$

$\frac{3}{3} = 1$

$\frac{4}{3} = 1\frac{1}{3}$

$\frac{5}{3} = 1\frac{2}{3}$

$\frac{6}{3} = 2$

$\frac{7}{3} = 2\frac{1}{3}$

To adults this seems so boring; to children who are learning the system of mixed numerals, this assignment is enjoyable because it makes sense.

A quick Internet search on changing improper fractions to mixed numerals provides rule-based instruction. Here's the summary that makes sense only to the most logical thinkers.

Converting Improper Fractions to Mixed Fractions

A. Divide the numerator by the denominator.

B. Write down the whole number answer.

C. Then write down any remainder above the denominator.

Example: Convert $\frac{13}{4}$ to a mixed fraction.
Divide $13 \div 4 = 3$ with a remainder of 1
Write down the 3 and then write down the remainder (1) above the denominator (4), like this—
$3\frac{1}{4}$.

If elementary mathematics only had this one rule, all students could eventually remember it. However, there are hundreds of rules and many, many give up on math way too soon. Many of our most successful math teachers do not teach rules. Instead, they provide patterned questions and the kids' job is to generate the rules.

> Many of our most successful math teachers do not teach rules. Instead, they provide patterned questions and the kids' job is to generate the rules.

PROVIDING FORMATIVE EVALUATION

Self-reported grades, above, was written, for the most part, about individual student progress. Formative evaluation is about the classroom as a whole. Hattie (2009) wrote, "The formative evaluations were effective across student age, treatment duration, frequency of measurement, and special needs status. When teachers were required to use data and evidence based models, effect sizes were higher than when data were evaluated by teacher judgment. *In addition, when data was graphed, effect sizes were higher than when data were simply recorded. (Italics mine) . . .* The major message is for teachers to pay attention to the formative effects of their teaching, as it is these attributes of seeking formative evaluation of

The reason effect size is higher when graphed versus recorded is because graphs are visible and recordings in a spread sheet stored on the computer and are basically out of sight—out of mind.

the effects (intended and unintended) of their programs that makes for excellence in teaching" (p. 181).

The reason effect size is higher when graphed versus recorded is because graphs are visible and recordings in a spread sheet stored on the computer and are basically out of sight—out of mind. Visible means visible to students, the teacher, parents, and the administrators. Teachers may feel uncomfortable with their progress, or lack of, being so visible. However, when the graph shows progress they want it visible. In addition, when the principals makes their progress visible, it helps teachers.

The student run chart tells the student and parents if the student is making adequate progress toward end-of-year standards. The class run chart, which is a total for everyone, informs the teacher of the same information for the whole class of students. The scatter diagram described in Chapter 15 displays learning gaps and is very useful for disaggregated data when posted beside the aggregated data on the class run chart.

Sometimes I hear, "LtoJ® is not working; my graph is not going up." This teacher misunderstood the purpose of the LtoJ® class run chart. The formative feedback is not a teaching method; it is a way for teachers to know if their teaching methods are working. So, the teacher who says "LtoJ® is not working" needs to know that LtoJ® is working perfectly. The students are not learning what the teacher is teaching, and the really good news is that the teacher knows before the year is over and has time to rectify the situation.

Not only do teachers use formative assessment to improve week to week and month to month, they also want to improve year to year. The annual goal is to outperform all prior years. Figure 11.2 is a class run chart from Codi Hrouda's fourth-grade classroom. The graph shows progress for mathematics quizzes. Each week students are quizzed on seven Grade 4 questions, two Grade 3 questions, and one Grade 2 question. The horizontal line at the top of the graph is the goal, which is to outperform prior years' students. The goal is *not* a number that has no meaning to the students. Even more important, the students and the teacher will not be caught between outperforming prior years and not meeting some arbitrary goal. There is no way I can capture the joy the students experienced when they had an all-time-best that was the best Mrs. Hrouda's classes had ever earned.

| Figure 11.2 | Classroom Annual Goal |

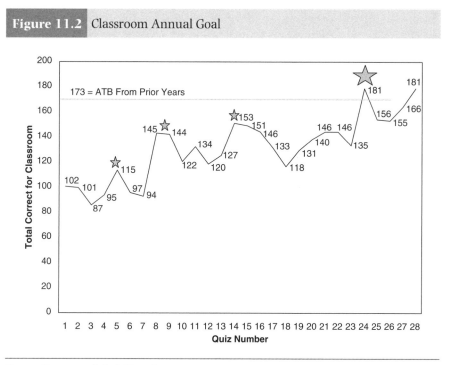

Source: Courtesy of Codi Hrouda.

MICROTEACHING

I am not writing here about the research quoted by Hattie. He writes about mini-lessons taught in the teacher education process with extensive feedback for the future teachers. What I am writing about is the power of mini-lessons as a part of regular classroom instruction. The practice relates to Chapters 5 and 15 with the random selection of key concepts throughout the year. When students are provided the year's key concepts and then given a non-graded quiz on a random sample of the key concepts, obviously some of the key concepts have not yet been taught.

The practice is for the teacher to give a thirty- to sixty-second mini-lesson on content yet to be taught and an estimate when the concept will appear in the curriculum. The statement from the teacher is something like this, "Here is an idea what the concept is about. I'll only take seconds to give you the essence of what you will learn in detail later. I estimate that we'll study this in depth in _____ (month)."

Sometimes, the preview can be an explanation from other students. Laura Walker wrote,

I believe that preview is extremely powerful. I taught a group of 12 high school students after school from 3–4:15 every day in the spring because they had failed their math class. They weren't the most 'school' loving students and hated being there on those pretty spring afternoons. LtoJ® quizzes were the most powerful. I was amazed that they would find excitement in trying to figure out one of the problems [when] they had yet to be exposed to that particular concept. When one of them figured it out, they would show it to the others. It was interesting that they liked this challenge and it wasn't about the grade. It led them to try to make connections from what they had been exposed to in order to be the one student to figure out the problem. These students also would ask more questions about the LtoJ non-graded quiz than they would the one that I actually recorded for a grade. It was fascinating! (personal communication, July 2014)

ACCELERATION

In schools, we can accelerate for all students and we can accelerate for higher achievers. Both are appropriate. Hattie's research shows strong academic gains from acceleration. The Common Core State Standards are an example of acceleration for all students. Much more can be expected and accomplished in our schools.

Recently, I was in a K–12 staff development meeting with teachers who had been asked to bring their math book, if they were teaching mathematics. If they were not teaching mathematics, they were asked to bring another textbook to the session. The teachers were asked to sit adjacent to the teachers assigned to the grade level one above their grade level. (Obviously teachers had to have two meetings; one with teachers teaching one grade below their grade level and another meeting with teachers responsible for one grade level above). The directions were for the teacher at the higher grade level to open up the math textbook to the table of contents and the teacher at the lower grade level was to check off what had already been taught. There was a lot of surprise in the room regarding how much content had already been taught.

There was a lot of surprise in the room regarding how much content had already been taught.

As I walked around the room observing the interaction I asked teachers if last year they finished all the chapters in their math book. Not one teacher said yes. Clearly one way to accelerate learning is for all to stop reteaching last year's and teach all of this year's content. It is not that we never review; it is review on demand instead of review because the math book reteaches last year's lessons for six or more weeks. Time for acceleration in the spring is possible for all, if schools start on the new curriculum in August.

With the LtoJ® process described in Chapters 5 and 15, acceleration also occurs when students have seven perfect quizzes in a row. The students "test out" and the class is given credit for the student's perfect score even though the student no longer takes the LtoJ® quizzes. The time formerly used for the quiz is utilized for acceleration or enrichment. Hattie's research shows little gain in learning from enrichment and thus we need to seriously consider the evidence. My advice is to lean strongly toward acceleration unless enrichment is focused upon creating a student expert. Remember experts know a lot and can do a lot. Helping a student become an expert in one aspect of the curriculum can be extremely valuable, whereas unfocused enrichment should be replaced with acceleration.

CLASSROOM MANAGEMENT

Obviously, students learn more in well-managed classrooms. Our current teachers, in their university years, had friends majoring in business. I can assure you that business majors need several promotions before they have twenty-five or more direct reports. Teachers are not so fortunate; the first day on the job, there are twenty-five or more direct reports. Some in society will want to discount this comparison because teachers' direct reports are so young. Not me—managing a classroom of students is not easy for most people.

Over the years that LtoJ® was developed, it has been found that one tool for managing behavior is the simple dot. Whatever teachers want to monitor can be counted and graphed. For example, if counting classroom interruptions, at the end of each day the total number of interruptions is graphed. The teacher and the students are all working to obtain an all-time-best, which would mean fewer interruptions than any prior day in the school year.

Various educators have graphed absences, minutes wasted due to tardiness, trips to the bathroom, weight of food wasted, and English spoken in the French classroom. I would never say that graphs are the answer to having better-managed classrooms, but I would say that graphing the class progress is one more tool to be used. It creates a team effect instead of the teacher versus the students. Figure 11.3 is a graph of trips to the bathroom, as an example.

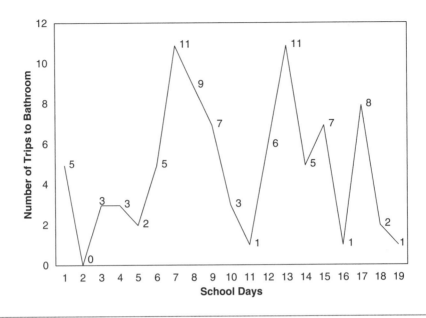

Figure 11.3 Trips to the Bathroom

TEACHER CLARITY

The brain is always attempting to make sense. Whenever I am struggling to learn, it is always a struggle to make sense of what is before me. Once I am able to make sense of the content, learning occurs instantly. The brain naturally disregards nonsense and gravitates toward sense. Teacher clarity, not surprisingly, is one of the most successful teaching strategies because our students need to make sense of the content in order to learn it.

From a continuous improvement perspective, teacher clarity begins with informing students what they will learn for the year.

From a continuous improvement perspective, teacher clarity begins with informing students what they will learn for the year. Student-friendly language is the key. Students have copies of these key concepts and dichotomous rubrics in their data folders. The next step for teacher clarity is to point out on the key concept list or rubrics what is being taught today. Every lesson is connected back to the year's expectations that were provided the first day of school. According to Hattie (2009), "One of the themes in this book is how important it is for the teacher to communicate the intentions of the lessons and the notions of what success means for these intentions" (p. 125).

Beyond these two steps, teacher clarity is a lifetime goal of educators. Day by day, month by month, and year by year, we are all learning how to make content more clear to students. The process never stops. When we ask a student to explain the content to another student, because we believe that the student may be able to explain more clearly, the job of the teacher is to listen to the student explanation.

FEEDBACK

When I present continuous improvement principles to educators, the first difficulty is helping people in the audience to know where to file the content I am presenting. Years ago, I read that the brain may be like a filing system with a place for both new and old content. We learn in three ways: (1) adding to an existing file, (2) starting a new file, and the quickest (3) connecting all the information in one file to another file.

Educators come to my seminars with a file for being evaluated by their boss and another file for evaluating students. Often educators do not have a file for listening to students as a group (feedback). They do have a file for 1:1 conversations with students, but not for listening to what the whole group is doing and thinking. The LtoJ® continuous improvement process, described in Chapters 5 and 15, is a feedback system, which often requires the establishment of a new file in everybody's brain. Feedback answers the question, "Are students placing in their long-term memory what I am teaching?" If not, it is very doubtful than any student experts are being created.

Hattie (2009) wrote, "I realized that the most powerful single influence enhancing achievement is feedback" (p. 12). "Visible teaching and learning occurs when learning is the explicit goal, when it is appropriately challenging, when the teacher and the student both . . . seek to ascertain whether and to what degree the challenging goal is attained . . . and engaging people . . . participating the act of learning . . . The remarkable feature of the evidence is that the biggest effects on student learning occur when teachers become learners of their own teaching, and when students become their own teachers" (p. 22).

> Feedback answers the question, "Are students placing in their long-term memory what I am teaching?"

In addition to the graphs showing student, classroom, and school learning, there are other very powerful tools to use. The plus/delta in Resource D is a simple tool, described earlier, to be used about once a month. Teachers merely ask students to write what went well this month under the + and to write what could make next month better under the delta. A brave teacher, Karen Fauss, from the Enterprise District in

Redding, California, provided parents a report card to fill out on her each time she sent home student reports cards. Now, that is taking feedback very seriously.

Vic Cottrell of Crown Global Consulting in Lincoln, Nebraska, designed a feedback form for teachers to provide students. My rendition of the form is included in Resource S. I have made a few revisions, but the concept is his. In order to use this feedback form, everyone must clearly understand the difference between feedback and evaluation. The students are not asked to evaluate the teacher but to give feedback; evaluation comes from the principal. Thus, the feedback forms are shared with the principal only if the teacher desires. In my work as a staff developer, I have people complete a feedback form at the end of the day. My purpose is to gain insight regarding how I can do a better job the next time I present. My feedback form is in Resource T. I fully recognize that the administrators who invited me to speak in their system are the evaluators; they determine if Lee Jenkins will ever return. Sometime these administrators ask the audience to help them by providing an evaluation questionnaire. The questions for evaluation are completely different than my feedback questions.

TEACHER-STUDENT RELATIONSHIPS

Relationships are developed through 1:1 conversations and by listening. This is true for adult-adult relationships and teacher-student relationships. These positive teacher-student relationships are essential for learning to occur.

How much do you learn from people you don't like? How much do students learn from people they don't like? At what age can people separate their attitude toward the teacher from their attitude toward the subject?

When I ask these questions to educators, the most common responses are that people learn what *not* to do from people they don't like. Even though there are myths about the mean teacher whose students excelled, most teachers did not have this teacher in their youth. Further, few people say they can ever separate their attitude toward the teacher from their attitude toward the subject. And if they ever can separate the two, it is as an adult, not a student in a K–12 classroom.

The students are not asked to evaluate the teacher but to give feedback; evaluation comes from the principal.

Figure 11.4 is from data collected in an elementary school. Students in Grades 1–5 were asked to place a happy face, sad face, or straight face after each school subject. The average happy faces were plotted on the graph. For the purposes of this chapter, I'd like readers to focus on the math and science in Grades 4 and 5. The student attitudes in Grade 4 are the same for both

Figure 11.4   Elementary School Happy Face Survey

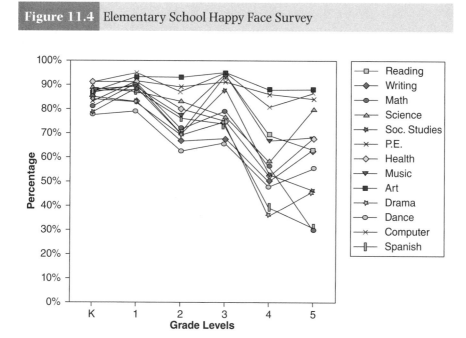

mathematics and science. In Grade 5, the science attitude is almost 90 percent happy faces and mathematics is below 40 percent happiness. What happened? This school departmentalized in Grade 5 for math and science. The students adored their science teacher and had nothing good to say about their math teacher. These students who answered the happy face survey most likely cannot remember the math teacher's name, can remember the science teacher's name, and almost certainly remember their attitude toward Grade 5 mathematics. Hopefully, a miracle worker of a teacher was able to turn around the math attitude in a later grade level.

So, since teachers don't need a twelve-year-old buddy, what is the key to developing positive relationships? As stated earlier, it is 1:1 conversations and listening. Teachers have much positive advice to give students, but step one is listening, not giving advice.

SPACED AND MASSED PRACTICE

John Hattie (2009) wrote, "It is the frequency of different opportunities rather than merely spending 'more' time on a task that makes the difference to learning" (p. 185). Let's take the learning of math facts as an example of massed practice that could be replaced with spaced-out practice. The normal practice is to provide students 100 addition facts and give students timed tests until they meet a certain standard of number correct in the specified time. Then it is assumed that addition is conquered and the process is repeated for subtraction. If, and when, the standard is met for subtraction, we start over with multiplication. Addition and subtraction are left behind. The other way we work with facts is with one factor at a time. Students take timed tests on the 2s and continue until mastery is met. Then they work to achieve mastery on 3s, and so on. I haven't used the term *massed practice* until reading Hattie's work, but it describes perfectly the normal process used in most schools.

Spaced practice is different. For example, the math fluency quizzes based upon the structures described in this book are very different when spaced practice is in place. The difference is students are provided, by grade level, a random set of math facts and the student aim is to answer more and more correctly in the specified time. Students are given credit for all-time-bests and the total math facts answered correctly are added up for the whole classroom. Details are contained in the e-booklet entitled "Let's Fix Math Fluency," with fluency quizzes written by Peggy McLean. Resource U is a sample two-minute math fluency quiz written by McLean. It is one of the twenty-eight Grade 7 math fluency quizzes that clearly follow the spaced practice advice given by Hattie.

There is no real good reason to stop practicing fluency at the end of elementary school. Sometimes, McLean's math fluency quizzes for Grades 7 and 8 and even used in high schools. Fluency with numbers is a lifelong skill that can continue to be developed on through secondary education. Each grade level would need to add some aspect of math fluency, such as exponents, square roots, and decimal, fraction, and percentage equivalents. The major point here for implementing Hattie's spread-out practice versus massed practice is that addition is never dropped. Because the students are not being given 100 math facts from one operation, there is ample time to keep everything in mind.

PRIOR ACHIEVEMENT

"What a child brings to the classroom each year is very much related to their achievement in previous years" (Hattie, 2009, p. 41). No surprise here. The bad news is that prior achievement is 14th of 138 factors influencing learning. The good news is that prior achievement is 14th of 138 factors influencing learning. Yes, prior achievement is a good predictor of current year achievement, but there are thirteen researched strategies within the power of educators to implement that

> Since prior achievement is such a strong predictor of future learning, educators must have the term *J curve* on the tip of their tongue as a driving force.

are better predictors than prior achievement. Hattie (2009) said it this way, "One of the most fascinating outcomes of this synthesis of meta-analysis is that there are measures that schools can implement that are more influential than this prior achievement effect" (p. 42).

However, since prior achievement is such a strong predictor of future learning, educators must have the term *J curve* on the tip of their tongue as a driving force. I wish I knew how to make education perfect and end up with an "I non-curve" on the histogram! I do not know how, but educators must internalize that the bell curve is for the middle of the school year, not for the end of the year.

Figures 11.5, 11.6, and 11.7 are combined histograms from the classrooms of Angela Willnerd, Heather Kroeger, and Kinsey Wernhoff who

---

Figure 11.5 First Grade Reading Histogram—Fall

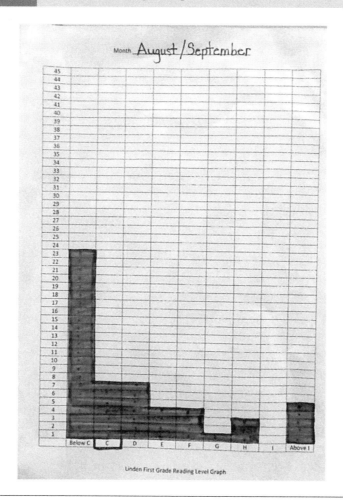

Source: Courtesy of Angie Willnerd.

Figure 11.6 First Grade Reading Histogram—Winter

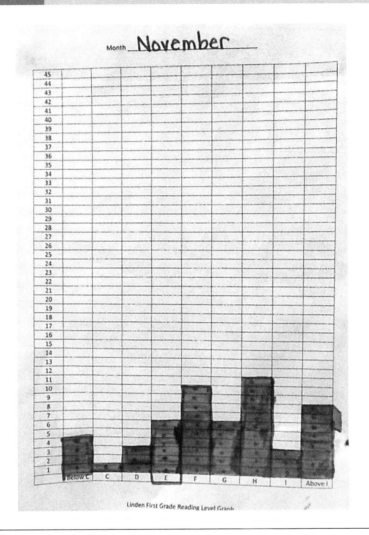

Source: Courtesy of Angie Willnerd.

teach first grade in Fremont, Nebraska. They show progress from fall to winter to spring. The y-axis is the number of students and the x-axis is reading level. The year started off with an *L*-shaped curve, progressed through the bell curve and ended with a wonderful *J*-shaped curve. They celebrated an incredible year and then established countermeasures to make next year even better.

The twin of the bell curve is grade inflation. It is often assumed that if too many students are successful there must be grade inflation. Pressure mounts to force the bell curve when grade inflation is suspected.

| Figure 11.7 | First Grade Reading Histogram—Spring |

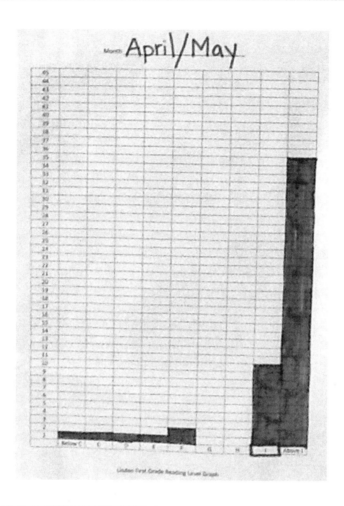

Source: Courtesy of Angie Willnerd.

This pressure is the perfect recipe to make sure prior achievement impacts future poor learning.

Education has the responsibility to distinguish between grade inflation and high success rate. Grade inflation is the result of low standards and few support this notion. Success is the marriage of high standards and high success rates. All should applaud teachers when they move their classroom from an *L* curve (high standards) at the beginning of the year on through the bell curve and finally at the *J* curve (high success rate) by year's end.

> *Education has the responsibility to distinguish between grade inflation and high success rate.*

VOCABULARY PROGRAMS

In his 2006 book, *The Knowledge Deficit*, E. D. Hirsch makes the case for vocabulary development versus reading skill. He relates that in the United States, students in Grade 4 do well on international reading exams but cannot perform nearly as well on future international reading exams. His premise is that the replacement of time teaching history, geography, civics, art, music, and science with more time on reading skills has actually damaged reading. The reason is that students do not have the background knowledge to comprehend what they are reading. They have no clue that Madagascar is a country much less know that it is an island about the size of California off the coast of Eastern Africa. So, when the word *Madagascar* appears in text, students can only think of a movie and thus do not comprehend what the writer has written. Repeat this over and over in US schools and one can easily understand why Hirsch calls this the knowledge deficit.

A school with only reading and a little of all the other subjects is a lousy school that will never create student experts.

What can schools do to develop vocabulary in their students?

1. Do not let reading sub-optimize the curriculum in elementary schools. When one element of an organization sub-optimizes the organization, this means that one aspect of the organization wins at the expense of the whole. A school with only reading and a little of all the other subjects is a lousy school that will never create student experts.

2. Urge teachers to use all vocabulary. Do not water down the words for children. For example, with pattern blocks, the teacher, even in kindergarten must use the words *trapezoid, rhombus, hexagon, triangle,* and *square* to describe the shapes. Red, blue, yellow, green and orange won't cut it. Teachers may say, "blue rhombus" or "tan rhombus" to distinguish between the two rhombuses in the set of pattern blocks. Evelyn Neufeld who introduced base ten blocks to me years ago would assign her first-grade students to the math problems in the lower right quadrant. The kids can handle it.

3. Ignore all readability formulas that have syllable counts as a part of their formula. Student interest trumps syllable counts.

4. Use organizational time to teach vocabulary. On my website, www .LtoJConsulting.com, under "Free LtoJ Support," are PowerPoints. Rhonda Johnston is from the Catholic School Division in

Lloydminster, Canada (SK and AB border). Her LtoJ® biology questions are on PowerPoint. The questions are randomly selected by students pulling out of a canis-

Student interest trumps syllable counts.

ter, a tongue depressor with an element from the periodic table written on it. The student who pulls the tongue depressor then goes up to the interactive screen and touches the corresponding symbol. Up pops a biology question that has nothing to do with the element. This is merely a way to select the question. No classroom time has been subtracted from biology to reinforce the periodic table. We can probably think of hundreds of ways to use organizational time to teach vocabulary without subtracting time from other curriculum.

REPEATED READING PROGRAMS

Sixteenth of the 138 influences on student achievement is repeated reading. Repeated reading makes perfect sense to both logical (Piagetian conservers) and nonlogical students. They understand the purpose is to become more fluent in reading, pausing at punctuation, and raising or lowering the voice just like the teacher does. When repeated reading is combined with self-reported grades, it is really powerful. Beginning readers are provided a story every Monday and asked to practice reading it all week. On Friday, their words-per-minute on the story are calculated and each student graphs their WPM. In addition, the total WPM for the whole class is calculated and graphed. The psychology behind repeated reading is solid. Students must hear themselves with their own ears sounding like a fluent reader. Over the years many children's books have been published with repeated reading in mind. Two of the best known authors are Bill Martin Jr. and Mercer Mayer.

BE YOUR OWN RESEARCHER

Included with Excel is the **Pearson Correlation Coefficient**. It helps us answer the question, "Are the results from my program or process highly correlated with my accountability responsibilities?" A correlation of .7 or higher is what we are after. We want to be assured that students who succeed in our classrooms have the knowledge to succeed on state or national assessments. The most well-known correlation in elementary schools is the correlation between reading fluency and reading comprehension. It is typically between .7 and .8. This means that for 70 to 80 percent of elementary students, if we know their fluency rate, we can accurately predict their comprehension ability. However, for 20 to 30 percent of students, the fluency rate will not predict comprehension skill.

The process for obtaining the Pearson Correlation Coefficient is located at Resource W. It will come in very handy when faculty members are debating the merit of a particular purchased program.

I have chosen to comment on the most successful strategies. However, readers knowledgeable of Hattie's meta-analysis in rank order will recognize that I have selected thirteen of the first sixteen in the ranking. I have not written about all 138 or taken all of the first sixteen; three were skipped. This is not because I discount the research, but because I have nothing meaningful to say about the skipped items.

A reminder: The reason that I placed these comments about Hattie's research in this book is to assist educators as they develop their counter-measures as described in Chapter 9. Initially, what to do to move the dot on the radar closer to 100 percent will not be that difficult. But after several years of continuous improvement, the question is, "Now what!?" Hattie's research can assist educators all along the way.

LOOKING AHEAD

The next chapter describes the dichotomous rubric. I have chosen to give this valuable tool its own chapter because accurate assessment of performance based student work is so important. Listen to student and parent complaints about a grade assigned by a teacher. Often it is the grade from a performance that is at the center of the grumbling. For background knowledge questions, most can agree on a wrong or right answer. Insert performance and it is all very murky. We can do better.

The Dichotomous Rubric and Performance Expectations

12

Measurements that are useful are often much simpler than people first suspect.

—Douglas Hubbard, 2010

Performance is measured in three ways: by counting, by checking off skills, and by scales of quality, typically labeled *rubrics*. Keyboarding speed, reading words per minute (WPM), and measures of fitness are some of the typical performance measures obtained by counting. The most common check-off performance systems are in computer science and other career tech courses. Automotive teachers know precisely what skills students are to master by the end of the course and check them off as students prove their new abilities.

The counting and check-off systems can be vastly improved through the student engagement of self-reported graphing. Two graphs, at a minimum are necessary. They are the student run chart and the class run chart. With typing speed, for example, students graph how many words per minute they typed and on the wall of the classroom is a graph of the total words per minute typed by the class as a whole. This simple counting and adding is repeated for fitness, reading fluency, and other performance standards measured by counting. Figures 12.1 and 12.2 are the student run chart and class run chart for a middle school keyboarding class with 40 WPM as the standard. The class size is 25, thus, 1000 words typed in a minute is used for the y-axis.

The same two graphs are necessary for check-off systems. If a welding teacher has twenty skills to be learned by the end of the course, then students have a student run chart that goes from 0 to 20. Each week students graph how many skills have been approved by the teacher. On the wall, with twenty students in class, is a graph that has a y-axis of 400. With twenty students and twenty skills, the class can achieve a score of 400 by the end of the course.

RUBRICS

The third aspect of performance, that cannot be easily counted, is scored on rubrics. The lowest numeral on the rubric is typically 1 and the most common rubrics are on a 1 to 4 scale, but the complexity of the topic determines how high the scale needs to go in order to capture all of the performance ability.

Any survey of the Internet will provide ample examples of rubrics. A common format is a 4 × 5 matrix. There are four levels of performance from beginner to expert and five different aspects being evaluated. These rubrics are written for adults, not students. The power of the **dichotomous rubric** is that it can be given to students to guide their work. Ideally, students can look at their work, compare it to the rubric, and arrive at the same score as the teacher.

The power of the dichotomous rubric is that it can be given to students to guide their work.

SIMPLICITY

The significance of the dichotomous rubric is the simplicity of the yes/no questions. Does the student work contain _____? Yes or no? Students can follow these questions and almost always arrive at the same rubric score as the teacher. Look at Resources I, Q, and V to see how simple dichotomous rubrics are for students to follow and for teachers to fairly assess. Continuous improvement in performance assignments is dependent upon accurate measures. If the student cannot understand what is expected and the teachers are unsure of the accuracy of their scoring, then continuous improvement will have no place in the performance-based curriculum. Simplistic accuracy is a must.

Figure 12.1   Keyboarding Speed Student Run Chart

Name _____

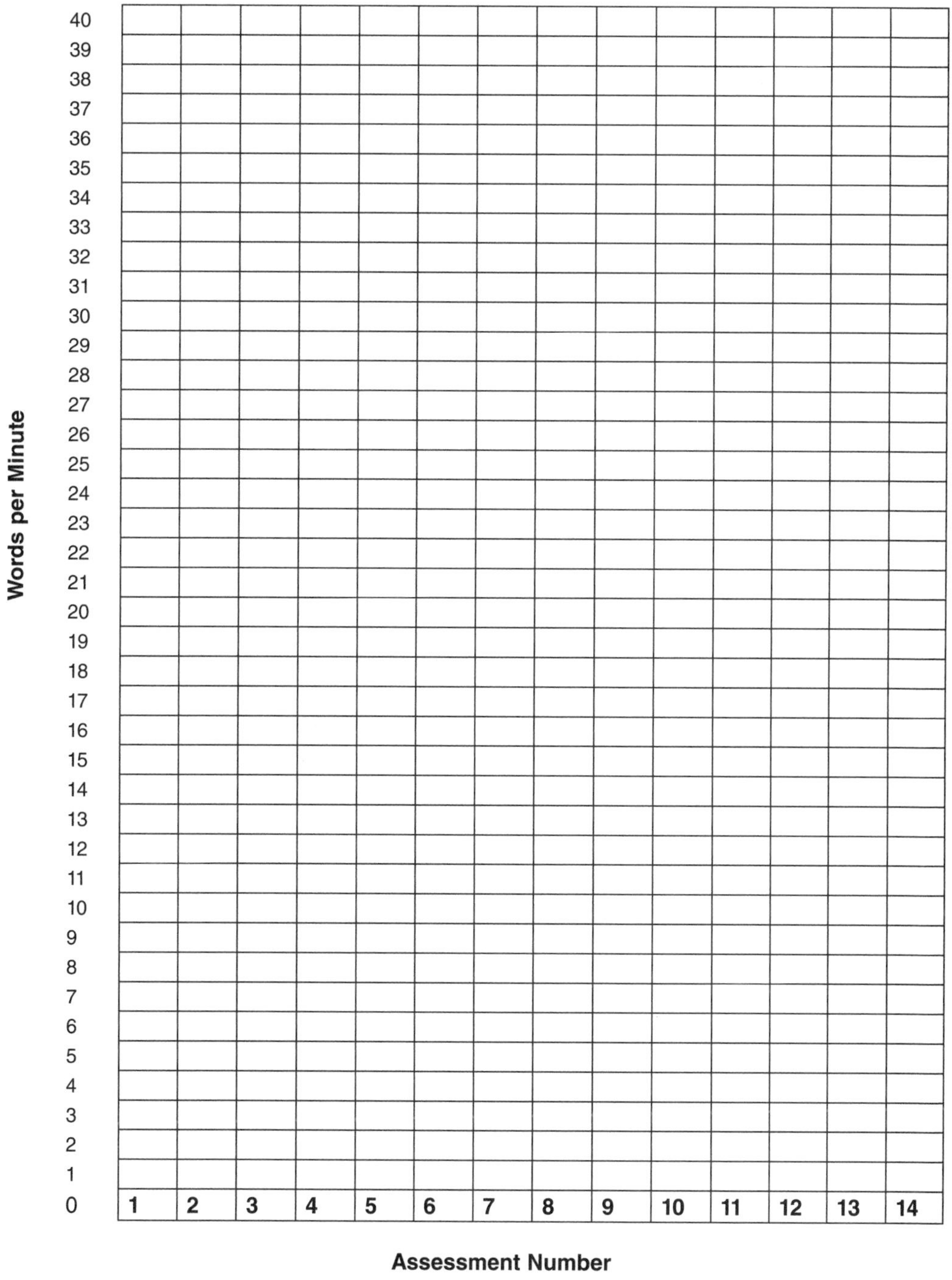

Source: © From LtoJ® Consulting Group, Inc.

Figure 12.2 Keyboarding Speed Class Run Chart

Period _____

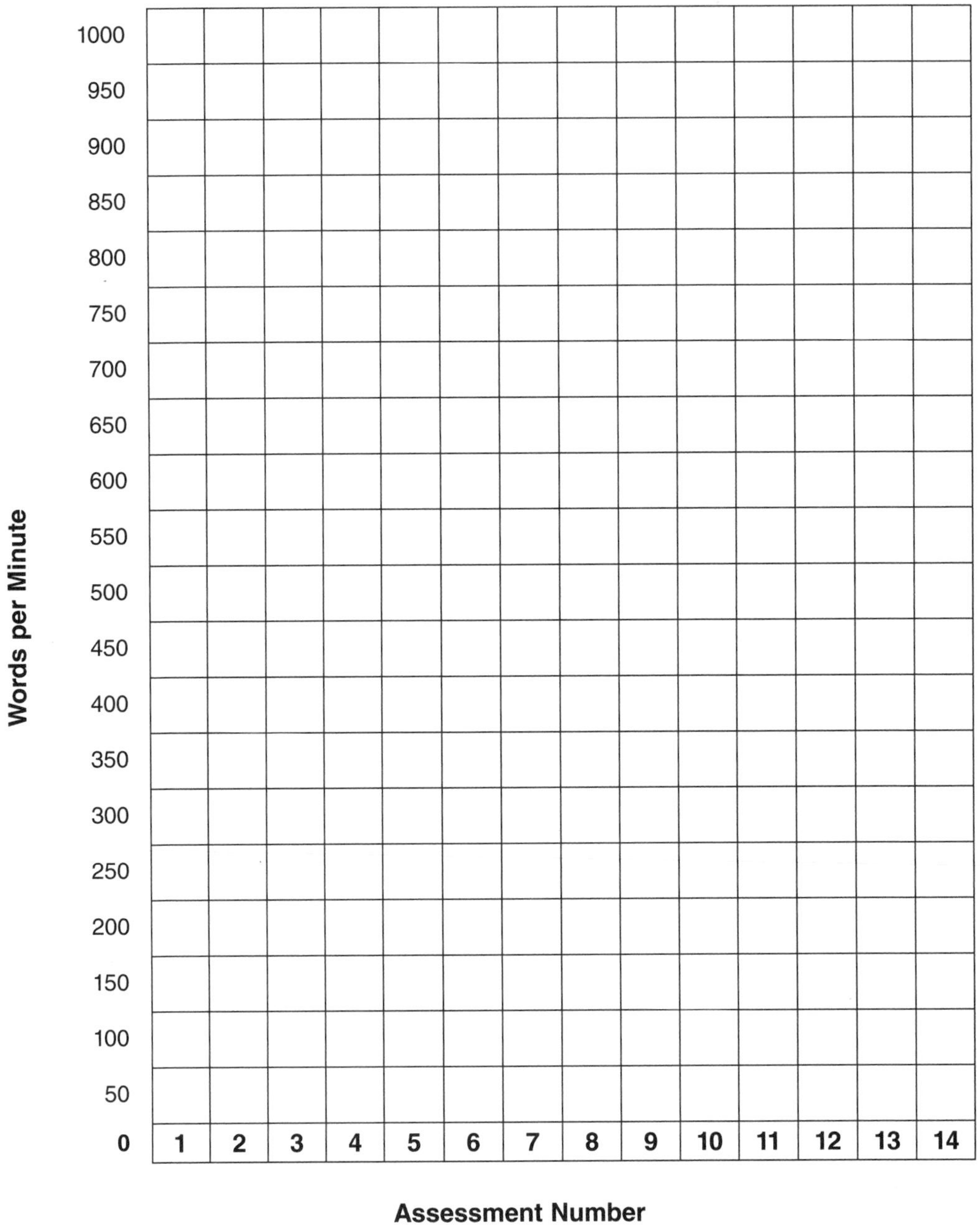

Source: © From LtoJ® Consulting Group, Inc.

SEEING PROGRESS

The graphing of progress in writing or any other performance based curriculum also involves two graphs: one for each student and one for the class as a whole. Two blank graphs are below (Figures 12.3 and 12.4): one for the student and one for the class as a whole. The large space at the bottom of the graphs is for recording the assigned project. An art teacher, for example, working with clay could have students record at the bottom of the graph, the assignments: stamp, pinch, fish, coil, and slab. The students and the teacher will know for each aspect of the art curriculum whether or not skill is improving and lessons from one aspect are being internalized and incorporated in future lessons.

CREATING DICHOTOMOUS RUBRICS

Once an educator has determined to assign a performance-based task that cannot be evaluated by counting or by checking off skills, the dichotomous rubric is essential. When creating the dichotomous rubric, the first task for the teacher is to decide what is most important in the project. This value judgment becomes the first question. Does the student work have _____? Yes or no?

On a number of occasions, I have worked with students who were given a tangram problem-solving writing assignment. The steps for the student were the following:

1. Select a tangram picture you wish to write about.
2. Solve the geometry puzzle by placing the seven tangram pieces on the tangram picture.
3. Reproduce the tangram picture with the tangram template. Include all interior lines to show the seven pieces.
4. Write a story about the picture.
5. The story is to include a problem and a solution to the problem.
6. Check the work for punctuation, spelling, and capitalization.
7. If desired, embellish the tangram picture with other art.
8. Attach the story to the tangram picture.

Figure 12.5 is a dichotomous rubric created for this assignment. Note the value judgments. I placed the geometry requirement first. If the tangram pieces are not correct, the student cannot obtain the top score. However, if the student has all the writing components correct, only one

Figure 12.3 Dichotomous Rubric Student Run Chart

Dichotomous Rubric Student Run Chart for _____

4																												
3																												
2																												
1																												
0																												

Rubric Score

Assignment

Figure 12.4 Dichotomous Rubric Class Run Chart

Dichotomous Rubric Class Run Chart

Rubric Total

100

80

60

40

20

0

Assignment

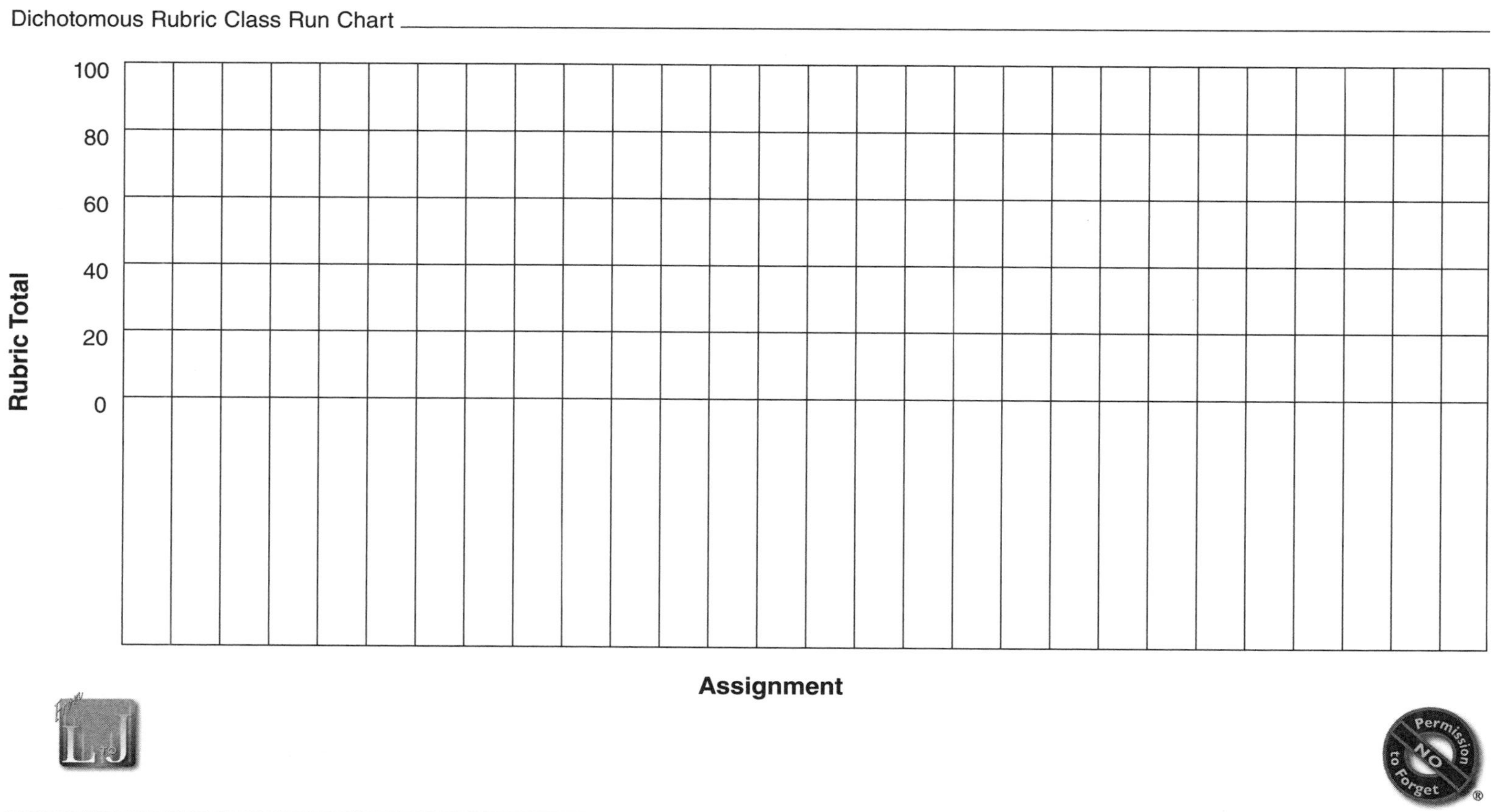

Source: © From LtoJ® Consulting Group, Inc.

Figure 12.5   Dichotomous Rubric: Tangram Problem-Solving Story

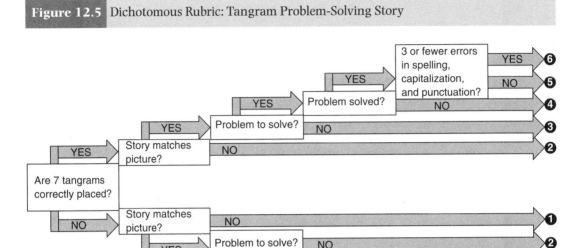

point is missed because of the geometry. Because there is a lot of thinking occurring while creating a dichotomous rubric, I have found it easier to create one with sticky notes prior to putting ideas in the computer for later printing. Long before I knew dichotomous rubrics existed, I gave this assignment to a first- or second-grade student. The child selected the letter Y to solve with tangram pieces and to write about. I really wondered what problem a child would give to a letter! Well, she had no problem with the writing assignment. She said the Y had a problem because he wished he was a Z. The Z agreed because he wanted to be a Y. So, they traded costumes. Problem solved. If I had known of the dichotomous rubric then, the score would have been a "5" because the student left out the square in solving the tangram geometry puzzle. The first question was a "no," but all the other questions on the rubric were a "yes."

The remainder of this chapter includes sample dichotomous rubrics because examples from various teachers at various grade levels with multiple subjects are probably the best way to understand the power of these rubrics. We need key concepts written in student-friendly language to help students gain background knowledge and we need dichotomous rubrics to help students gain proficiency with performance expectations. Documents that are written only for teachers tend to stay on shelves or in the computer. Key concept lists and dichotomous rubrics are for student and teacher use. Dichotomous rubrics are always distributed widely. For example, Resource X, a dichotomous rubric for reading, is of great help to parents of beginning readers.

Nicole Trovillion of Massac County Schools in Metropolis, Illinois, jumped all over the dichotomous rubric because of her frustration with the ambiguity of typical rubrics. She attended an after-school, one-hour workshop on dichotomous rubrics and two days later was explaining them to students. She wrote,

> After teaching seven years and using a variety of rubrics, I have found that the dichotomous rubric takes the guesswork out of rubric use. Some traditional rubrics can be so subjective that the decision between one level of achievement and the next is based solely on the teacher's choice. When grading students' work with a traditional rubric, I find myself saying, "Maybe they earned a 3? Or maybe they earned a 4?" It's confusing because the rubric does not set clear expectations. The dichotomous rubric is more user friendly because you answer yes or no questions. There are no "maybes."

Figure 12.6 is one of her six rubrics for writing. Figure 12.7 is the student run chart with 5 possible rubric points. All of these materials are on the website www.LtoJConsulting.com under "Free LtoJ Support" and then "Dichotomous Rubrics." The dichotomous rubric is essential for the

---

Figure 12.6 Writing Dichotomous Rubric

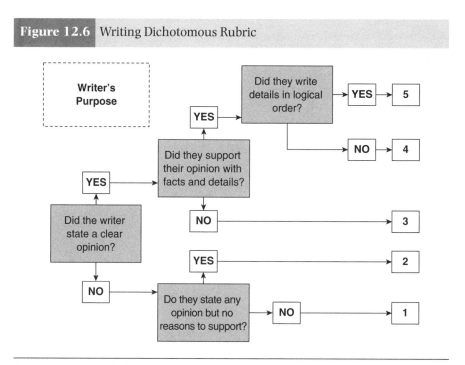

Source: Created by Nicole Trovillion.

Figure 12.7 Writing Dichotomous Rubric Student Run Chart

Six Traits Writing Student Run Chart for _____

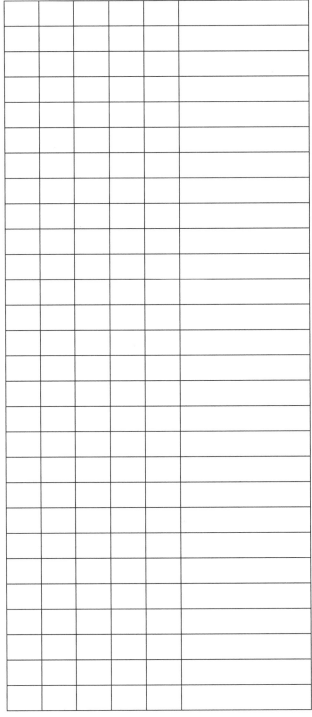

Rubric Score

5

4

3

2

1

0

Trait

Source: © From LtoJ® Consulting Group, Inc.

teacher, servant leader because when students understand what is expected, they ask for the teacher's help. The leader provides the rubric and the servant leader helps the student attain a higher rubric score.

LOOKING AHEAD

This chapter concludes the section of the book on instruction and next is a close look at continuous strategic improvement in personnel. It takes very talented people to optimize the whole system by implementing the principles and practices outlined in this book.

PART IV

Optimizing Human Resources and Finance

13 *Human Resources*

Need to investigate the "dead wood" procurement policy.

—W. Edwards Deming, 1992

S o far I have written about schools having great instructional
strategies; this chapter is about having great people. "The search for
excellence requires both exceptional people and great processes. . . . Some
companies have neither and are simply struggling to get by. More typically,
a company that has been around for a while has succeeded on the backs
of some exceptional people who have prevailed in spite of poorly organized processes . . . We also know of companies with very strong engineering departments that have developed well-designed processes but see the
people who operate them as a necessary evil. People are interchangeable
parts, and there is relatively little investment in developing them . . . Only
companies with excellent processes *and* excellent people will truly excel"
(Liker & Franz, 2011, p. 41). Schools must have the aim of educating
students with superb adults and excellent processes. Both are essential.

HOW TO EVALUATE THE HR DEPARTMENT

One of the most difficult departments in a school district to measure is the
personnel department. If the payroll staff is included in HR we can, of
course, count errors on payroll warrants and then strive to reduce errors.
The more important issue, however, is measuring the two major responsibilities of HR: hiring well and removing ineffective employees. When
measuring performance, educators use rubrics and it seems that a rubric

Figure 13.1 Teacher Evaluation Summary on Dichotomous Rubric

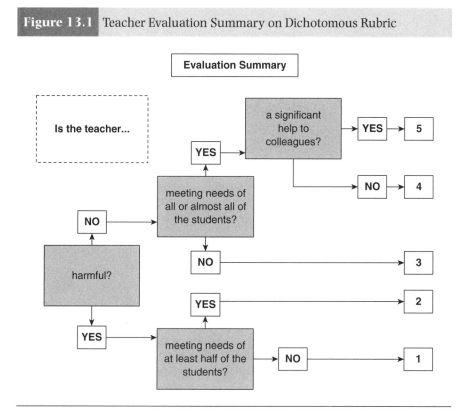

for the HR department is necessary to track improvement. Figure 13.1 is a dichotomous rubric for teacher performance.

We are after a clearly described standard that everybody can aspire to, rather than a sorting of people. "Employees generally begin a new job with enthusiasm, full of hope for a bright future. It takes effort for us to turn these high hopes into feelings of apathy, despair, frustration, cynicism, disgust, or outright rebellion" (Liker & Meier, 2007, p. 217). The assessment system can be used to create these negative feelings or it can continue to inspire employees. We can focus on health and prevention or illness and cures with our personnel practices.

CONTINUOUS STRATEGIC IMPROVEMENT IN HR

Continuous strategic improvement in HR means more teachers at levels 4 and 5 and fewer teachers at levels 1, 2, and 3. I understand that value judgments are utilized with this dichotomous rubric; it is true for all rubrics. "The lack of having an exact number is not the same as knowing nothing" (Hubbard, 2010, p. 69). Performance is not nearly as precise as measuring factual knowledge (Did you arrive at work on time?). Nevertheless, the senior administrators and the school board have the right and responsibility to know if the personnel department is improving along with the rest of the district. The HR department can celebrate all-time-bests (ATB) along with everybody else, although it is recognized that much of what a personnel department does is confidential. The ATB celebrations occur when there are fewer 1s, 2s, and 3s plus more 4s and 5s than ever before.

LEVEL 1

The attitude of the employees has everything to do with their level of performance. Mark Murphy (2012) writes, "We know that attitude, not skill, defines high and low performance" (p. 1). He further states, "I don't care how many billboards you rent and television spots you buy, all the marketing in the world can't help you if your employees are undermining your brand every day" (p. 7). Attitude is a crucial aspect of any quality rubric of employees.

District leaders and principals know who the 1s are. They attempt to motivate students through sarcasm and put downs, they take pride in their high failure rates and clearly would enjoy teaching much more if there were no students. In Murphy's words, these are the low performers. Murphy describes four categories of employees. Some are the low performers with poor attitudes and poor skill. Then there are the poor attitude people with great skill. These he calls *talented terror*. The opposite of talented terror are those with great attitudes and poor skills. He calls them *bless their hearts*. Of course the employees we all want have both great attitudes and great skill. Regarding these Level 1 employees, he writes, "The general rule of thumb is people who are incompetent *and* unpleasant can usually be safely classified as low performers. (They have lousy skills and bad attitudes). These folks are pretty easily identified in the interview process and are not a giant problem for hiring managers" (p. 14).

LEVEL 2

Level 2 teachers are actually more prevalent that one might think. They are often at the regional and state events with their high performers. They write glowing letters for the university admission's departments and actually stay in contact with prior graduates for quite a number of years. The problem is they are harmful to far too many students telling them, "You'll never amount to anything."

LEVEL 3

Level 3 teachers are the hardest to recognize. I gained this insight from a conversation with Vic Cottrell, founder and former president of Ventures for Excellence in Lincoln, Nebraska. In one week, four parents approached me to provide their opinion on a particular teacher. Two oozed praise and two spouted condemnation. I called up Vic and asked, "What do I do with this feedback?" and immediately he responded, "You have an average teacher meeting the needs of half of the students; all four parents are telling you the truth." I did have an average teacher and had no one to blame but me; I hired him.

Level 3, average teachers, can be classified there either because of poor skills or poor attitudes. According to Murphy (2012), "Some people have great attitudes, but terrible skills. Others have stellar skills but bad attitudes . . . You don't want to make the mistake of hiring either of them" (p. 14). He continues, "We call the people who have great attitudes but lousy skills as the Bless Their Hearts . . . Someone with a great attitude . . . who repeatedly fails to get the job done right isn't an 'almost' high performer . . . and no amount of amazing attitude is going to make up for it. And no low performer should be admitted to the elite club that is your organization" (p. 15).

A common word heard from Level 3 teachers is *opportunity*. They proudly state, "I gave the students the opportunity to learn and those students over there rejected the opportunity I provided." Sometimes this means, "Those students over there never took the opportunity to do homework, so they deserve to flunk." These are the talented terrors, in Murphy's words, who should be in a career behind a desk and not given the privilege of educating the next generation of adults. Murphy writes, "When they're at their worst, these people are like emotional vampires. And while they won't actually suck your blood, the frustration of dealing with them will suck the life out of you" (p. 16). "Talented Terrors are by far the most difficult kind of low performer to detect in interviews" (p. 16). This is probably because it is so easy to be blindsided by charm and talent.

LEVEL 4

Level 4 teachers are far beyond *opportunity*. They have replaced this word with *persuasion, caring, honoring, serving,* and are sometimes *in your face.* They clearly are the leader in the classroom AND the servant of all,

Level 4 teachers are far beyond opportunity. They have replaced this word with persuasion, caring, honoring, serving, and are sometimes in your face. They clearly are the leader in the classroom AND the servant of all, including the struggling student.

including the struggling student. They are not content until all students are successful, and if they meet the needs of almost all the students, instead of all students, they do not shrug their shoulders and blame the kid. They recognize no teacher is perfect, but that doesn't keep them from trying. In Murphy's words, they are the high performers. He writes that they are recognized by their understanding, caring, persistence, objectivity and sincerity. In Cottrell's words, these learning specialists are "always building positive and collaborative relationships, they have a mission of service for the growth and development of students, they are always facilitating the learning process with students, and keep a shared focus on progress toward results. They continually look for ways to extend the learning beyond the classroom" (personal communication, October 2014).

LEVEL 5

Level 5 teachers are just like Level 4 teachers with the additional quality of great assistance to colleagues. The department or even the whole school is improved because of these talented teachers. Somehow the staff knows where to go to ask the hard questions. Administrators would be wise to ask these Level 5 teachers, "In your experience, what separates our great attitude people from everyone else in the organization" (Murphy, 2012, p. 21). The collection of answers will be of great assistance in hiring and developing Level 4 people.

A MAXWELL RUBRIC

John Maxwell (2007) wrote a four-point rubric for employees that is not specific for education. It is worth looking at as the HR department completes its assessment of all staff. Further, this rubric can apply to all employees—administrators, teachers, and support staff.

When it comes to initiative, there are really only four kinds of people:

1. People who never do the right thing, no matter what.

2. People who do the right thing when told more than once.

3. People who do the right thing when told.

4. People who do the right thing without being told.

A four-point rubric, which could be combined with Maxwell's rubric that focuses directly on attitude is

1. People who are always blaming others for their problems.

2. People who follow rules mindlessly.

3. People who are problem solvers. They see the problems just like others but always think about solutions.

4. People who implement solutions for themselves and others.

Murphy (2012) obviously had influence on this rubric, with his insight, "You can roughly categorize people into two groups: problem bringers and problem solvers . . . problem solvers can't even think of a problem without instantly generating possible solutions" (p. 45).

THE HR BOTTOM LINE

So, what are continuous strategic improvement responsibilities of the HR department? In simple terms, it is to assist the superintendent and board in providing "great people surrounded by a system that mandates the need for such talent" (Liker & Meier, 2007, p. xix). I am only outlining six responsibilities as they relate to teachers, but obviously there are administrators and support staff responsibilities also.

Responsibilities

1. Hire Level 4 teachers.

2. Assist the development of Level 4 teachers to become Level 5 teachers.

3. Remove Level 1 and Level 2 teachers from the district.

4. Never allow any new Level 3 teachers to achieve tenure.

5. Provide assistance plans for tenured Level 3 teachers.

6. Remove tenured Level 3 teachers who fail to become Level 4 teachers.

These jobs are not accomplished by fiat or by legislated intensive evaluations of teachers. We must avoid "complex evaluation schemes designed to weed out the worst performers, and destined to demoralize everyone else" (Ripley, 2013, p. 85). Nevertheless, it is completely reasonable for a school board to expect continuous improvement from year to year with fewer 1s, 2s, and 3s and more 4s and 5s, understanding that the school system will never be perfect.

The strategic aspect of continuous strategic improvement in the Human Resources Department is the set of countermeasures to meet the six requirements above. The process is the same as the strategic planning for instruction: problem, root cause(s) and a countermeasure to be tested.

Strategic Plan for HR

1. Hire Level 4 teachers. Problem: We have hired some Level 1 and 2 teachers in the past. Possible root cause: We were fooled by charisma.

2. Assist the development of Level 4 teachers to become Level 5 teachers. Problem: We have no plan for this development. Possible root cause: We never saw this as a responsibility of the HR Department.

3. Remove Level 1 and 2 teachers from the district. Problem: We have relied on retirements to solve this problem. Possible root cause: Documenting a tenured teacher and leading a school, at the same time, is very difficult.

4. Never allow Level 3 teachers to achieve tenure. Problem: Too many teachers are tenured that should never have achieved tenure. Possible root cause: We hire principals with a great caring attitude for all people and they struggle with this responsibility.

5. Provide assistance plans for tenured Level 3 teachers. Problem: We never considered that Level 3 teachers needed assistance plans. Possible root cause: Some Level 3 teachers pride themselves with their high standards without realizing the need is for high standards *and* high success rates at the same time.

6. Remove tenured Level 3 teachers who fail to become Level 4 teachers. Problem: Level 3 teachers, in the past, have received satisfactory evaluations. Possible root cause: Administrators and teachers accepted meeting the needs of half of the students as satisfactory.

I will now suggest possible countermeasures that can be written for each of the six responsibilities, but clearly there are many more possibilities.

COUNTERMEASURE 1

Hire well, which means hiring at Level 4. I utilized the services of Vic Cottrell during my superintendent days. I became a very strong supporter of the structured interview and a centralized process of placing teacher candidates into a hiring pool from which principals and their staffs could select. Vic put together his structured interviews by asking various educators to identify, in their opinion, the most talented teachers in their district.

After a number of people in the same school district named the same person, he interviewed that teacher in depth. The answers to every question were recorded and analyzed for consistent patterns. The structured interview is composed of the same questions he used in his research, and the answers given by these outstanding teachers. Murphy (2012) states that asking interview questions without knowing the answer you are looking for is like giving an exam without knowing what answers you expect. Mark Keen, superintendent of Indiana's Westfield Washington Schools credits his eighteen-year history of hiring with Cottrell's system for the district's incredible results on the PISA (Program for International Student Assessment) exam. They outperformed all other tested countries and areas except Shanghai, China, and Singapore in mathematics and all other tested countries and areas except Shanghai in science and reading. This, obviously, includes outperforming the highly successful country of Finland.

He states, "Our student success on PISA simply reinforces the results we are getting from other assessments. What is useful about these scores is that it is an international, not simply local, state or national measure. Our students will compete internationally, so knowing how they measure up is significant. We have used the same structured interview process for 18 years, and the staff that we identify and select are the primary reason that our students score so well. Yes, we have alignment, staff development etc., but we also have staff internally wired to move mountains to provide meaningful and engaging learning opportunities for students" (personal communication, August 2014).

It is amazing how these teachers all think in very, very similar ways but utilize their own vocabulary to express the thoughts. The two companies carrying out Cottrell's legacy are Crown Global Consulting with Paul Berggren, located in Lincoln, Nebraska, and TargetSuccess, Inc. with Peter Pillsbury, located in Walnut, California. The websites are www.crown globalconsulting.com and www.TargetSuccess.biz. Cottrell can be reached through Crown Global Consulting. The first time I worked with Vic, he had the assembled administrators calculate the complete cost of typical teachers over the span of their career. It was well over $1 million (25 years times $40,000, at a minimum; in 2015, total salary for teachers, over career, is well over $2 million in many locales). He then asked us how much time we spend designing a $1 million construction project. Then came the clincher, "What will be the most value to students—the $1M building or the $1M teacher?" We all knew we were caught not acting out our priorities. There are experts that can help districts hire much better and they are not as expensive as architects. Every time a hiring mistake is made, the person hiring

> *It is amazing how these teachers all think in very, very similar ways but utilize their own vocabulary to express the thoughts.*

correctly sees the strengths of the candidate. However, the weaknesses are not discovered until too late.

Advice from others can be quite helpful in this most important of responsibilities. Maxwell (2007) wrote, "When people achieve great things, others often explain their accomplishments by simply attributing everything to talent. But that is a false and misleading way of looking at success. If talent alone is enough, then why do you and I know highly talented people who are not highly successful?" (p. vii). HR departments can be fooled by talent just they can be fooled by charisma. Jim Collins (2009) wrote, "People often ask, 'How do we get people to share our core values?'

Every time a hiring mistake is made, the person hiring correctly sees the strengths of the candidate. However, the weaknesses are not discovered until too late.

The answer: You don't. You hire people who already have a predisposition to your core values and hang onto them" (p. 159). Two more business quotes are lifted from Collins' work. He makes the point that attitude cannot be taught, but the skill on the job can be taught. "DiMicco (Nucor Steel) and his team retained the philosophy that it is better to hire people with the right work ethic and character and to teach them to make steel than to hire people who know how to make steel but lack the Nucor work ethic and character traits" (p. 169). "We (Nordstrom) can hire nice people and teach them to sell, but we can't hire salespeople and teach them to be nice" (p. 174). The problem I have with these quotes is that teaching is so much more complicated than being a salesperson. I haven't ever made steel, but I worked four years in college selling women's shoes. I know how much harder teaching is than being a salesperson. On the other hand, when I have hired a talented teacher that absolutely does not know how to develop positive relationships with students, I have made a hiring mistake! Murphy (2012) states, "Rare is the small business owner who takes the time to sit down and review all of the hiring successes and failures" (p. 29). The continuous strategic improvement annual report of 1s, 2s, 3s, 4s, and 5s demands this review.

COUNTERMEASURE 2

The second responsibility is assisting Level 4 teachers on their path to becoming Level 5 teachers. These are teachers with deep knowledge in one aspect of education and also an above average understanding of many other aspects of education. This second knowledge is enough to hold a conversation but is not deep, expert knowledge. A vertical strategy is sending teachers to the state and national conference for their area of expertise. Colleagues recognize this talent, respect this teacher, and want their advice. I can't but help think of

Peggy McLean, an elementary teacher who majored in science for elementary teachers. People liked her and so they were most willing to listen to her advice on the teaching of science. A horizontal strategy might be transferring a teacher to a different level of schooling, such as intermediate to kindergarten, high school to middle school, or elementary to high school, and so on. A staff development opportunity for teachers who are moving from Level 4 to Level 5 might be helping improve a process in one of the best schools or classrooms. This will strengthen them more than being asked to help a struggling location because a study of excellence is such a powerful learning experience. Jeffrey Liker and Gary Convis (2012) wrote, "Trainees were asked to engage in kai-zen (continuous improvement) to improve a process at one of the best plants in the company." (p. 19). I like what Peter Drucker (2009) wrote on this sub-ject regarding the desire to have senior teachers who are not counting the days until they can retire but are still meeting the needs of students and col-leagues. "People who manage the second half of their lives may always be in a minority. The majority may 'retire on the job' and count the years until their actual retirement. But it is this minority, the men and women who see a long working-life expectancy as an opportunity for themselves and for society, who will become leaders and models" (p. 41). Let's help those in the second half of their career all be at Level 5.

COUNTERMEASURE 3

The third responsibility is to remove Level 1 and 2 teachers. It is here that formal evaluation systems and attorney advice is essential. Since I am not an attorney or an expert in formal evaluation, I'll leave this to others. I do want to offer a strategy, however, that may be of significant help to districts in this area of responsibility. I suggest hiring retired administrators, on a per diem basis, to assist in evaluation. These retirees can spend all day in the classroom of Level 1 and 2 teachers and truly document in detail what is occurring. The full-day observations continue on a regular basis until attor-neys state one has the documentation to proceed. Principals rarely can operate their school and devote the time necessary to document in this way. The organizing of retired administrators and providing them updated inser-vice on evaluation can be organized by a regional service agency.

COUNTERMEASURE 4

The fourth responsibility is the hardest. Everyone knows this probationary, Level 3 teacher is more talented than the tenured Level 1 and 2 teachers down the hallway. Further, the probationary teacher has made a lot of friends and has college loans. The responsibility of the HR department is to not allow this teacher to obtain tenure! Principals will need a great deal of assistance here; it is hard. Collins' advice here helps a lot. He wrote, "The moment you feel the need to tightly manage someone, you might have made a hiring mistake" (2009, p. 139). If there is a difference between what a teacher said in the interview and what they actually do on the job, there is a problem. Maxwell (2007) states, "Fred Smith Sr. . . . says that a linguist with Wycliffe Bible translators told him that in twenty of the world's most primitive languages, the word for *belief* is the same as the word for *do*. It is only as people become more 'sophisticated' that they begin to separate the meaning of one word from the other" (p. 10).

COUNTERMEASURES 5 AND 6

Educators know how to provide assistance plans. However, the assistance plans are often how to improve lessons or behavior and these two are not always the issue. The clear message has to be, "I believe you have it in you to meet the needs of all or almost all the students, but my assessment is that you are meeting the needs of only half of the students. I further believe, that if you follow the assistance plan that I've written, you can improve to meet the needs of all or almost all students. We'll give this a try during the next school year." The first step in writing this assistance plan is to determine if the teacher has an attitude or skill problem and then write accordingly. At Toyota, "The student and the trainer would go to the workplace to observe the work being done by a skilled person" (Liker & Meier, 2007, p. 260). I suggest a department head or an administrator go together to see, and listen, how another teacher is able to have both high standards and a high success rate. Many Level 3 teachers are convinced that the only way to have a high success rate is to lower standards. Visiting together can be a powerful countermeasure.

Readers who have followed any of W. Edwards Deming's teaching know that he taught that "driving out fear" was one of the major jobs of leaders. Obviously, if a teacher has an assistance plan to help them move from Level 3 to Level 4, there is fear in place. What Dr. Deming meant by "driving out fear" was using blanket fear over the whole organization as a motivation tool. "If you don't raise test scores, half of the teachers and the principal will be fired," is an example of blanket fear over everyone. Dr. Deming was not speaking against removing incompetent employees, which may involve some individual fear.

The sixth responsibility is to admit and communicate that the assistance plans in the fifth responsibility did not work and to set up a strategy to remove this teacher from the school district.

NO RANK AND YANK

The HR department does not need a radar chart because there are not forty or more categories to measure. The replacement for the radar chart is a column graph with results shown year by year. The strategic plan consists of countermeasures written as hypotheses to increase Level 4 and 5 teachers and decrease Level 1, 2, and 3 teachers. Remember, not all countermeasures will result in success, but expect enough of them to work so that HR can show continuous improvement. A similar record of progress will need to be created for administrators and for support staff.

In summary, "We want to achieve the most efficient work with the least amount of waste, performed consistently and flawlessly with highly trained people" (Liker & Meier, 2007, p. 122). People performing at Levels 1, 2, and 3 are wasting time, student enthusiasm, and financial resources. Balancing this responsibility of eliminating Level 1, 2, and 3 teachers is resisting every attempt to rank the employees. Never will there be a document with all the teachers in the district and their rubric score. Also, "never demand that some arbitrary percentage of the workforce be unilaterally rated unsatisfactory. Never! (In the trade this is called 'rank and yank.')" (Bogle, 2009, p. 173). My whole career I have heard "education needs to be more businesslike." I have rejected this advice and often asked, "Which business?" We can all learn what to do from places like Toyota and learn what not to do from Enron. "The ranking system [was] advanced by Skilling as the best method to reward Enron's top talent. The competition was intense. Rankings were one through five—ones being worth fat bonuses and big promotions, fives needing to get their act together and move on" (Eichenwald, 2005, p. 212). No rubric was necessary at Enron; the opinion of the boss, if HR and finance agreed, was sufficient. Why finance? Since the aim was to give out fat bonuses, Enron couldn't have too many rated as top talented people. Another Enron quote gives a more complete picture of what "being more businesslike" can mean. "Even if his entire staff consisted of modern-day Einsteins, Kaminski [a supervisor] would be forced to brand the performance of most of them as average or worse . . . If everyone did a good job, the only way to move ahead was by undermining a colleague, but analysts needed to work as a team to get the best answers" (p. 462).

Seth Godin (2010) wrote, "Let me be clear: Great teachers are wonderful. They change lives. We need them. The problem is that most schools don't like great teachers. They're organized to stamp them out, bore them, bureaucratize them, and make them average" (p. 29). If this is true, it is true for almost all organizations, not just teachers. Years ago, I read about a hidden camera documenting the employee interaction when some workers had their pay tripled because of high productivity. The other employees intimidated the highly paid workers so much they went back to average production. So, how can we help with this problem? One way is for admin-istrators to make it clear that their desire is to have *all* teachers at Level 5.

Bill Watkins, superintendent of the Marcola School District in Oregon, reviewed the rubric in this chapter and then sent me his rubric for obser-vations. He wrote, "When I observe instruction—a 4 is meeting the needs of all students (or all students are engaged), a 3 is meeting the needs of 50% or more of the students, a 2 is meeting the needs of less than 50% of the students, a 1 is meeting the needs of no students but the teacher is still teaching. A "0" is the teacher sitting at the desk or not teaching and the students are unengaged" (personal communication, August 2014).

Reading Michael Lewis' (2003) book, *Moneyball*, I was struck by this observation: "If gross miscalculations of a person's value could occur on a baseball field, before a live audience of thirty thousand, and a television audience of millions more, what did that say about the measurement of performance in other lines of work?" (p. 72). So, even though I believe this chapter can be a great assistance to superintendents and HR departments, nothing is perfect.

PROMOTIONS

A final responsibility of the HR department, superintendent, and school board is determining who is promoted. "The promotion process spends as much time looking at *how* results are achieved . . . as at *what* results are achieved" (Liker & Convis, 2012, p. 35). Clearly, as stated in the beginning of this book, the purpose is to meet the accountability standards society deserves while leading with a servant leadership mindset. Of course, as an educator, my favorite quote regarding who is promoted at Toyota is, "Being able to teach others all of the above" (Liker & Convis, 2012, p. 53). Top leadership lists the quali-ties they desire to see in their future leaders, but most of all, they have to be able to teach adults how to do a better job in order to be considered for a promotion. Sometimes, people think administra-tors have left teaching. Not true. They have left full-time teaching of chil-dren and are now full-time teachers of adults.

> They have to be able to teach adults how to do a better job in order to be considered for a promotion.

TOO SIMPLISTIC

Every time I share the contents of this chapter in a seminar, it generates more discussion than any other topic. In the review process of the manuscript, this chapter generated the most comments. The reason is that personnel evaluation involves legal ramifications, union negotiations, tenure, and so on. I am not suggesting that the dichotomous rubric provided in this book IS the evaluation. I am suggesting that the use of the rubric, either as a cover sheet to the legal evaluation, or a separate conversation, can be of help to both principals and teachers. (Other dichotomous rubrics can be created for similar dialog with principals/bosses and support staff/bosses.) Further, leaders in HR need to be accountable for their decisions just like everyone else. A servant leader in HR wants to know if the district is improving from year to year

Leaders in HR need to be accountable for their decisions just like everyone else.

and wants the superintendent and board to have this knowledge. Figure 13.2 is the Optimization Matrix again with personnel added.

The Optimization Fishbone (Figure 13.3) has added personnel to the list of all-time-best celebrations. It is a great deal of work for a school system to have more Level 4 and 5 teachers and fewer Level 1, 2, and 3 teachers PLUS create similar documents for administrators and support staff. When improvement occurs, it is worth a time to relax and celebrate.

Figure 13.2	Optimization Matrix

		SYSTEM Sub-Optimize	**SYSTEM** Optimize
PEOPLE	Optimize	All students are honored for improving in depleted curriculum. All employees know how they contributed to success of system. Some subjects rob time from other subjects. Teachers at Levels 4 or 5 desire the implementation of the Personnel Dichotomous Rubric. No success.	All students are honored for improving in rich curriculum. All employees know how they contributed to success of system. No subject can rob time from other school subjects. All teachers not at Levels 4 or 5 are either being documented or on assistance plan.
	Sub-Optimize	Some students honored in depleted curriculum. Some employees know their contribution to success of system. Some subjects rob time from other subjects. Personnel dichotomous rubric is rejected; excuses abound.	No subject can rob time from other school subjects. Some students honored in rich curriculum. Some employees know their contribution to success of system. Strong hiring evaluation, hiring system is undermined by some administrators.

Figure 13.3   Optimization Fishbone

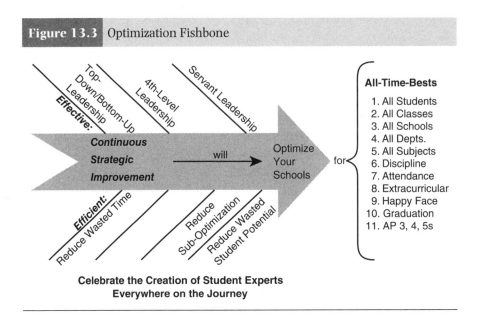

Celebrate the Creation of Student Experts
Everywhere on the Journey

LOOKING AHEAD

The same focus utilized in this chapter for HR will now be applied to school finance. The value judgment is classifying expenditures into those that assist student learning directly, assist student learning indirectly, and those that don't assist student learning. This will be easier than rubrics for employees.

14

Finance and Operations

Cutting costs without improvement of quality is futile.

—Joyce Orsini (quoting Deming), 2013

The fiscal assets of a school system must be managed: cash flow, accounts payable, accounts receivable, bond repayment, and so on. In my 2008 book, *From Systems Thinking to Systemic Action*, I list four finance questions in rank order of importance. The first two are management of money and the last two have to do with money leadership. That is the proper sequence; first of all the school system has to pay its bills. Management includes, for example, making sure the finance office and personnel office records match. This chapter, however, is not about managing the finances; it is about fiscal, continuous improvement, leadership.

FISCAL LEADERSHIP

What is fiscal leadership? It is a continuous record, year after year after year, of fewer expenditures that do not positively impact student safety or student learning. One example is spending more money on musical instruments and less money emptying the dumpsters. "Cutting costs without improvement of quality is futile" (Orsini, 2013, p. 8). Leadership is required to make these

> *What is fiscal leadership? It is a continuous record, year after year after year, of fewer expenditures that do not positively impact student safety or student learning.*

gradual adjustments in expenditures. The teaching staff will see CPAs who continually add funds to the instructional budget and subtract funds from accounts that add no value to learning as servant leaders. Again, Enron gives us a business example of what not to do. Enron was becoming anything and everything; "Executives who found investments—particularly deals that brought quick profits—were virtually guaranteed fat bonuses. There were no rewards for holding down costs" (Eichenwald, 2005, p. 169).

STEP 1: THREE CATEGORIES OF EXPENSES

Step 1 in reducing costs from a continuous strategic improvement perspective is dividing every expense into one of three categories: (1) The expenditure does not assist with student safety or student learning; (2) the expenditure may assist with learning or safety, but if so, it is indirect support; or (3) the expenditure is a direct support for student learning or safety. An example from the first category is legal expenses, an example from the second is electricity, and an example from the third category is teacher salaries.

The various state accounting codes are far too broad for this purpose; they work fine for fiscal management but are useless for fiscal leadership. The examples of this point are below:

State Accounting Category	No Help Category 1	Indirect Help Category 2	Direct Help Category 3
Substitutes	Jury duty	Sick leave	Staff development
Bus transportation	Removal of used oil, tires, batteries	Home to school	Field trips
Conferences	New laws	New evaluation	History/civics
Maintenance	Vandalism repair	Snow removal	Book displays

Reducing costs is a never ending job requiring the creativity of all support staff and many, many certificated staff members. Jeffrey Liker and Timothy Ogden (2011) wrote, "The idea was to ruthlessly cut any expenses that did not have an impact on customers or on the company's future growth prospects—that's why layoffs and large R&D cuts were off limits" (p. 41). In education, the concept is to cut any expenses that do not impact student

In education, the concept is to cut any expenses that do not impact student learning or safety.

learning or safety. Liker (2004) asked many different Toyota managers "if cost reduction is a priority and they just laughed. Their answers amounted to 'You haven't seen anything until you've experienced the cost consciousness of Toyota—down to pennies'" (p. 72). The focus of continuous strategic improvement in finance is cost reduction and an all-time-best (ATB) in finance can be as little as one penny less per student on attorneys. "Lots of small efforts, rather than a few big cuts made by senior executives, added up to big savings" (Liker & Ogden, 2011, p. 39) is the idea and this cannot be implemented October 15th when the state legislature announces a 5 percent cut for the current year. The teamwork described earlier in classrooms and instructional leadership can be duplicated in fiscal matters. The people actually see savings per pupil in nonacademic expenditures. "You actually accomplish results. Nothing else counts. And when you do get somewhere, the energy that is released enables the group to go places they never thought possible. Once they experience that, they will never go back" (Fullan, 2011, pp. 7–8).

STEP 2: COST PER STUDENT

Step 2 with Continuous Strategic Improvement in finance is calculating the **cost per student** for all district expenditures in the first two categories. This will include those that do not add to learning or safety and those that indirectly impact learning and safety. Cost per student is what makes continuous strategic improvement in finance possible. Enrollments and budgets change from year to year, so actual dollars are not an ideal metric for gauging improvement. However, cost per student can accurately measure expenditures year after year. Cost per student has two other significant advantages over raw numbers: (1) The accounting department can manage district finances with spreadsheets full of large numbers. However, fiscal leadership requires the intelligence and commitment of large numbers of people. Everybody understands cost per student, but few can work with the large numbers of a district's total finances. All react the same when they discover that the district spent more money per student emptying the dumpsters than per student on library books. This was certainly true when the Centennial District (Portland, OR) calculated they spent $12.85 per student for garbage versus $8.30 per student for library. (2) Districts of varying sizes can compare notes and learn from each other. This takes away the problem of trying to learn from a school system that is three times smaller or larger. Cost per student is the common denominator of school finance.

> Cost per student can accurately measure expenditures year after year.

STEP 3: SPREADSHEET(S)

Step 3 of continuous strategic improvement in finance is placing all the cost per pupil records on two pages—one for each of the two categories of expenses that do not directly impact student learning. Figure 14.1 is a sample spreadsheet. I am suggesting one spreadsheet for each of the two categories, but business office personnel may prefer only one spreadsheet for cost reduction.

Cost per student is the common denominator of school finance.

Regarding business, John Bogle (2009) wrote, "[Financial institutions] have a large incentive to favor the complex and costly over the simple and cheap, quite the opposite of what most investors need and ought to want" (p. 72). In this instance, tax payers are investors and seeing cost per student when deciding how to vote on a referendum speaks volumes about school system leadership.

| **Figure 14.1** | Sample Spreadsheet for Finance |

Cost per Student (CPS) for Expenditures
That Do Not Assist Student Learning or Safety

	2015 CPS	2016 CPS	2017 CPS	2018 CPS
Empty dumpsters				
Dispose of used oil				
Dispose of old tires				
Dispose of old batteries				
Auto insurance				
Bus insurance				
Worker's comp insurance				
Fire insurance				
Attorneys				
Subs for jury duty				
Travel for New Laws Conf.				
Vandalism				
Attendance reports				
Annual floor waxing				

CONTINUOUS STRATEGIC IMPROVEMENT FOR FINANCE AND OPERATIONS

The strategic aspect of continuous strategic improvement is the same in finance as with instruction and personnel—determine the problem, then the root causes of the problem, and then select one of the root causes for a countermeasure as a hypothesis. What do we think, if carried out successfully, will reduce costs per student without harming learning or safety? If the problem is overtime for payroll staff, and if one root cause of this expense is payroll errors, then a countermeasure will be a hypothesis for reducing payroll errors. If the problem is maintenance expenses are not improving learning or safety, and one root cause is replacing broken windows, a further study will be necessary to determine why there are so many broken windows. It might be discovered that one cause of broken windows is lawnmowers kicking up rocks. A countermeasure is then written to counter the broken window costs.

Every employee must be involved in reducing costs that do not add to learning or safety. Why everyone? Seth Godin (2010) says it well: "Artists are people with a genius for finding a new answer, a new connection, or a new way of getting things done. That would be you" (p. 8). Every employee can provide ideas for reducing costs that do not add to learning or safety.

LONG-TERM VIEW

The purchasing department needs direction from senior executives that long-term savings is more important than quick savings. An Australian mining operation never received this message. "There were five drill rigs on the site, and each was a different make and model, with different performance characteristics. Apparently, when they were purchased, over time, the corporate procurement department had gone for the lowest cost units" (Liker & Franz, 2011). The quick savings in purchasing made parts inventory nearly impossible which resulted in increased maintenance costs. Costs per pupil, year after year, give employees a long-term view of finance.

Two practices must be in place for employees to embrace cost savings: (1) Nobody loses their job because of these savings—a different job maybe, but not "no job"; and (2) employees must see the benefits to students because of their efforts. The landscaping staff can deliver the new trombone to the band that was purchased with window replacement savings. The kitchen staff can deliver new equipment to the family consumer science staff that was purchased with savings in workers compensation insurance claims by having safer shoes in the kitchen

Figure 14.2 Optimization Matrix

	SYSTEM Sub-Optimize	**SYSTEM** Optimize
PEOPLE Optimize	All students are honored for improving in depleted curriculum. All employees know how they contributed to success of system. Some subjects rob time from other subjects. Teachers at Levels 4 or 5 desire the implementation of the Personnel Dichotomous Rubric. No success. Some employees are cost conscious, but no support from system.	All students are honored for improving in rich curriculum. All employees know how they contributed to success of system. No subject can rob time from other school subjects. All teachers not at Levels 4 or 5 are either being documented or on assistance plan. No employees harmed by system's effort to reduce expenses that are not directly helping students.
PEOPLE Sub-Optimize	Some students honored in depleted curriculum. Some employees know their contribution to success of system. Some subjects rob time from other subjects. Personnel dichotomous rubric is rejected; excuses abound. Nobody cares about fixed costs. When a problem cut staff.	No subject can rob time from other school subjects. Some students honored in rich curriculum. Some employees know their contribution to success of system. Strong hiring evaluation, hiring system is undermined by some administrators. Worry about losing work hampers system effort to put more money in classrooms.

(spilled soup is slippery). Everybody assists in savings and everybody knows when their countermeasure worked.

The finance department becomes tenacious in regard to reducing what used to be called *fixed costs*. Expenditures are not fixed and can always be reduced. Leadership does not replace good management of resources but does bring the finance office much closer to the learning process.

Our updated Optimization Matrix is Figure 14.2 and our updated Optimization Fishbone is Figure 14.3. The fishbone addition is at the very bottom as reducing wasted money and at the far right as an ATB celebration with fewer dollars spent than ever before on items that do not directly impact student learning.

Figure 14.3	Optimization Fishbone

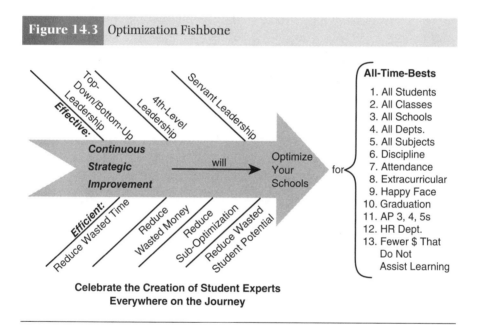

**Celebrate the Creation of Student Experts
Everywhere on the Journey**

LOOKING AHEAD

Thus far I have written many suggestions regarding continuous strategic improvement. They can all be implemented over time, but the deeper issue is creating a culture of continuous improvement. The next three chapters describe what districts look like and believe when they have a culture of continuous strategic improvement. First is a chapter of teacher expertise with the LtoJ® process (Chapter 15), then principal expertise (Chapter 16) and finally an ABC reflection upon the values described in this book (Chapter 17).

PART V

Creating a Culture of Continuous Strategic Improvement

15

Classroom
Teacher Experts in Continuous Strategic Improvement

In many US schools priorities were muddled beyond recognition.

—Amanda Ripley, 2013

In Chapter 5, I described the basics of continuous strategic improvement for classrooms and schools. In this chapter, I will explain the additional graphs for classrooms and what each provides for the teacher and the students. Each of the graphs has a distinct purpose and communicates over and over a clear priority for the class as a whole. Everyone will know if the class is on the path of creating experts. Remember, students are creating all of the graphs, not the teacher.

THE BASICS

The basics explained in Chapter 5 are (1) students are provided at the beginning of the school year or course precisely what they will learn; (2) students are assessed on a non-graded quiz almost weekly on their progress toward meeting end-of-year standards; (3) student graph their individual progress; and (4) some students are assigned the responsibility of graphing the total for the whole class, grade level, department or school. These graphs of classes and schools are almost like a scoreboard at an athletic event, except there is no opponent. The goal is to outperform results from past quizzes, or performance measures, rather than outperform an opponent.

Further, in Chapter 5 the histogram was introduced. I placed the histogram in this chapter because it is the histogram that shows the movement from the L curve through the bell curve onto the J curve. Resource Z shows how a set of histograms can be displayed for the whole year. It is easy, when all of them are on one page, to follow the journey as the classroom moves from the L to the J.

In the 21st century when people think of data, they almost always think of computers. Rarely do we see data that has not been generated by some software. Educators do need software to create the necessary graphs for results (summative) data that arrives annually. However, for process (formative) data, no software is needed; we have kids to do the work. Educators cannot complain about a lack of engagement when the computer is doing all the work. In addition, it is the teacher that is entering the data into the computer. Please, no. The students do the work. I explained in Chapter 5 that the students are completing the run charts for themselves and their classrooms. Next is the explanation for creating the other graphs.

> *Educators cannot complain about a lack of engagement when the computer is doing all the work.*

THE SCATTER DIAGRAM

The **scatter diagram** is not to be confused with the scatterplot. They are very similar, with one key difference. If three students score ten correct on a quiz, a scatter plot has one dot at 10, whereas a scatter diagram has 3 dots at ten. It is the scatter diagram that means so much to teachers and students. Figure 15.1 is a sample scatter diagram showing the dots for each of the quizzes.

When I first learned about the scatter diagram in 1992, I did not want it displayed in the classroom because of the fear of embarrassing students. However, it was teachers who convinced me of the power of the scatter diagram and how much students like it. They reported no negatives because of embarrassment. So now, I recommend that the scatter diagram be a central aspect of continuous strategic improvement. Students and teachers alike receive joy from seeing the dots gradually move from the lower left of the graph to the upper right of the graph.

Figure 15.1 Scatter Diagram

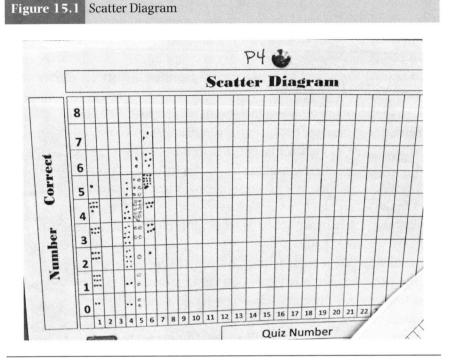

The collecting of the information for the scatter diagram varies among teachers. Methods I have observed are

1. One student per row or table places the dots on the classroom scatter diagram.

2. One student is assigned the responsibility to score the papers and to place the dots on the scatter diagram as scoring is completed.

THE HISTOGRAM—SOME DETAILS

The histogram has the same information as the scatter diagram except that each week is a separate graph and has the advantage of displaying the L, bell, and the J curves. Further, the histogram is engaging for students as they become quite creative in their artwork on the histogram. Even in kindergarten, students understand that they are working toward the J curve as a team of learners.

Figure 15.2 is a histogram from the second week of school in Karen Toenjes' Phoenix Grade 4 classroom learning Latin and Greek prefixes, suffixes, and root words. It is a beautiful L showing that the standards are high.

Figure 15.2 Histogram of Latin/Greek

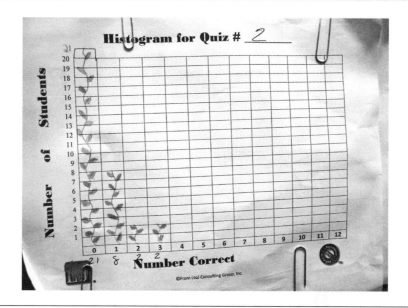

I have observed five different ways that teachers display the histograms:

1. A booklet is made with each subsequent histogram being placed on top of the prior histogram. This makes it possible for people to flip through the histogram booklet, as one would a cartoon type booklet, and observe the movement from *L* to *J*.

2. The first histogram is displayed along with the most recent histogram (Figure 15.3).

3. All the histograms are displayed above the whiteboard telling the full story of the year.

4. Often secondary teachers utilize one bulletin board for all the graphs from all of their classes. In this structure, only the most recent histogram is displayed.

5. Some teachers prefer to display all of the histograms for the year to tell the story of success (Figure 15.4). On the website, www .LtoJConsulting.com, under "Free LtoJ Support" and then "Blank Graphs," are histogram masters designed to be enlarged in school systems that have poster makers. This allows all twenty-eight histograms to be displayed on one poster.

Figure 15.3 *L* to Bell Histograms

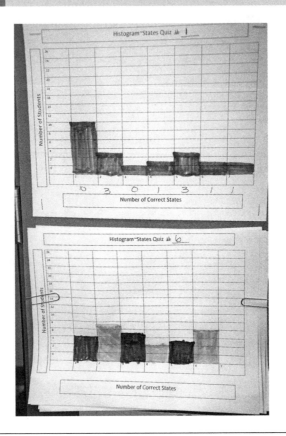

Figure 15.4 Histogram Story

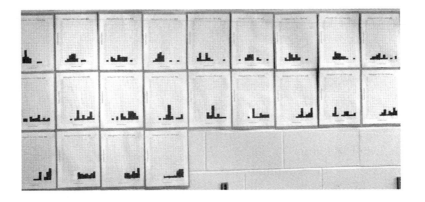

Some teachers have used the histogram as the method for collecting all of the classroom data. The histogram is passed around the classroom and each student colors in one cell. When this is all complete, the data is available for the class run chart and scatter diagram.

THE SCATTER OVERLAY

The **scatter overlay** combines the scatter diagram and the student run chart (see Figure 15.5). It is *never* used as a display on the wall, but its best use is for IEP (Individualized Education Program) meetings when the question, "How did the student do compared to the rest of the class?" is asked. It is a perfect picture of an individual student's progress compared to the progress of the class as a whole. There are no privacy issues because the scatter diagram has no names. Both teachers and principals tell me how much time is saved in IEP meetings when everyone can observe the same scatter overlay.

Figure 15.5   Scatter Overlay

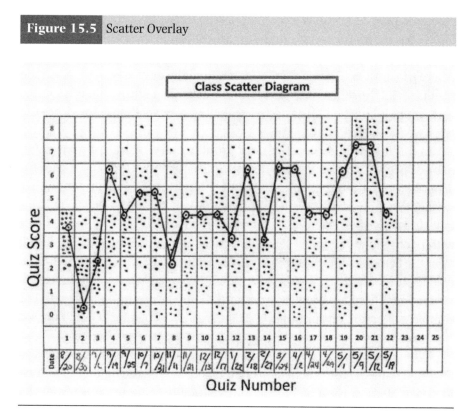

There are four ways I have observed the construction of the scatter overlay:

1. Copy the scatter diagram and reproduce the student run chart by hand on the scatter diagram.

2. Make a transparency of the class scatter diagram and place the transparency over the student run chart.

3. Project the scatter diagram on the interactive whiteboard. Connect the dots for the one student and print.

4. Photograph the scatter diagram and load into a computer. Draw the student run chart on this photo and print or print the scatter diagram directly from a smartphone and then connect the dots for the student scheduled to have the IEP.

ITEM ANALYSIS

The item analysis graph is merely recording the errors from most errors to fewest errors. All the other graphs count correct answers; the item analysis graph counts errors. Why? The students and teachers need to know where the most errors are occurring because the only way to increase the results on all the other charts is to decrease errors. Figure 15.6 is a sample item analysis chart created in a Grade 4 class with spelling errors from the prior week's spelling quiz.

In this instance, the teacher Codi Hrouda, had one student write down missed spelling words and then pass the paper around the room while students had other assignments. In about ten minutes, each student either wrote down new words or placed a tally mark by the word if some student had already written that particular word. Remember, this spelling quiz was with twenty-four randomly selected words at the time of the quiz, selected from the complete list of over 400 words for the year. The students and the teacher know if missed words are review words that have been taught previously, or if they are preview words yet to appear in the curriculum. For complete direction on continuous strategic improvement with spelling, see "Let's Fix Spelling" located at http://LtoJconsulting.com/e-books/.

When the item analysis chart is presented to the teacher by the assigned student, the teacher has two responsibilities. The first is to look at review items missed by far too many students. One response from the teacher is, "Well, the way I explained this the first time didn't stick. So, I am going to think about a better way to explain this tonight and we'll deal with this item first thing tomorrow." The second responsibility is to

Figure 15.6 Class Item Analysis

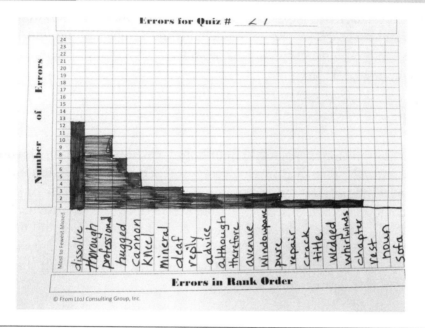

Source: Courtesy of Codi Hrouda.

look at preview items missed by very few students. If a topic has not even been taught yet but most of the class answered the question correctly, then the pacing of the year will be adjusted.

Sometimes, teachers do not introduce the item analysis chart at the very beginning of the school year. If most students are missing most of the questions, then the chart is rather useless. Some teachers save the item analysis until the class run chart plateaus. Typically, the run chart increases regularly in the beginning of the school year and then it flatlines. At that time, the teacher introduces the item analysis chart to figure out a way to get the class run chart back on an improvement trajectory.

RESOURCES

The blank graphs teachers need are on the website, www.LtoJConsulting .com, under "Free LtoJ Support" and then "Blank Graphs." For LtoJ® quizzes on background knowledge, teachers need to determine how many questions they will ask per quiz and then download the quizzes for that number. For example, if a teacher was quizzing students on recognizing the US states, and since there are fifty states, there would be seven questions per quiz, because the square root is the approximate number of questions for each quiz. Thus the teacher would download the blank graphs for seven questions. Five graphs are in the file: student run chart, class run chart, scatter diagram, histogram, and item analysis. In addition, sample LtoJ® graphs are posted at http://LtoJconsulting.com/free-ltoj-support/sample-graphs/. The advantage of looking online at the graphs is they are in color.

TIME

Who has time for twenty-eight quizzes per year? Everybody who is running out of time during the year to teach all of the standards. Establishing a system that continually requires students to retrieve information from prior lessons actually saves time. Teachers then eliminate practices such as review time in class prior to quizzes and many even eliminate chapter tests. The focus completely changes from short-term memory for grades to long-term memory for life. Much time is saved in this significant strategy change.

ESTABLISHING A CULTURE OF CONTINUOUS STRATEGIC IMPROVEMENT

While I have described the five graphs utilized in classrooms where continuous strategic improvement is occurring, implementing graphs is not the most difficult job. Yes, there is a learning curve for everyone to figure out how to schedule the quizzes, how to assign students to the jobs, and how to make sure the process is efficient and doesn't take unnecessary time. However, having a school or school district where everyone is striving to do better than ever before is a big deal! We have been trained to think 100 percent is the ideal; it is not. The ideal is to have challenging work that nobody can earn 100 percent on the first of the school year and then everyone strives to get better and better. The reward for getting better is internal, with a "thank you" from the teacher.

Establishing a system that continually requires students to retrieve information from prior lessons actually saves time.

LOOKING AHEAD

For every organization, "The tools are the easy part; the culture change is the hard part" (Liker & Hoseus, 2008, p. 5). This requires a principal with a deep understanding of continuous strategic improvement visualizing an optimized school for all.

The Role of the Principal With Continuous Strategic Improvement

16

Praise that was vague, insincere, or excessive tended to discourage kids from working hard and trying new things. It had a toxic effect . . . To work, praise had to be specific, authentic and rare.

—Amanda Ripley, 2013

William Hatfield, former superintendent of Massac County School District in Illinois, was visiting a pre-kindergarten classroom. This classroom was implementing the LtoJ® process with mathematics, as described in Chapter 5. A class run chart was posted on the wall showing the total number of questions answered correctly, week by week, on the random math quizzes. The teacher had a can of labeled tongue depressors, each representing one of the year's math concepts. A different student was asked each week to draw out five of the sticks for the weekly 1:1 questioning. Bill visited the classroom a week when the class run chart plummeted and had the following conversation with a four-year-old student:

Bill:	What happened on your class run chart for math? Why did it go down?
Four-year-old:	Josh did it!
Bill:	What did Josh do?
Four-year-old:	He drew all shapes! (tongue depressors randomly drawn from the can; the corresponding questions all about naming shapes)
Bill:	*What are you going to do about this?*
Four-year-old:	We have a lot of work to do with shapes!

I have italicized the key question for administrators in this conversation. What is your hypothesis to make the learning better and get the run chart back on an improvement trajectory? The job of the principal is not to come into the classroom to make sure the teacher is doing what they were told (unless on an assistance plan). The job is to know (1) if progress is being charted and posted for students and parents to see, and (2) to know that when the chart goes into a valley or it plateaus, the teacher and her students all know what hypothesis is being tested to increase learning. The administrator, through the seeking of hypotheses is constantly working to establish problem solving as the key element of the work culture. Otherwise, organizations turn sour as described by Jeffrey Liker and James Franz (2011): "Without a problem-solving culture . . . we were the proverbial drowning person. All the workers could do . . . was get angry and either accept the frustration . . . or blame others" (p. 249).

> *The administrator, through the seeking of hypotheses is constantly working to establish problem solving as the key element of the work culture.*

EXPERIENCE, MENTORS, AND HYPOTHESES

If experience were the best teacher, we would not need hypotheses or each other's mentoring; keep on covering chapters and all will be fine. However, all is not fine in education land, so we must learn from each other and from testing hypotheses. Thus, a wonderful response from a teacher when asked what hypothesis is being tested is, "I learned from a colleague in our grade-level meeting about this idea. I shared it with my students and they wanted to try it out. So I told them that we'd test this hypothesis for three weeks. If it didn't work, we'd have a class meeting and try something else." Another wonderful response from a teacher to her principal was, "In the meeting, we saw that all of our classes were having the same problem. We brainstormed hypotheses and agreed that each of us would test this idea for three weeks." The point is that the principal is asking, "What is your hypothesis?" and is involved at a deep level. Many principals were themselves superb teachers and have become highly admired by their staffs. These principals have suggestions for hypotheses. They say, "This process worked for me, but it may not work for you or for this set of students. Why don't you try this out for three weeks and see if it works. I'll check on you later to see if the class run chart shows progress." Three weeks is long enough to know if a hypothesis is going to bring about improvement. Further, "a series of experiments is required to discover the main causes of trouble" (Orsini, 2013, pp. 241–242). Liker and Franz (2011), reporting on continuous improvement implementation in business wrote, "The scientific method . . . was a huge cultural change to start to apply this to daily problems rather than simply jumping to solutions" (p. 231). Hypothesis testing is constant. This is exactly what some in business experienced. "I also learned the meaning of 'in your face' problem solving. Unless the problems are 'in your face,' they tend to get ignored or pushed out to another day" (p. 272).

ADDITION

The most overlooked tool for principals is addition. How is the school doing as a whole? Add it up. Figure 16.1 is a graph from Central City Middle School in Central City, Nebraska. The total correct for the whole school is posted weekly with the all-time-bests clearly designated. Simple addition. The principal must be deeply involved in the success of student learning or else the staff see

The most overlooked tool for principals is addition.

chart making as another administrative or legislative mandate that wastes time. Figure 16.2 is from the Centennial Elementary School in Columbus, Nebraska. The graph is only for mathematics, but this chart has an annual goal—to outperform all prior years; it is the top line indicating the best week ever for the school.

The employees perceive correctly that the task of posting and celebrating student body success is an aspect of servant leadership. The principal is celebrating along with the students and staff but is also helping teachers figure out what to do when the graph plateaus. Because every student and every teacher wants the total correct in the school to increase, any help provided by the principal is correctly perceived as servant leadership. If the principal desires something different than the teachers desire, the

| Figure 16.1 | Schoolwide Run Chart for All Subjects in Middle School |

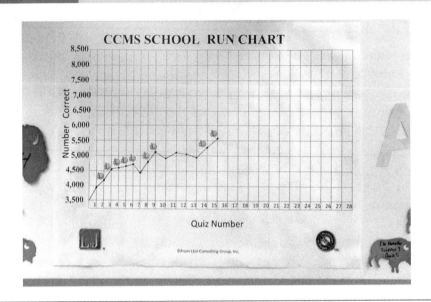

Source: Courtesy of Darron Arlt.

| Figure 16.2 | Schoolwide Math Run Chart |

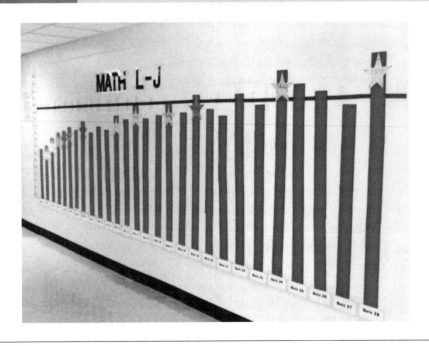

principal's work is considered pressure. But when the staff and principal desire the same outcome, the principal's work is considered servant leadership. Totals correct for the whole school is a superb tool for our servant (principal) leader.

The same attitude is true in all organizations.

An investigation showed the supervisors and management in the successful departments responded to the indications on the charts. They encouraged workers to make changes and monitored the effects with the charts. The other departments made, but ignored the charts. No changes were made to operating practices. Workers had to keep the charts, but nothing came of their efforts. They complained about doing the extra work for nothing. (Ha, 2002, p. 148)

FREE

We have everybody involved in determining hypotheses, giving non-graded assessments, and celebrating individual, classroom, grade-level, department-, and schoolwide improvement. I hope readers have picked up that continuous strategic improvement is basically free. Yes, there are staff development costs, but there is no software, no hardware, and no expensive licenses to procure. Telling the student body how proud you are of them is free and when there is a graph on the wall to support the principal's pride, the students and staff know it's not vague, but genuine praise. Remember, "Our approach is not a slave to data collection and statistical analysis; rather it uses data and direct observation for root-cause analysis and to assess interventions" (Liker & Franz, 2011, p. 240).

I know principals want to be deeply involved in student learning and continuous strategic improvement gives them even more opportunities. They need to look for the weeks that the school had an all-time-best (ATB), but just barely, by a question or two. Principals know which students are really struggling. They may not know all students, but they know who these students are. When the school barely has an all-time-best by one or two questions, find a struggling student who also had an all-time-best. Let the student know that you, as principal, know that the school had its ATB because of this struggling student's improvement. If he had answered two fewer questions correctly, the whole school would not have been able to celebrate.

This same conversation can also be held with a class that previously plateaued. They started to overcome the problem, increased their score by a few over prior weeks, and thus the school had an all-time-best. Powerful and free.

In Norman, Oklahoma, Principal Chris Crelia posts panther paws to build a chain of paws on the walls of the school (Figure 16.3). Each paw represents a student or a class with an all-time-best. When a student has an ATB, the paw has the name of the student, date, and subject. No number is posted. When a class has an ATB, the total correct for the class can be added. Teachers report to me that this is the most powerful practice they have ever done for special education students. Under the traditional mastery concept, students need 80 percent or higher to have public recognition and many special education students never make it. However, when ATBs are posted and announced, everybody is recognized for getting better. Again, it's free and we do not give candy and other extrinsic incentives. We publicly say "Thank you; I'm proud of you."

> *Teachers report to me that this is the most powerful practice they have ever done for special education students.*

I wrote in *Permission to Forget* students in the USA normally receive over 10,000 incentives from kindergarten through grade twelve. Five times a day, times 180 days, times thirteen years, equals 11,700 incentives. In the elementary grades, incentives are typically stickers, erasers, popcorn

---

Figure 16.3 ATBs in Hallway

Source: Courtesy of Chris Crelia.

parties, and more recess time. In secondary schools, the incentives are typically grades, video, and food. If incentives worked, this book would not be necessary (Jenkins, 2013). Daniel Pink (2009) in his book *Drive* reports a great deal of evidence

Five times a day, times 180 days, times thirteen years, equals 11,700 incentives.

on this topic. He wrote, "Only contingent rewards—if you do this, then you'll get that—had the negative effect. Why? 'If then' rewards require people to forfeit some of their autonomy" (p. 38). He uses the term *rewards* for both bribes and thank yous. My preference is to use the term *celebration* as a thank you for a job well done. Principal pictures are often on the front page of the newspaper for giving if-then rewards. "If you kids read this many books, I'll shave my head," is an example. We would be far better off to track learning and when students have an all-time-best to merely say, "Thanks, I'm so proud of you!" Further, the message for students is that learning is not so much fun, so we have to do something extra to get you kids to learn. The result is that "adding certain kinds of extrinsic rewards on top of inherently interesting tasks can often dampen motivation and diminish performance" (Pink, 2009, p. 37). "Rewards can perform a weird sort of behavioral alchemy: They can transform an interesting task into a drudge. They can turn play into work. And by diminishing intrinsic motivation, they can send performance, creativity, and even upstanding behavior toppling like dominoes" (p. 37). One of the key advantages of continuous strategic improvement is that the principal has daily opportunities for real compliments, not vague and superficial ones.

Stuart Albert (2013) wrote, "Ask a team to report when they think they are half done" (p. 73). The principal can say to every grade level and every department in secondary schools, "Let me know when your grade level or department has 25 percent, 50 percent, and 75 percent correct. Further let me know your highest percentage for the year." Teachers must know that their principal cares about student growth, shares in the joy when the benchmarks are reached, and can help hypothesize with teachers ways to improve even more. It is especially rewarding for the principals when a team reaches a benchmark early. For example, half way through the school year is typically week 18. Did the department or grade level hit 50 percent correct on end-of-year expectations earlier than week 18?

I call this calculation the "Hope Calculator." Determine perfect. If every student answered every question correctly, how many questions would be correct? Next determine the percentage of the year that has transpired or what percentage of the quizzes have been used out of the twenty-eight. Then determine the percentage correct for the student body. Is the student body ahead of schedule? If so, shout the "speeding" results loud and clear to parents, staff, and students. An example in math fluency comes from Mark Twain Elementary School in Colorado Springs. Math specialist, Melinda McConnaughey, leads the schoolwide effort along with her principal. Here is the data:

Possible correct for whole school: 10,310

Percentage of quizzes utilized: 10 of 28, which is 36%

Number correct on quiz 10: 5347

Percentage correct on quiz 10: 53%

"Speeding gap": 17%; which is 53% – 36% = 17%

What servant leader wouldn't want to congratulate all the student body for their math fluency work?

BUSINESSLIKE

I know well that education is being pushed to be more "businesslike." So, since business seems to be successful with bonuses, shouldn't education follow suit? Not so fast. "Reporting the results for the Federal Reserve Bank of Boston, the researchers wrote, 'In eight of the nine tasks we examined across the three experiments, higher incentives led to worse performance" (Pink, 2009, p. 41). Mark Murphy (2012) wrote about success without bonuses: "The sales force is noncommissioned. Yes, you read that right—sales engineers without traditional commissions grew sales 56 percent in 2011 at a billion-dollar company. They have bonuses tied to worldwide sales goals, but not the individual incentives you'd typically see" (p. 34).

I want principals to recognize that if one tries "to encourage a kid to learn math by paying her for each workbook page she completes—and she'll almost certainly become diligent in the short term and lose interest in math in the long term" (Pink, 2009, p. 39). Principals are key leaders in negating this harmful practice occurring in our homes and classrooms.

One of the problems with children and with young adults is they can often be manipulated with the promise of a reward. The younger people are often insulted but do not have the money or maturity to fight back. Not so with Joe Torre, former manager of the New York Yankees. When asked why he quit as the Yankees manager he replied, "I could get the money back if we won this, that, and the other thing. I was insulted that they thought I needed to be motivated financially" (Brady, 2010, p. 96).

THE PRINCIPLE TEACHER

One of my favorite examples of the principal becoming the principle teacher comes from the Maple Glen Elementary School in Westfield Washington School District near Indianapolis, Indiana. Principal Joe Montalone implemented what you have read earlier in this book: almost weekly quizzes on the year's standards, graphing results from students, classrooms and grade levels and he extended item analysis to the grade level. Then, the principle teacher, Joe Montalone, took the process one step further. He organized packets for parents to have over the summer.

He wrote,

Maple Glen Parent,

As summer approaches, the one question that is most often asked is, "What can I do as a parent to help my child retain the information that was taught over the course of the year?" Throughout this school year, your child has taken weekly quizzes (Reaching for the Stars) that helped reinforce the most important concepts taught. Each question on the quiz corresponds to a specific concept. By assessing students multiple times on the same concept, profound long term learning takes place. So what can you do? We are encouraging you to continue to use these quizzes to help reinforce these concepts throughout the summer. In the binder provided, you will find the following items: 10 weekly quizzes and answer key, previous graph from reaching for the stars, and an empty graph. The following process will take only 20–25 minutes once every week:

- **Step 1:** Give your child the weekly quiz #1 in a quiet setting (10–15 minutes).
- **Step 2:** Using the answer key, go over the answers.
- **Step 3:** Graph how many questions were answered correctly on the blank graph that is provided.
- **Step 4:** If the same numbered question is missed consecutively from week to week (example: Question number 2 is missed three times in a row) then go to the school website (www.mges.k12.in.us) and there will be some lessons that can be given to help reinforce the concept.
- **Step 5:** Repeat this same process the following week using quiz 2, 3, 4, etc.

Just a few minutes a week can make a profound difference in your child's ability to retain the information that they've learned throughout the year. If you have any questions, please don't hesitate to contact me or your classroom teacher.

The leadership example has many elements. The superintendent, Mark Keen, suggested that his principal read *Permission to Forget*. Joe Montalone garnered the help of two teachers, Libby Baud and Laura Melling, to experiment in their classroom and then expanded their success to the whole school. Lastly, Joe experimented again. Basically, he said that the continuous improvement process described in Chapters 5 and 15 worked, but the school still had room to grow. In other words, the school was not perfect. Instead of purchasing a new program, he expanded what was already successful and most parents continued the continuous improvement process during ten weeks of summer. And the final good news is our principle teacher assessed the students to see if the summer project helped. He compared the results from posttest results in the spring to the first pretest the following year. While the students did not do quite as well in the fall as in the spring, it was almost as good. Teachers reported to Joe Montalone that they were accustomed to spending six to seven weeks of review in the fall and the review was now down to six to seven days. If all schools added twenty to twenty-five days a year onto the school year, the cost in the United States alone would be approximately $60 billion. Look what was accomplished for free. The students scored almost as well in the fall as they did in the prior spring. In fact, there was no significant difference between the spring score and the next fall's score. The combination of taking away permission to forget during the school year and extending quizzes over summer stopped the summer educational loss. Amazing.

> *If all schools added twenty to twenty-five days a year onto the school year, the cost in the United States alone would be approximately $60 billion.*

"At Toyota teaching is considered the central part of any manager's job" (Liker & Meier, 2007, p. 7). Implementing this responsibility in education is difficult with legislators using their power to communicate that evaluating is considered the central part of a principal's job. Nevertheless, I am going to finish this chapter with advice for the principle teacher—the principal.

The principle teacher is to help the staff look for common problems instead of thinking everything is unique. Our best servant leaders help solve common problems. Students forgetting week to week and over the summer is certainly a common problem. "Most people tend to look at any situation and first consider the unique or creative aspects rather than the common and teachable aspects" (Liker & Meier, 2007, p. 28). My work described in *Permission to Forget* is designed to assist administrators in looking for and removing common problems. This will take a great deal of teaching—a lifetime of teaching. When confronted with a problem, the principal needs to start with Deming's assessment that 94 to 97 percent of the problems come from the system and very, very few are unique and caused by the students or their parents. The same percentage works in business. Liker and Franz (2011) writing about one of the companies that hired them wrote, "I marveled that incredibly smart professionals were impeded daily by even more incredibly broken processes" (p. 265). Once this fact is established, the problem solving leadership process can begin.

Principals are to let staff know that bringing problems to the surface is expected and burying them is frowned upon. Why? Every problem is "an opportunity to develop people" (Liker & Meier, 2007, p. 3). The leader can be very successful when the leader understands "when bad news is brought up, you cannot react negatively, or you will inevitably lose the trust of people when it comes to bringing up any further bad news" (Liker & Franz, 2011, p. 304). And this attitude of digging into root causes to help people is for the long haul. "Studies have found that experts in various fields take 10 years to reach a high level of performance, with thousands of hours of deep practice in that time . . . most companies have moved onto a different program before they reach their 10-year anniversary" (p. 386).

> *Principals are to let staff know that bringing problems to the surface is expected and burying them is frowned upon.*

After the principal has established a practice of listening to staff, without negative reactions, and developed the habit of using problems as an opportunity to teach, the next step is formal listening in addition to 1:1 listening. Formal "listening" comes from data and from asking everyone. The radar chart was described in Chapter 8 for the school district or division. However, principals need their own radar chart. It won't have as many vectors as the district radar chart, but certainly enough to keep everyone busy. The same process as described in Chapter 9 is then used for the school plan. Why is this listening? It is for two reasons: (1) The data screams out the waste or gaps between perfect and where we are now; and (2) the staff, by writing their countermeasures are communicating with their principal regarding what they believe will be of the most help in closing the gaps.

LISTENING

Three tools for asking everyone are the plus/delta, nominal group technique, and priority matrix. With the plus/delta (Resource D) the principal asks "What went well in our school this past month?" and "What could

I change to make things better next month?" This will work if the principal promises to probably make only one change a month and then follow through. The Nominal group technique is asking staff to rank their choices on a particular topic. First place obtains 3 points, second place 2 points and third place 1 point. Points are added up to see the staffs' priorities. A third formal listening tool is the priority matrix (see Figure 16.4). It is set for ten variables. However, the explanation below is with five variables in order to make the explanation simpler.

The priority matrix has one line for each item under consideration. Let's say the faculty was helping the principal understand the biggest time wasters. They brainstormed five, so there would be five lines in the priority matrix.

1. Grading Papers
2. Lesson Plans
3. Staff Meetings
4. Interruptions
5. Practice State Exams

Figure 16.4 Blank Priority Matrix

										Number of	
1	1	1	1	1	1	1	1	1	1	1s	______
	2	3	4	5	6	7	8	9	10		
2	2	2	2	2	2	2	2	2		2s	______
	3	4	5	6	7	8	9	10			
3	3	3	3	3	3	3	3			3s	______
	4	5	6	7	8	9	10				
4	4	4	4	4	4	4				4s	______
	5	6	7	8	9	10					
5	5	5	5	5	5					5s	______
	6	7	8	9	10						
6	6	6	6	6						6s	______
	7	8	9	10							
7	7	7	7							7s	______
	8	9	10								
8	8	8								8s	______
	9	10									
9	9									9s	______
	10										
10										10s	______
Total											

After Grading Papers the following numerals are typed: 1/2; 1/3; 1/4; 1/5.

The numerals after Lesson Plans are 2/3, 2/4, and 2/5.

The numerals after Staff Meetings are 3/4 and 3/5.

The numerals after Interruptions are 4/5.

No numerals are after Practice State Exams.

The job of the teachers is to circle one numeral in each pair of numerals. For example, after Grading Papers 1/2, the teacher asks himself, "What is the bigger time waster? Number 1 or number 2? If grading papers is the bigger time waster, the teacher circles 1. The process continues with comparing 1 to 3, 1 to 4, and 1 to 5. On the next row, the teacher compares 2 to 3, 2 to 4, and 2 to 5.

After each row is completed, the teachers count up the number of 1s circled on the whole page, the number of 2s circled, the number of 3s and 4s circled, and finally, the number of 5s circled. This page is turned in and the totals for the whole faculty are added up. With this data, the principal knows which of the five time wasters to tackle first. The priority matrix gives everybody a voice and also requires a comparison of every item to every other item.

LISTENING TO THE WHOLE STUDENT BODY

Four of the many questions asked by PISA (Program for International Student Assessment) at the end of their academic exams are below. They are great questions with the students stating strongly agree, agree, disagree, or strongly disagree for each of the twenty or so questions.

1. I was able to try new things without worrying about embarrassment.

2. I do my personal best when working for something for myself or others to see.

3. I was able to express what I learned in many ways.

4. I understand what I was taught.

These are great questions and principals do care about the results. The only problem with results data is that the results come to the principal when the year is over. The solution is to ask questions multiple times during the year, but who has time to take all of these surveys and tabulate the results? Surprise. Sampling is the solution.

The steps are

1. Randomly select students from the whole student body. The square root of the student body is the number of students to randomly select.

2. Bring these students to a separate location.

3. Ask the students to write down the names of five friends. Tell the students you will not collect the names of the students.

4. Then ask your questions. "How many of your five friends would say they understand what the teacher is teaching?" How many of your five friends will try new things without being afraid of embarrassment?" "How many of your five friends do their best almost all of the time?" "How many of your five friends are able to express what they are learning in different ways?"

Results data is typically all the information, from all the people. A final exam, for example, is a complete set of questions for all students. Process data throughout the year is a sampling of questions and/or a sampling of students. When process sampling, data is collected regularly throughout the year, it is very accurate. With process data, as described above, the principal can have enough information to make adjustments prior to the collection of the results, final data.

Reflection

The continual total for the whole school is one of the most powerful tools a principal can ever use. The hurdle, however, is getting started. What data is the school now collecting that could be used to make the first schoolwide graphs? Could reading fluency work? What about the total number of office referrals for discipline posted each week?

LOOKING AHEAD

Continuous strategic improvement is for the superintendent and board also, not just for the teachers and principal. When people lead with continuous strategic improvement, many of the problems swirling around can be mitigated or solved. It took intrinsic motivation to read this book; my hope is the concepts presented will help readers utilize the intrinsic motivation within the students and adults they are leading. Twenty-six principles to help readers reflect on their continuous strategic improvement journey are next. When principals and other administrators implement these principles, their schools will move much closer to optimization.

Reflection   **17**

Improvement of education, and the management of education, require application of the same principles that must be used for the improvement of any process, manufacturing or service.

—W. Edwards Deming, 1994

C ontinuous strategic improvement puts the wheels on servant leadership. Think of this chapter as a time to reflect upon the spokes. Even if you skip this chapter for now, take time later to reflect upon these spokes as you ramp up your commitment to servant leadership and continuous strategic improvement.

A IS FOR *ALWAYS*

There is always a better way. No matter what is implemented this year and no matter how much closer the system comes to perfection, there is always a better way. The better way could be (1) better results or (2) the same results in less time or with less cost. If time is saved, then it can be used to improve other areas of the system. For example, if the assistant principal took care of the same number of discipline referrals as in prior years but was able to accomplish the procedures in half of the time, then this better way provides time for improving other aspects of the school. If cost is saved, well there is no end to the possible uses. We can always fine-tune the processes we now have. It will be good to also remember, "There is *always* more than one way to solve *any* problem" (Liker & Meier, 2006, p. 356).

B IS FOR *ALL-TIME-BEST*

The simple idea that students and adults are working to outperform their prior best rather than meet some arbitrary goal is a game changer. Every student, every employee, and every school can be a winner. These people and schools are not winners because they outperformed somebody else, but because they outperformed their prior best. This idea is powerful for struggling students who can see their record of all-time-bests (ATBs) and it is powerful for the best students who can no longer relax and collect their *A*s. They are challenged to collect ATBs like everyone else.

C IS FOR *CONTINUOUS*

People are accustomed to seeing two data points—this week and last week. What happened two weeks ago? Nobody knows. Continuous means that the graphs are long and narrow showing growth over time. The focus is on long-term gains instead of short-term events.

D IS FOR *W. EDWARDS DEMING*

He wrote that the number one job of a leader was to create more leaders. Toyota has put this into practice by having a goal of one leader for every five people. "The aim is to provide enough teachers and coaches to support each employee so that actual development of employees and leaders can take place" (Liker & Convis, 2012, p. 107). This advice is contrary to what American administrators are often told is the ideal; the flat organization is set up as the ideal. However, if leadership development is taken seriously, then grade-level chairpersons in elementary schools and department chairpersons in secondary schools are natural positions for initial leadership development. A ratio of 1:5 is not so far from possible and payment for this extra work is far superior to payment for test scores.

E IS FOR *EVERYBODY CONTRIBUTES*

No employee in the school district is expected to mindlessly carry out their responsibilities. So, when a new employee is hired, the directions are two-fold: (1) This is how we complete these tasks; and (2) when you have an idea how we can improve upon what we've told you, let us know. Nobody can say, "I just work here." If a school is to be optimized, then every student and every employee must contribute to the establishing of countermeasures and to their success. Further, everybody can be a part of the celebrations; they are not reserved for a select few.

F IS FOR *FRONT AND CENTER: THE CLASSROOM*

Small improvements in the classroom, year after year, add up to greatness. Jeffrey Liker and Gary Convis (2012) report that hundreds of visitors observe Toyota plants. They want to know how such superb excellence was achieved. Visitors are told that what they see is the result of years of small changes made by people doing the actual work on the assembly lines. They often do not believe it; they want to hear the story of some brilliant CEO who had a major epiphany and mandated a whole new method and upended the current method to create what the visitors now observe. In education, we must remove the word *steal* from the description of one teacher learning from another. The greatness of one classroom must be transferred to everybody year after year.

G IS FOR *GOAL*

The goal is to move closer to perfection. Do not arbitrarily establish a quota. No, the goal is to come closer and closer to perfection in a year after year process. We don't start over and over and over with new programs, based upon somebody else's research. No, we strive to move closer to perfection by fine-tuning what we are doing. Time is allocated for determining which countermeasure we believe will move us the closest to perfect, but no time is wasted on numerical goal setting (quota). The goal is a constant: moving closer to perfect, getting better and better.

H IS FOR *HYPOTHESIS*

The question to ask people is, "What hypothesis are you testing in an attempt to make it better?" When the question is asked and the response is, "I don't have any hypothesis; I'm just counting and graphing because I'm told to do this," there is a problem. It is not a problem when an employee tests out a hypothesis and finds out it doesn't make things better. We do not ask people what their goal is; the goal is common sense—get better. If the best week a school has ever had is four office referrals, then the goal is three office referrals in a week. If the best month in payroll is eleven errors, then the goal is ten errors. Goal setting should not be a macho activity of how high we can reach. It is all about establishing and testing countermeasures to improve.

I IS FOR *INVENTORY*

"Inventory hides problems" (Liker, 2004, p. 29). When I first read this, I wondered what this had to do with education other than the district warehouse (which could cost more than it saves). Then it dawned on me where education has inventory—it is the review the first weeks or months of every school year. At Toyota, the part that is to be installed on the car is delivered the day it is needed. No inventory. If

> A leader's job is to know gaps, which is the waste between perfect and current reality.

the part does not show up on the designated day, there is a problem to solve. If education started every school year with the new content for the current year, instead of review time, problems would immediately surface and they would need to be solved. As long as schools spend weeks or more in review and over-lap (inventory), many, many problems are hidden, and thus never solved.

J IS FOR *JOB TO KNOW GAPS*

A leader's job is to know gaps, which is the waste between perfect and current reality.

In the head of every principal and central office administrator is cemented the knowledge of the gaps. Yes, there are forty-five vectors on the instruction radar chart, there are employees at Levels 1 to 3 on the personnel rubric, and we spend a lot of money that has no positive impact on student learning. This is a lot to have on the tip of one's tongue, but educational leadership is a big job.

K IS FOR *KAIZEN*

Improvement is the aim—not change. The Japanese word *kaizen* is often used as a synonym for continuous improvement. *Kaizen* actually means change plus good. The purpose of continuous strategic improvement is not to create change, but to create positive change, moving closer to perfection.

L IS FOR *LEADER*

"In Toyota, the terms *sensei* (teacher) and *leader* are almost synony-mous" (Liker & Convis, 2012, p. 90). Our very best teachers should con-sider moving into administration as the primary job of administrators is teaching adults versus the former job of teaching young people.

Do you receive the same joy from teaching adults you used to receive from teaching children? If so, you are in the right job. If not, well . . .

> *The primary job of administrators is teaching adults versus the former job of teaching young people.*

M IS FOR *MOTIVATION*

The most powerful motivation is intrinsic. Students begin kindergarten with all the intrinsic motivation they need for life. We must use every strategy at our disposal to protect this motivation. The waste of student enthusiasm is one of education's biggest problems and it can be solved. Further, it is servant leaders who are operating at the fourth level of leadership who are able to maintain their staffs' enthusiasm for teaching.

N IS FOR *NON-GRADED QUIZ*

It is counterintuitive that 50 percent of students are motivated by graded exams and 90 percent are motivated by non-graded quizzes, as described in Chapters 5 and 15. It is amazing, but true. Students like keeping a record of their own improvement and contributing to the success of the whole classroom and whole school. This doesn't mean that grades disappear from schools; it does mean, however, that grades as a motivation tool only work for half of the students.

O IS FOR *OPTIMIZE AND SUB-OPTIMIZE*

If education is ever going to reach its potential for good in society, the sub-optimization where some people and some activities and some academic disciplines continually win over others must stop. The strategies in this book are all written so that schools can be optimized. Until some parents write the principals and say, "It's OK for my kid to be the loser kid," we must optimize the system for everybody. Until society says, "Who cares about _____ (academic subject)?" Schools must be optimized for all academics.

P IS FOR *PERMISSION TO FORGET®*

At a Christmas party in 2014, I was speaking with a very successful businessman who told me how stupid he often feels. The reason, he related, is that he crammed and forgot throughout K–12 and university. He really wishes he could remember the answers he put correctly on the exams.

No country can ever hope to have student experts graduating from their schools when "permission to forget" is the norm. The cram/get-a-grade/ forget cycle that starts with first-grade spelling and continues on through chapter tests and finals must stop now.

Q IS FOR *QUALITY*

"The quality of a product is the responsibility of management" (Deming, 1994, p. 16). As should be obvious to readers of this book, I am writing from the perspective that quality in instruction, HR, and finance are all necessary for a quality education. So, are there school superintendents who are experts in all three major aspects of operating a school district? There may be some, but not 16,000—one for every US school district. The continuous strategic improvement process taught in this book clearly places the responsibility on the superintendent for quality, but all have to bring their brain to work and write countermeasures. The top-down aspect from the superintendent is setting up the process; the bottom-up aspect is everybody's contribution.

R IS FOR *REMOVE*

Remove the non-value-added activities. There are ample opportunities for administrators to remove activities that waste time, student enthusiasm and money. Employees regain much hope for the organization when they witness the removal of these non-value-added activities. Sometimes, the non-value-added activity is legislated. In these cases, the responsibility of leadership is to determine where the compliance with this law is done in the least amount of time and share the processes with the admonition, "There is always a better way; see if you can improve even more on what I've shared with you."

S IS FOR *STABILIZE*

"One must standardize, and thus stabilize the process, before continuous improvements can be made" (Liker, 2004, p. 142). First comes alignment of the curriculum and then the essential step of stabilizing the curriculum. Stabilization is the agreements made with faculty regarding the formula for assessments. What percentage of every graded and every nongraded quiz will be content from prior grade levels and courses? No course is allowed to be an island unto itself. Even the career-tech courses that seem like they are 100 percent new content must be stabilized. They rely upon prior instruction and must be a part of the stabilization agreements.

T IS FOR *TEAMWORK*

I believe that educators understand the power of teamwork. The problem is that the total for the team is not a part of the culture of education. The students work together, for example, on a writing assignment, but the total rubric scores for the students are never posted. The students and the teacher do not know if the team improved or not. Teamwork is essential for all of the various elements of a school and school system to be optimized. The class run charts, the radar charts, and other displays all focus upon the results of the team. This never means that students do not track their individual progress. It is not individual versus team; it is individual *plus* team.

U IS FOR *UNRELIABLE FIGURES*

"Wherever there is fear, there will be wrong figures" (Deming, 1994, p. 43). I am not excusing the cheating that has taken place on tests in various parts of the United States. What Dr. Deming wrote is that in business and government, when bosses manage with fear, the numbers will be unreliable. When I heard Dr. Deming in 1992, he related the story of a company owner who promised that if the workers ever made 10 percent defective in one day, he would close the factory. The inspector, who had many worker friends, made sure there was never 10 percent defective. People resent their boss managing by fear and then these same people often turn around and manage their direct reports by fear. More unreliable figures passed down.

V IS FOR *VISIBLE*

Progress must be visible. In every classroom and by every office should be posted the current results of improvement efforts. The graph must be simple such as the number of payroll errors per month, the number of discipline referrals per week, or the number of classrooms with no substitute available per week. "What people are working on and when should be clear, simple, and visual. They should be able to walk you to the actual workplace, perhaps refer to documentation on the wall, and easily explain what they are working on" (Liker & Franz, 2011, p. 69).

W IS FOR *WASTE*

Removing waste is the fastest way to improve. The mindset of educators is often switch programs and textbooks, purchase the latest technology, restructure the schedule or calendar, and, of course, apply pressure. Removing waste is direct and based upon insights gained from studying the system and data. Why did only 75 percent of the students participate in extracurricular activities? Why did only 90 percent of our second graders read at 100 words per minute? We spent the money and time for 100 percent but did not achieve 100 percent. What "waste" can we attempt to remove next year? I know *waste* is a harsh word and maybe some would prefer the word *gap*. I do believe, however, that over time educators can embrace the word *waste* as long as the board and superintendent understand that since we will never be perfect, there will always be some waste. At Toyota, "All managers . . . go on regular 'waste walks'" (Liker & Franz, 2011, p. 131).

X IS FOR *EXPERT STUDENTS*

The best result from the optimization of schools is the creating of student experts. The students are *in* the system; the adults are responsible for working *on* the system. The structures described in *Optimize Your School* are all for working *on* the system to optimize for the good of everybody.

Y IS FOR *RANK AND YANK*

The opposite of optimize is "rank and yank," which means we grade on the curve, discourage a few more each year, and the students yank themselves out of the system. We blame the students by calling them *dropouts*. Optimization of schools will not make them perfect and eliminate all dropouts but will provide guidance and evidence of moving closer and closer to perfect each year.

Z IS FOR *ZZZZZZZ*

Each year a few more students lose their enthusiasm for school; they would rather sleep in. When one or two students per class of twenty to thirty students lose their enthusiasm for school, few are left after thirteen years. Optimized schools greatly reduce this tragedy. In this book, I have not blamed educators for the problem but have blamed the system created over decades of decisions designed to sub-optimize everything.

PART VI

Results

18 Data and Statistics

From a Continuous Strategic Improvement Perspective

The entire industry of statistical analysis seems unconcerned with practical accessibility.

—Douglas W. Hubbard, 2010

The body of knowledge for trend data has a number of heroes beginning with Walter Shewhart, Joseph Juran, and W. Edwards Deming. Donald Wheeler is probably the most prolific author writing today. Educators who venture off into a commitment to improvement and trend data may be charting new territory for education but certainly do not need to create the statistics.

Data-based decision making has been a topic of interest in education for a number of years. It seems that more and more data is being mined each year adding to the overload of figures and spreadsheets. In order to provide some statistical guidance for data-based decision making, I have included this chapter, which is basically a review of the statistical tools utilized throughout this book with some additional background information. My hope is that somewhere, someplace, professors in educational leadership and educational statistics will follow Hubbard's advice and help us all create data that is accessible and useful. Learning how to use trend data is the best place to start.

School administrators typically have two statistics courses—one in the master's degree program and one for the doctorate. The statistics is essentially the same for both degrees with the master's and doctoral students often in the same course. The universities have the statistics correct for the doctorate; the aim is to write an approved dissertation. The statistics course in the master's degree is often not designed for on-the-job assistance. Master's students ask, "Why do we need this course? We are not working on a dissertation." The professor replies that administrators need this course so they can interpret research done by others. This reasoning is wrong on two counts: (1) The life of school administrators is far too hectic to analyze research and (2) educators such as Bob Marzano and John Hattie have done a superb job of interpreting research for us. We need to listen to John Bogle (2009) who wrote, "We ignore the diamonds of simplicity, seeking instead the illusory rhinestones of complexity" (p. 23). More to the point, Douglas Hubbard (2010) wrote, "The limitations of statistics textbooks are part of the problems for managers seeking solutions to measurement challenges. The entire industry of statistical analysis seems unconcerned with practical accessibility" (p. 140).

IMPROVEMENT OR LUCK?

The answer to the question, "Was our increase in test scores a result of improvement in the school or was it luck because smarter kids moved into our school or some other kids moved away?" How does one know? The answer comes from middle school flip of the coin probability. When a school has two years of data, there is no way to know if it was luck or actual improvement. The probability is 50/50. If a school has its baseline data and then improves the next two years, the probability is now 25 percent luck and 75 percent chance of improvement. Each year the probability of luck is cut in half—12.5 percent to 6.25 percent to 3.12 percent, and so forth. We could use the statistical term *levels of confidence* to explain these percentages. Research results are often stated "at the .05 or .01 level of confidence." A .05 level of confidence means that there is a 95 percent chance the hypotheses was accurate and a 5 percent chance it was wrong. A .01 level of confidence is thus 99 percent chance the hypotheses was accurate and a 1 percent chance it was wrong. If we apply this typical explanation to trend data, we can say that after five years of continuous improvement there is a .03 level of confidence and after seven years of continuous improvement, there is less than a .01 level of confidence. "A useful criterion for recognition of outstanding performance is unquestionable demonstration of improvement year by year over a period of seven or more years" (Orsini, 2013, p. 28).

THE MASTER'S DEGREE

The statistics for the master's degree for school administrators should be improvement/trend statistics. Administrators need to be able to quickly and simply analyze their own school or school district's data. Some data will be weekly, some monthly, some quarterly, and some annually. To start this process, universities could use the book, *Quality Control for Dummies* or *The Book of Statistical Process Control.* The only problem with these books is the lack of education examples. The books are written for industry.

> *The statistics for the master's degree for school administrators should be improvement/trend statistics.*

THE COMPOSITE GRAPH COMES FIRST

Probably the first assignment in the new master's degree statistics course for future administrators is to create the **composite chart**. It displays the percent of exams taken in the school or school district where students met or exceeded state standards. The graph is a composite—all exams from all subjects and all grade levels. If education were a business, this would be called the *bottom line.* Educators are very used to disaggregating or averaging but are not used to aggregating. Many people, including the public, the school board, and all the employees want to know the answer to the simple question, "Did the district improve? Did the district have an all-time-best?"

Figure 18.1 is a composite graph from a school district showing the percentage of exams with students meeting or exceeding state standards, plus the percentage of exams with students exceeding standards. This tabulation is updated annually.

The composite graph does not answer questions such as "How did students perform in reading?" "How was Grade 8?" "What about science?" The composite graph is the view from 30,000 feet that answers the question, "How did our team do?" The composite graph is what helps system leaders implement what Michael Fullan (2011) wrote about. His desire is that everyone take pride in whole-system accomplishments and reach out to help others whenever it is called for.

One of the problems with the composite graph is changing standards. If the state boards of education change the standards each year, then how does one really know if improvement occurred? Place an asterisk adjacent to any year's data where the state changed standards.

We create the composite graph utilizing Excel. Each exam is listed in a row along with the number of students who took each exam and the number of students who met or exceeded state standards. A grand total is

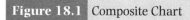

Figure 18.1 Composite Chart

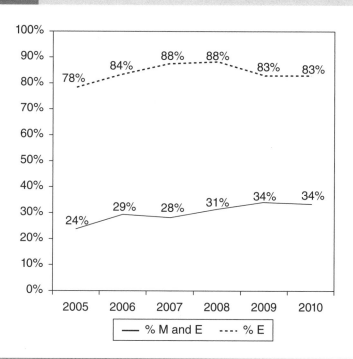

calculated for the total number of exams administered and the total number of exams where students met or exceeded standards. There will be one, and only one, numeral for each academic year. Figure 18.2 is a sample spreadsheet created to calculate this one numeral.

THE DUAL COMPOSITE GRAPH COMES SECOND

The first disaggregation comes by separating results into two groups: students above standards and students below standards. One line is percentage of exams where students exceeded standards and the second line is percentage of exams where students were below standards. It is an exciting day when the two lines cross. See the **dual composite chart** example in Figure 18.3.

RADAR CHART

After the two composite charts are created, naturally people will want to know about each grade level/each subject. This data is displayed on the radar chart described in Chapter 8. The two composite charts plus the

| Figure 18.2 | Spreadsheet for Calculating Composite Chart |

Divide 15965 by 12508 for % of exams with students meeting or exceeding standards.

	Number Tested	Percent Meeting Standards	Percent Exceeding Standards	Percent Meeting or Exceeding Standards
Reading 3	787	77%	9%	677
Math 3	787	52%	30%	645
Reading 4	780	74%	15%	694
Math 4	780	55%	28%	647
Reading 5	867	68%	13%	702
Writing 5	760	66%	8%	562
Math 5	872	43%	43%	750
Soc. St. 5	869	33%	44%	669
Science 5	871	55%	29%	732
Geog. 7	879	64%	25%	782
Reading 8	795	72%	17%	708
Writing 8	793	66%	3%	547
Math 8	892	50%	33%	740
History 8	798	58%	18%	606
Science 8	796	65%	24%	708
Alg. 1	904	20%	23%	389
Eng 2	904	23%	54%	696
US Hist.	963	59%	9%	655
Bio 1	868	47%	22%	599
TOTALS	15965			12508

radar chart give a very complete picture of the school or school district. The most powerful radar chart I have seen comes from the Department of Education in Nebraska. One is placed in the commissioner's office and one in the room where the State Board of Education meets. The radar chart is printed on a 4' by 4' poster. Each vector has a composite number for five

Figure 18.3 Dual Composite Chart

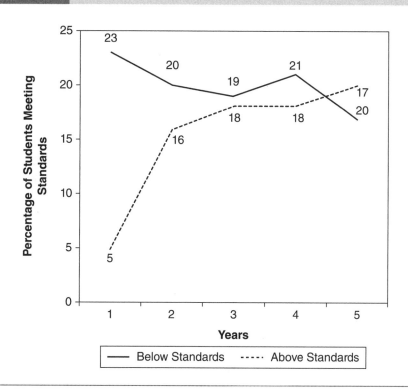

years for each of the 250 school districts in Nebraska. Adjacent to each district name is either nothing, * or **. A ** indicates All-Time-Best while a * indicates a tie with prior results. The Commissioner of Education, Matt Blomstedt, thus is communicating to school superintendents that he wants districts to outperform their prior best, not to outperform some other school district. The 2014 radar chart can be observed at www.ne .gov/COMMISH/2014NebraskaRadarChart.pdf. Readers of this book, in later years, can probably find the most recent radar chart by using the same URL but changing the year.

CULTURE AGAIN

If Nebraska leadership can convince the press, the federal Department of Education, the State Board of Education, the legislators, and the school superintendents that the aim is for everybody to have a record of continuous improvement, and not to look for ranking as a pressure tool, then we will all be reading about Nebraska's success.

ANALYSIS OF DATA

In addition to the three enumerative graphs described here, two analytical tools have been explained. They are the Pareto Chart in Chapter 4 and the computation of correlation in Chapter 11. Together, the three enumerative graphs and the two analytical tools can provide leaders with the simple tools necessary to create even better measures.

LOOKING AHEAD

The final chapter of this book delivers a challenge along with a summary.

Conclusion and Challenge

19

Everyone starts to identify with the success of the system. Everyone takes pride in whole-system accomplishments and reaches out to help each other whenever it is called for.

—Michael Fullan, 2011

The challenge before educators is to surrender or to optimize. Schools can be optimized for the good of everyone or educators can surrender to the pressures to completely sub-optimize education into thousands of different directions. Everybody doing their best in a sub-optimized system is not a recipe for success.

I understand why there are so many arguing to sub-optimize schools. For at least four decades the prevailing education theory was bottom-up leadership. The most popular name for bottom-up was *decentralization*. After considerable dissatisfaction with the results from bottom-up, the power was transferred to top-town. The most popular name for top-down is *fidelity*. Somebody else has figured education out; do everything as they say. Further, inspectors visit on a regular basis to assure your fidelity.

People can dream of a return to bottom-up, but I do not see this occurring. Thus the millions of educators, who are discouraged by the failures of top-down, are tempted to surrender and count the days until retirement. They have never experienced top-down/bottom-up, fourth-level, servant leadership and surrender is very tempting.

Optimize Your School: It's All About the Strategy is written for these very educators who are discouraged with the failure of top-down, realize that bottom-up is not returning and are fighting the temptation to surrender. "Everyone takes pride in whole-system accomplishments" (Fullan, 2011, p. 55). This is their book.

The strategy taught throughout the book is the same no matter the particular chapter. The leader of continuous strategic improvement has top-down responsibilities as do the employees have bottom-up responsibilities.

TOP-DOWN DIRECTIVES

1. Every division of the school system is to write down each of their responsibilities.

2. Next for every responsibility, the staff must write down what perfect is.

3. For each responsibility, the current reality is calculated.

4. The problem is written down. This is the gap (often called *waste*) between perfect and current reality.

5. Staff development is provided in root cause analysis. People learn how to dig down below the surface to find the root cause of problems. They learn that root causes are not blame statements but aspects of education that educators have the power to improve.

6. Each division of the organization writes down root causes of problems. *Permission to Forget: And Nine Other Root Causes of America's Frustration with Education* will help.

BOTTOM-UP IS NEXT

1. After the root cause analysis, staff members select one of the root causes to address.

2. A countermeasure is agreed upon for this root cause.

3. The organizational decisions are made to truly test this counter measure.

4. The bottom-up work is collected. It includes the problem, root cause analysis, countermeasure and any other organizational decisions made to test the countermeasure.

TOP-DOWN AGAIN

Bosses are on the lookout for sub-optimization. No division is allowed to have a countermeasure that harms another division of the school system. Other than sub-optimization, or possible legal problems, bosses allow the people closest to the action the ability to test their own countermeasures.

THE FOUR LEVELS OF LEADERSHIP

> No division is allowed to have a countermeasure that harms another division of the school system.

The organization is composed of many different teams of people working together to move closer to perfect. All through the year, the teams have posted data so all know if adequate progress is being made. Level 1 to 3 leadership won't work with continuous strategic improvement.

> Level 1: I'll just do the job by myself.
>
> Level 2: I'm in charge; do it the way I tell you.
>
> Level 3: I'll meet with you in the beginning of the year to agree upon your objectives. Then I'll meet with you again near the end of the year to see if you met your objectives.
>
> Optimization requires Level 4: We are a team working together toward a common aim which we believe will move us closer to perfect.

OPTIMIZATION REQUIRES SERVANT LEADERSHIP

Bosses are doing everything possible to assist staffs as they carry out their countermeasures. They may try to persuade staffs to adjust their countermeasure when adequate progress doesn't seem to be forthcoming. They certainly energize their staffs when they applaud progress, but most of all, staff members witness their boss assisting them with the implementation of their countermeasures. The "servant" and the "leadership" are equally present.

ALL-TIME-BEST

At the end of the year, data is collected from each division. Everyone knows if the organization had an all-time-best (ATB) as a whole (composite graph in Chapter 18) and where ATBs occurred as displayed on the radar chart (Chapter 8). Since no organization is perfect, it is very doubtful that every vector on the radar chart will document evidence of an ATB. Bosses need the mindset of the first-grade girl who consoled a teammate who did not achieve at ATB. She said, "It's OK Adam, you helped the team. Good job."

No boss, however talented, can ever carry out these steps for all aspects of schooling. Top-down/bottom-up is the only choice. Our servant leader is to lead the teams of people carrying out the strategy described throughout *Optimize Your School*. When a school system is optimized, all functions will be following the same process. For the first time ever, maintenance, transportation, food services, payroll, HR, finance, and instruction will all be able to help each other as the work to optimize their respective responsibilities. "Individual schools cannot get on—or if they do, cannot stay on—the moral track unless the whole district is working on the problem" (Fullan, 2011, p. 39).

Great communicators (leaders) give help and hope; poor leaders give hoops and hype. Leaders who commit to optimize their schools must provide the help described here. The results will create great hope as people all across their system realize their countermeasures worked. Further when these employees observe hoops (waste) being removed hope is piled up on hope. Lastly, hype is buried. Hype is an initiative in a school system for which nobody knows the result. "Did the initiative work? Nobody knows?" There was no baseline data collected, so it is impossible to know if improvement occurred. The enemy of hype is baseline data. Maxwell is right; great leaders give help and hope. Optimized schools are full of visible hope.

Figure 19.1 is inserted one last time as a visualization of the optimization strategy.

Surrender, NO. Optimize with continuous strategic improvement, YES.

Figure 19.1 Optimization Fishbone

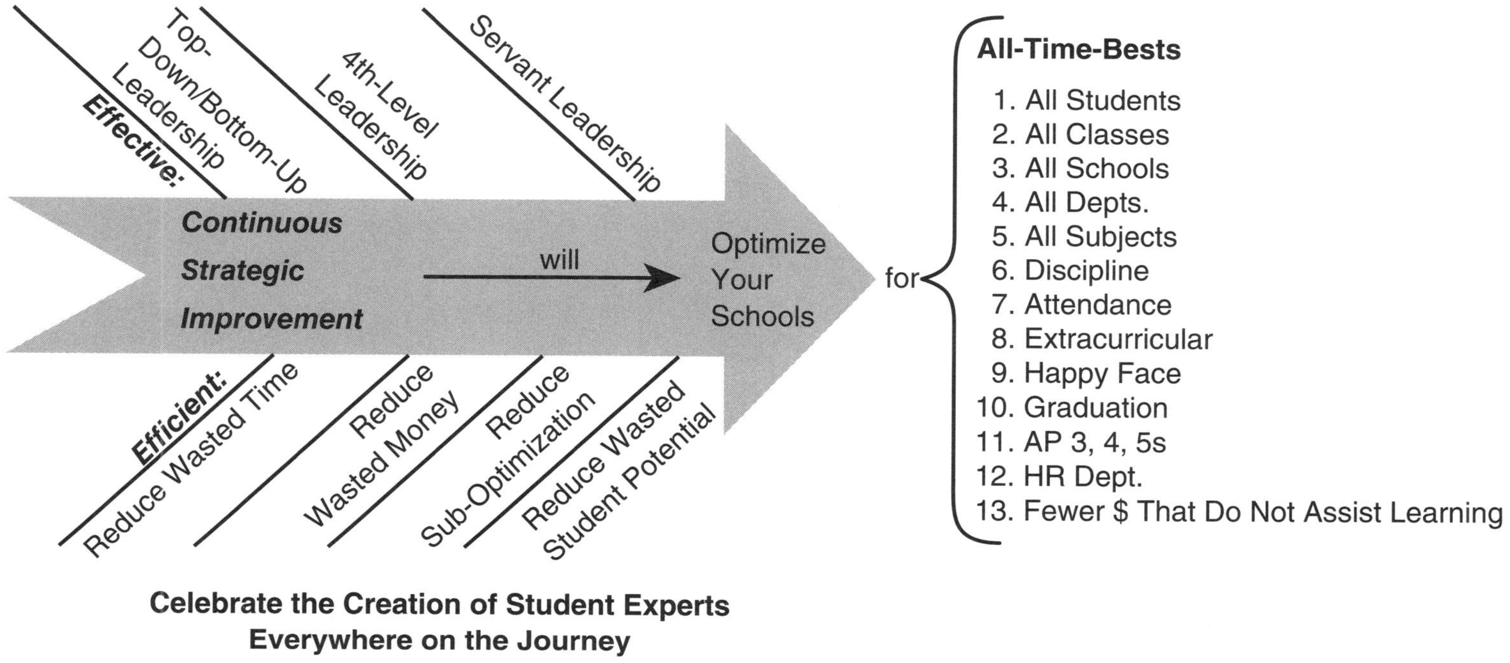

All-Time-Bests

1. All Students
2. All Classes
3. All Schools
4. All Depts.
5. All Subjects
6. Discipline
7. Attendance
8. Extracurricular
9. Happy Face
10. Graduation
11. AP 3, 4, 5s
12. HR Dept.
13. Fewer $ That Do Not Assist Learning

for

Optimize Your Schools

will

Continuous Strategic Improvement

Effective:

Top-Down/Bottom-Up Leadership

4th-Level Leadership

Servant Leadership

Efficient:

Reduce Wasted Time

Reduce Wasted Money

Reduce Sub-Optimization

Reduce Wasted Student Potential

Celebrate the Creation of Student Experts Everywhere on the Journey

Resources

Resource A: K–12 Loss of Enthusiasm

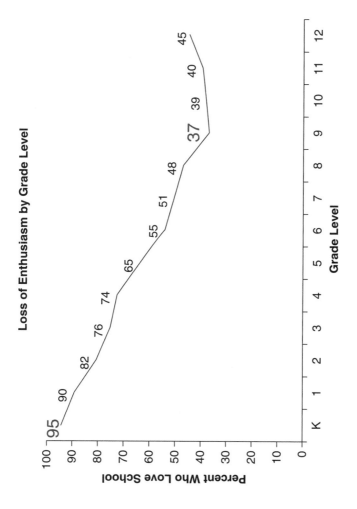

Loss of Enthusiasm by Grade Level

Resource B: Happy Face Survey

	😊	😬	☹	N/A
Reading				
Writing				
Math				
Science				
History				
Geography				
Art				
Music				
Agriculture				
Physical Education				
Spanish				

Resource C: Monthly Enthusiasm Graph

Monthly Enthusiasm Feedback for Teachers

Name _____

	August	September	October	November	December	January	February	March	April	May	June
Love it											
Like it											
OK											
Dislike it											
Hate it											

Note: Thanks to Jeff Burgard.

Resource D: Plus/Delta Expanded

Plus/Delta

+	Δ

I could volunteer to implement this idea.

Name _____

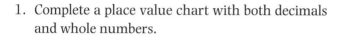

Resource E: Mathematics Key Concept List

Grade 5 Key Math Concepts

Number

1. Complete a place value chart with both decimals and whole numbers.

2. Multiply and divide by 10.

3. Use exponents to denote powers of 10.

4. Read, write and compare decimals to the 1000th place.

5. Write decimals in expanded form.

6. Round decimals to the nearest 1000th.

7. Divide with two digit divisors.

8. Add, subtract, multiply, and divide decimals.

9. Add and subtract fractions (including mixed numerals) without common denominators.

10. Determine if fraction problem answers are reasonable.

11. Interpret a fraction as division of the numerator by the denominator.

12. Solve fraction multiplication problems by completing an array.

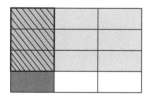

> Multiplication is the rectangle or square formed by the intersection of two fractions. Here $\frac{3}{4}$ is overlapped with $\frac{1}{3}$. The answer is $\frac{3}{12}$, the portion where the $\frac{3}{4}$ and $\frac{1}{3}$ overlap.

13. Understanding that multiplication by a number larger than 1 increases the size of the answer, whereas multiplying by a number smaller than 1 decreases the size of the answer.

14. Create equal multiplication problems by scaling factors (e.g., $12 \times 80 = 6 \times 160$).

15. Solve fraction multiplication word problems with mixed numerals.

16. Divide a whole number by a fraction and a fraction by a whole number ($4 \div \frac{1}{3} = 12$; $\frac{1}{3} \div 4 = \frac{1}{12}$. Use egg cartons to understand).

17. Solve division of fraction word problems.

Operations and Algebraic Thinking

18. Use parentheses and brackets in numerical expressions.

19. Write simple verbal expressions as number sentences.

20. Find the prime factors of numbers between 2 and 50.

21. Complete function tables and graph on coordinate plane.

Measurement and Data

22. Convert different-size standard measurements within a given measurement system (e.g., $\frac{1}{15}$ hour = 4 minutes).

23. Interpret the line plot to find mean, median, mode, and range.

24. Use 1 cm^3 cubes or 1 cubic inch cubes to measure volume of rectangular prisms.

25. Solve volume word problems.

Geometry

26. Plot points on a coordinate plane.

27. Solve word problems with a coordinate plane.

28. Classify polygons.

29. Classify polyhedra.

Resource F: Spanish Vocabulary

Nombre _____

1. La corona—Joya para la cabeza usada por reyes y reinas (CROWN)

2. Bandera—Insignia de un país (FLAG)

3. El marino—Persona que trabaja en un navío o barco (SAILOR)

4. La tripulación—Grupo de personas que trabajan en un barco (CREW)

5. Las carabelas—Barcos (CARAVEL)

6. La desembocadura—Donde un rió llega al océano (OUTLET)

7. Redondo—Circular (ROUND)

8. El globo—Mapa del mundo (GLOBE)

9. Conquistadores—Personas que llegaron a América (CONQUEROR)

10. Desembarcar—Bajar de un barco (TO DISEMBARK)

11. Imprescindible—Necesario (NECESSARY)

12. Renombrado—Famoso (RENOWNED)

13. El apoyo—La ayuda (SUPPORT/HELP)

14. El robo—Un asalto (ROBBERY)

15. El crimen—Ofensa, romper la ley (CRIME)

16. Quitar—Tomar algo de alguien (TAKE AWAY)

17. La cartera—Billetera (WALLET)

18. Bolsillo—Donde pones cosas en tu ropa (POCKET)

19. El carterista—Persona que roba carteras (PICKPOCKET)

20. Cortar—Romper (CUT)

21. La comisaría—Estación de policía (POLICE STATION)

22. El truco—Lo que se hace para engañar (TRICK)

23. El colectivo—Bus, camión (PUBLIC VAN)

24. El chofer—La persona que conduce un coche (CHAUFFEUR)

25. El bautizo—Ceremonia religiosa (BAPTISM)

26. El infarto—Ataque cardiaco (HEART ATTACK)

27. La demora—La tardanza, el retraso (DELAY)

28. El riesgo—El peligro (RISK)

29. El aumento—El incremento (INCREASE)

30. Reducir—Disminuir (REDUCE)

31. Aprobar—Autorizar (APPROVE)

32. Fracasar—No tener éxito (TO FAIL)

33. Las llamas—Rayos de fuego (FLAMES)

34. El navío—El barco (SHIP)

35. Hundirse—No poder mantenerse a flote (TO SINK)

36. El naufragio—Cuando una nave se hunde (SHIPWRECK)

37. El maleante—Delincuente, criminal (CRIMINAL)

38. La madrugada—Las primeras horas de la mañana (DAWN)

39. Los damnificados—Las víctimas de una catástrofe (VICTIM OF A DISASTER)

40. Destruir—Causar la destrucción (DESTROY)

41. Sobrepasar—Exceder (EXCEED)

42. Ocasionar—Causar (TO CAUSE)

43. Fallecer—Morir (TO DIE)

44. Rescatar—Salvar (RESCUE)

45. Apoderarse de—Tomar algo ajeno (de otro) (TO SEIZE)

46. El desconocido—Persona que uno no conoce (STRANGER)

47. El parentesco—La relación familiar (RELATIONSHIP)

48. El ascenso—Una promoción en el trabajo (PROMOTION)

49. El eje—El centro de algo (AXIS)

50. La deshonra—El deshonor (DISHONOR)

51. Lanzarse—Tirarse (TO JUMP)

52. Girar—Dar vueltas (TO SPIN)

53. Compartir—Dividir, repartir (TO SHARE)

54. Recoger—Tomar a un niño, recolectar (TO PICK UP/TO HELP)

55. Hacerse cargo de—Tomar la responsabilidad de algo (TO TAKE CARE OF)

56. Los trapos—Ropa vieja (RAGS)

57. La gota—Pequeña porción de agua (DROP)

58. El mendigo—Persona que pide dinero en la calle (BEGGAR)

59. El pelado—Persona que no tiene dinero (PENNILESS PERSON)

60. Las monedas—Tipo de dinero (COINS)

61. Adivinar—Predecir (GUESS/ PREDICT)

62. Agradar—Dar gusto (TO PLEASE)

63. Dar vergüenza—Sentir humillación (TO BE ASHAMED)

64. El carnet—Documento de identificación (ID)

65. La bondad—Acto de hacer el bien (GOODNESS/KINDNESS)

66. El presupuesto—Dinero asignado para los gastos (BUDGET)

67. Perpleja—confundida (CONFUSED)

68. Guía—Persona que guía (TOURIST GUIDE)

69. Inflexible—No flexible (NOT FLEXIBLE)

70. Rehusar—Decir que no (REFUSE)

71. Marcharse—Irse (TO LEAVE)

72. El afecto—La devoción, sentir aprecio (AFFECTION)

73. El cargo—La responsabilidad (CARE/CONTROL)

74. El trayecto—La distancia (DISTANCE)

75. Autorizar—Permitir (AUTHORIZE)

76. Proponer—Hacer una propuesta (PROPOSE)

77. Terminantemente—Categóricamente (CATEGORICALLY)

78. El toreo—Deporte lucha con un toro (BULLFIGHTING)

79. El torero—Persona que practica el toreo (BULL FIGHTER)

80. Las venas—Por donde corre la sangre en tu cuerpo (VEIN)

81. La casta—La calidad o clase de un animal (CASTE/CLASS)

82. La tontería—Una cosa estúpida o tonta (FOOLISHNESS)

83. El poder—La fuerza, la energía (POWER)

84. La afición—El amor por algo (A LIKING)

85. Elegir—Seleccionar (TO SELECT)

86. Vengar—Tomar venganza, vindicar (TO AVENGE)

87. Fluir—Correr un líquido (TO FLOW)

88. Heredar—Recibir de los padres o familiares (TO INHERIT)

89. Estar dispuesto—Estar listo (TO BE READY TO)

90. Asemejarse—Ser parecido (TO RESEMBLE)

91. Extrañar—Sorprenderse (TO BE SURPRISED OF)

92. Aportar—Dar contribuir (TO CONTRIBUTE)

93. Taurino—Relacionado con el toreo (ABOUT BULLFIGHTING)

94. Los alimentos—La comida (FOOD)

95. El pescado—Animal marino (FISH)

96. El enfermero—Persona que asiste a un médico (NURSE)

97. El médico—El doctor (DOCTOR)

98. Inscribir—Matricular (TO SUBSCRIBE/TO REGISTER)

99. Estatal—Del estado (STATE, ADJ.)

100. Diario—De cada día (DAILY)

101. Alimenticio—De alimentos (RELATED TO FOOD)

102. Pesquero—Del pescado (FISHING, ADJ.)

103. Un examen médico—Una revisión hecha por un doctor (CHECK-UP)

104. Tomar una radiografía—Tomar rayos X (TAKE X-RAYS)

105. Tomar el pulso—Revisar los latidos del corazón (TO CHECK THE PULSE)

106. Caminar—Andar (TO WALK)

107. Tomar la tensión arterial—Tomar la presión (CHECK BLOOD PRESSURE)

108. La jeringa—Objeto para aplicar una inyección (SYRINGE)

109. Exigir—Pedir (DEMAND)

110. Estar de buena salud—Gozar de buena salud, estar bien (TO BE HEALTHY)

111. Pulmonar—De los pulmones (LUNG, ADJ.)

112. Cardiaco—Del corazón (HEART, ADJ.)

113. El aula—Salón de clase (CLASSROOM)

114. La cantina—La cafetería (CAFETERIA, LUNCHROOM)

115. La vajilla—Los platos y vasos, etc. (DISHES)

116. Las tapas—Lo que cubre un envase (LIDS)

117. Las pinzas—Objeto para tomar un objeto (TWEEZERS)

118. El acuerdo—El pacto (PACT)

119. Los docente—Los profesores (TEACHERS)

120. Consumir—Usar (USE/CONSUME)

121. Los envases—Recipientes (CONTAINER)

Source: Courtesy of Liliana Velasco.

Resource G: US Constitution Key Concepts

Section 1—History of the Constitution

1. The Constitution was written and signed in Independence Hall in Philadelphia, PA. This is also where the Declaration of Independence and Articles of Confederation were written.

2. The United States has had two written Constitutions in its history: the Articles of Confederation, which provided for a weak central government, and our present Constitution of the United States. An example of the weakness of the Articles is that it did not provide for a court system.

3. The framers who wrote the Constitution originally met to revise the Articles of Confederation but then scrapped it and started all over.

4. Of the seventy men chosen to meet and revise the Articles of Confederation, only about fifty-five attended on a regular basis and only thirty-nine of these signed the final product. Rhode Island chose not to send any delegates to the convention.

5. The Bill of Rights, as it is called, is the first ten amendments. The Bill of Rights was added to the Constitution in 1789 and was ratified in 1791. There were actually twelve proposed, but one of them never became a part of the Constitution and the other wasn't added for 201 years, becoming the 27th Amendment.

6. John Adams, one of the most influential of the framers, went on to become the first vice president of the United States and the second president.

7. According to the Constitution, if no candidate gets a majority of the electoral votes, the president is chosen by the House of Representatives. Thomas Jefferson is the only president to be chosen by the House.

8. The Constitution was completed and signed on September 17, 1787. September 17 is now celebrated as Constitution Day for our nation.

9. One of the delegates elected to serve at the convention from Virginia was Patrick Henry. He refused to attend saying that he "smelt a rat."

10. James Madison, who showed up in Philadelphia with an entire draft for a proposed Constitution, is now called the "Father of the Constitution."

11. Benjamin Franklin, at 81 the oldest delegate, was considered the "Sage of the Constitution." His mind was sharp but his body was deteriorating as he had to be carried into the hall on a chair by four men.

12. The largest city at the time of the writing of the Constitution was Philadelphia, with 40,000 population. America had only four million population at that time.

13. The first African American to serve on the Supreme Court was Thurgood Marshall. He was confirmed in 1967.

14. The first woman to serve on the Supreme Court was Sandra Day O'Connor, appointed in 1981.

15. Franklin D. Roosevelt tried to "pack" the Supreme Court with his own nominees. He did not succeed. Although there were six justices when the Court began its proceedings under the new Constitution, there are now nine; one chief justice and eight associate justices.

16. The two parties vying to either ratify or defeat the new Constitution were the Federalists and the Anti-federalists. The Federalists were in favor of the proposed Constitution and the Anti-federalists were opposed to it.

17. Roger Sherman of Connecticut proposed what became known as the "Great Compromise." That compromise dealt with how the states would be represented in Congress and is said to have saved the Constitution.

18. Thomas Jefferson, one of the founders of our country, thought that the Constitution should be rewritten every generation.

19. God is mentioned only once in the US Constitution. It is found in Article 7 where it says, "the Seventeenth day of September in the Year of our Lord one thousand seven hundred and eighty seven ..."

20. A series of essays written jointly by James Madison, Alexander Hamilton, and John Jay encouraging citizens to ratify the Constitution, were called the Federalist Papers.

21. In order for the Constitution to become the law of the land, two-thirds of the states or about nine states had to ratify (approve) it. All thirteen states eventually ratified it with Rhode Island being the last to do so.

Section 2—The Document

22. The introduction to the Constitution is called the *Preamble*. It begins with the words, "We the People of the United States" because that is

where the power for the Constitution is derived. This concept is called *popular sovereignty*.

23. There are seven articles in the Constitution and twenty-seven amendments have been added to it since 1788, the year it was ratified.

24. The first ten amendments were added all at once in 1791 and are collectively called the *Bill of Rights*.

25. Article 6 of the Constitution states that it is the highest law of the land. No state or local law can be greater than the Constitution. For example, no state may allow slavery since the 13th Amendment to the Constitution (a higher law) forbids it.

26. The original Constitution document is kept at the National Archives in Washington, DC.

27. The United States Constitution is the shortest and oldest written constitution of any government in the world today.

28. The Constitution guarantees to every state a republican form of government.

Section 3—The Law of the Land

29. US representatives must be at least twenty-five years of age, have lived in the United States for seven years, must be a US citizen and of the state they represent, and serve a term of two years.

30. US senators must be at least thirty years old, must have lived in the United States for nine years, must be a US citizen and of the state they represent, and serve a term of six years.

31. The president must be a natural born citizen of the United States, must have lived in the United States for fourteen years, and must be at least thirty-five years old. He serves a term of four years. He is elected by winning a majority of the electoral votes.

32. Representatives are elected every two years. One-third of senators are elected every two years.

33. Article 1 of the Constitution describes the powers and duties of the legislative branch. Article 2 describes the powers and duties of the executive branch, and Article 3 describes the duties and powers of the judicial branch.

34. Congress (legislative branch) makes the laws, the president (executive branch) enforces or carries out the laws, and the Supreme Court (judicial branch) interprets and explains the laws.

35. No holder of a public office can be required to take a religious test. Congress cannot make "ex post facto" laws which make an act illegal after it has been committed. Neither can Congress pass "Bills of Attainder" which are acts that declare someone guilty without a trial.

36. Among the powers of Congress according to Article 1 are the following: tax, borrow, regulate commerce, coin money, establish post offices, declare war, impeach the president or a Supreme Court justice, maintain a military, admit a new state, and many more. These powers are called *enumerated powers*.

37. According to the Constitution, Congress must meet at least once each year.

38. The number of representatives a state gets is determined by population. Each state has two senators so that one house has equal representation. This was the essence of the Great Compromise.

39. The president is elected by the Electoral College. The number of electors each state gets is equal to the total of its representatives and senators.

40. The president is the commander in chief of all armed forces of the United States.

41. The Constitution states that neither house of Congress, while in session, may adjourn for more than three days without the consent of the other house.

42. The president is elected on the first Tuesday after the first Monday in November every four years. He or she is sworn in on January 20 at noon following the election.

43. The president must get the "advice and consent" of the Senate for treaties with foreign countries and it must pass by a two-thirds vote. Senate approval for nominees to federal offices need only a majority vote.

44. The Constitution states that no one may be convicted of treason against the United States without the testimony of two eyewitnesses.

45. An oddity of the Constitution is that the vice president (a member of the executive branch) presides as the president of the Senate (the legislative branch). When he is not there to preside, the president pro tempore of the Senate presides.

46. After a bill has been sent to the president, it becomes a law if he does not send it back after ten days while Congress is in session. If the president takes no action on a bill while Congress is adjourned, this is called a *pocket veto* and the bill fails.

47. Supreme Court justices are nominated by the president and confirmed by the Senate. They hold office for life or as the Constitution phrases it, "during good behavior."

48. The Constitution provides for separation of powers and checks and balances. Separation of powers means, for example, that only the Congress can make the laws and the other branches cannot. Checks and balances mean that the other branches have some power over the decisions of the other branch. An example would be when the Supreme Court declares a law passed by Congress to be unconstitutional.

49. The Congress and the President share the responsibility of establishing foreign policy for the United States.

50. A controversial part of Article 1 in section 8 is called *the elastic clause* because it allows Congress to make laws that reflect changing conditions in our nation.

Section 4—The Principles of the Constitution

51. The power of the government comes from the consent of the governed. This is called *popular sovereignty*.

52. The Constitution divides the powers of government among the three branches. This is called *separation of powers*.

53. The powers of government are also divided between the national government and the states. This is called *federalism*. Powers that are shared between the federal and state governments are called *concurrent powers*. Powers given only to the federal government, such as the power to coin money, are called *delegated powers*.

54. Each branch of government has some power over the others. This is called *checks and balances*. An example of this would be when Congress overrides the veto of a bill by a two-thirds vote.

55. The Constitution strictly forbids the Congress to award titles of nobility, pass "ex post facto" laws, or "bills of attainder."

56. The Constitution says that Congress can bring formal charges against a government official, such as the president, for crimes committed in office. This is called *impeachment*. Only two presidents have been impeached, Andrew Johnson and Bill Clinton and both were acquitted. Charges are brought by the House of Representatives and the trial takes place in the Senate with the chief justice presiding as judge.

Section 5—The Bill of Rights

57. The First Amendment contains five of our most precious rights. These are freedom of religion, speech, press, assembly, and the right to petition the government if we have grievances against it.

58. The Second Amendment grants the right to bear arms (guns) to citizens and to establish a well-regulated militia.

59. Before and during the American Revolution, the British were forcing Americans to house (quarter) its soldiers. This resulted in our Third Amendment known as "the Quartering Act" which forbids such action.

60. The Fourth Amendment protects people against unreasonable search and seizure by government officials. This is why law enforcement officials must obtain a search warrant upon "probable cause" that there is evidence of a crime.

61. The Fifth Amendment contains rights for people accused of crimes. These include the right not to be tried for the same offense twice (double jeopardy), not compelled to be a witness against himself (self-incrimination), not to be held in jail without a charge (writ of habeas corpus), and not to be deprived of life, liberty, or property without "due process of law."

62. The Sixth Amendment guarantees rights to a fair trial for persons accused of a crime. These include the right to a speedy and public trial, the right to face one's accusers, an impartial judge and jury, to call witnesses on one's behalf, and to have the assistance of counsel for their defense.

63. The Seventh Amendment grants the right to a jury trial for persons being sued for more than $20.00. While this amendment is obviously outdated since no one would call for a jury trial if being sued for only this amount, it remains a part of the Constitution.

64. The Eighth Amendment prohibits cruel and unusual punishment, such as torture, and excessive bail and fines.

65. The Ninth Amendment says that the listing of certain rights in the Constitution does not mean that other rights, not mentioned, are not retained by the people.

66. The Tenth Amendment says that powers not given to the United States and not prohibited to the people are retained by the people and the states.

Section 6—Beyond the Bill of Rights

67. The Thirteenth, Fourteenth, and Fifteenth Amendments were all passed after the Civil War and gave rights to African Americans that were formerly denied them. The Thirteenth banned slavery in the United States; the Fourteenth made African Americans citizens of the United States (reversing the Dred Scott decision), and ensured that all citizens are entitled to due process of law; and the Fifteenth gave African Americans the right to vote.

68. The Sixteenth Amendment allowed Congress to tax incomes (income tax) and the Seventeenth Amendment moved the election of senators from state legislatures to the people.

69. The Eighteenth Amendment banned the manufacture, sale, and consumption of alcoholic beverages in the United States (Prohibition). This amendment became the only one to be repealed, done by the Twenty-First Amendment.

70. The Nineteenth Amendment gave women in all states the right to vote in federal elections including voting for the president and vice president. This amendment joined the Fifteenth in the movement toward "universal suffrage" (allowing all citizens to vote). Later the Twenty-Third Amendment would give the people of Washington, DC, the right to vote for president, the Twenty-Fourth Amendment would prohibit "poll taxes," and the Twenty-Sixth Amendment would give eighteen-year-olds the right to vote in national elections.

71. Amendments Twenty, Twenty-Two, Twenty-Five, and Twenty-Seven all have to do with presidents, senators, and members of the House of Representatives:

    • The Twentieth Amendment shortened the time between the election and the beginning of presidential and congressional terms.
    • The Twenty-Second Amendment limits the president to two terms in office. He can also serve up to two years of another president's term and still be elected twice on his own.
    • The Twenty-Fifth Amendment handled the matter of who succeeds the president if he resigns, is removed from office, is temporarily unable to fulfill the duties of his office, or dies. If any of these happen, the vice president takes over.
    • The Twenty-Seventh Amendment states that, if Congress votes itself a raise, it cannot take effect until after there has been a general election. This gives the people a chance to vote them out if they feel they are not doing a good job and don't deserve a raise.

This was the original Twelfth Amendment proposed along with the Bill of Rights, but it wasn't ratified until 201 years later.

Section 7—Landmark Supreme Court Cases

72. *Marbury v. Madison* (1803): This landmark decision made sure, once and for all, that the Supreme Court had the final say about whether a law passed by Congress agreed with the Constitution. This is called *judicial review*.

73. *Dred Scott v. Sandford* (1857): Dred Scott was a slave who had moved with his master to the free state of Illinois, becoming free, and then back to the slave state of Missouri. He sued for his freedom but Chief Justice Roger Taney said that he was never free at all because slaves were not citizens and could not sue in court. This is widely considered the worst court decision in American history.

74. *Brown v. Board of Education* (1954): This unanimous decision stated that segregated schools for the races were unequal and unconstitutional. This began what is called the modern civil rights movement.

75. *Miranda v. Arizona* (1966): In this case, the court decided that Ernesto Miranda had not been told that he had the right to remain silent and it struck down his conviction. As a result, police must now inform a suspect of his or her rights including the Fifth Amendment right to remain silent and not incriminate themselves.

76. *Roe v. Wade* (1973): One of the court's most controversial decisions, it struck down a Texas law that forbade Norma McCorvey from getting an abortion and set guidelines for when states could restrict abortions.

Section 8—Constitutional Odds and Ends

77. The Constitution calls for a census to be taken every ten years. This determines how the states will be represented in the House of Representatives.

78. If Thomas Jefferson had been strictly following the Constitution, he could not have purchased the Louisiana Territory from France.

79. The so-called "Three-Fifths Compromise" at the Constitutional Convention determined how slaves would be counted for purposes of representation.

80. Whichever presidential candidate wins the popular election of a state gets all of that state's electoral votes in forty-eight states and

Washington, DC. Nebraska and Maine have systems for a proportional allocation of the electoral votes.

81. Today there are 435 members of the House of Representatives and 100 senators. That number could change in the House with increases or decreases in population and in the Senate if a new state were to be added to the Union.

82. The only Constitutionally mandated duty of the vice president is to take over for the president if he cannot continue.

83. Any and all bills regarding spending must begin in the House of Representatives. All other bills can start in either house.

84. A proposed amendment to the Constitution can begin in Congress or in the states but it must be ratified by three-fourths of the states within seven years.

85. All state and federal office holders must take an oath to support the Constitution of the United States.

86. Article IV of the Constitution calls for each state to give "full faith and credit" to the laws and acts of all other states. This, for example, is why you do not need a separate driver's license for each state you drive into.

87. There is no mention in the Constitution of the vice president receiving compensation or pay whereas, for the president, it specifically states that "The President shall . . . receive for his services a compensation . . ."

88. Although the Constitution provides only for the vice president to take over if the president should die, resign, or become unable to fulfill his duties, the Presidential Succession Act of 1947 allows for a line of succession should both the president and the vice president die. Next would be the Speaker of the House of Representatives.

89. In order for a proposed amendment to the Constitution to become law, three-fourths of the states must ratify it within seven years or it will fail. A proposed amendment may begin in Congress or in the states. No amendment has ever begun in the states so far.

90. The only time a writ of habeas corpus can be suspended is during a time of rebellion or invasion. Habeas Corpus is an order making a jailer show good reason why a man is in jail.

91. Congress can remove a member of either house for "disorderly behavior" but it requires a two-thirds vote.

92. Traditionally, the chief justice of the United States administers the oath of office to a newly elected President.

93. The right to vote is guaranteed only to citizens (natural born or naturalized) of the United States.

94. The original Constitution did not contain term limits for the president. It is because George Washington voluntarily stepped down after two terms that it became a tradition for all future presidents to do so. The Twenty-Second Amendment, however, now limits the president to two terms.

95. The word *democracy* does not appear anywhere in the text of the US Constitution.

96. Once an amendment to the Constitution is ratified, the only way it can be changed is by a new amendment. Such was the case with the Nineteenth Amendment (Prohibition) and the Twenty-First Amendment (repeal of Prohibition).

97. The Constitution does not mention political parties. George Washington is the only president not to have any political party affiliation.

98. The term *bicameral* means a two-house legislature. The US Congress is bicameral, consisting of the House of Representatives and the Senate. The only state not to have a bicameral legislature is Nebraska. Theirs is a unicameral legislature.

99. Presidential succession beyond the Speaker of the House is as follows: president pro tempore of the Senate, secretary of state, secretary of the treasury, secretary of defense, attorney general, secretary of the interior, secretary of agriculture, secretary of commerce, secretary of labor, secretary of health and human services, secretary of housing and urban development, secretary of transportation, secretary of energy, secretary of education, secretary of veterans affairs, secretary of homeland security.

100. Prior to the Twenty-Second Amendment, the only president to be elected to two more terms was Franklin Delano Roosevelt who was elected in 1932, 1936, 1940, and 1944 (four times). After taking office for his fourth term in 1945, he suffered a stroke and died, making Harry Truman the president.

Source: Created by Dan McCaulley, author of *Continuous Improvement in the Social Studies Classroom* (designed to accompany From LtoJ® US Constitution PowerPoint).

Resource H: Sample Grade 5 Math Quiz

Name _____ Grade 5   Week 6

Grade 3: (19) Started the race at 12:15 p.m. and ran for 23 minutes. What time did the race end?	**Pictorial Representation** *(circle and a rectangle with a colon)*	**Solutions**
Grade 4: (17) Compare. Use > < or =		.67 .7
Grade 4: (22) How many units?	How many ounces = 1 pound _____? How many grams = 1 kg _____?	
Number: (13) Place > < or = in each of the number sentences.		$\frac{3}{5} \times 275$ _____ 275 $1\frac{3}{5} \times 275$ _____ 275
Number: (9) Add and subtract.		$\frac{4}{5} + \frac{2}{3} =$ $\frac{4}{5} - \frac{2}{3} =$
Number: (14) Find the missing factor.		$32 \times 14 = 7 \times$ _____ $16 \times 14 =$ _____ $\times 28$

Number: (4)	Pictorial Representation	Solutions
Write the numeral for 7 and 49 thousandths.		

Operations and Algebra: (21)

Complete the table and graph.

X	Y
1	7
3	9
5	
7	

Measurement and Data: (25)

The sidewalk will be 6" thick by 3' wide by 18' long. How many cubic yards of concrete are needed?

Geometry: (26)

Solar panels were being set up in a hexagonal pattern. Four of the panels were placed at (8, 8), (10, 6), (3, 6), and (5, 4). Where do they need to place the last two panels?

_____ & _____

Resource I: Mathematics Dichotomous Rubric

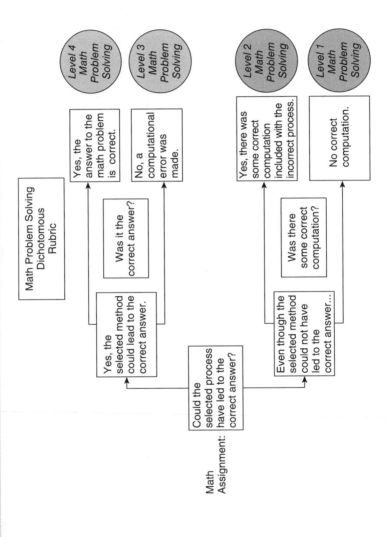

Resource J: Important Words for Four First-Grade Students

Steven	Troy	Brock	Karen
Tyrannosaurus Rex	Cheeta	prehistoric	mother and daddy
Diplodocus	leopard	Africa	angels
Edaphosaurus	bobcat	America	church
Elasmosaurus	black panther	world	Bible
Allosaurus	snow leopard	solar system	God
Trachodon	lion	volcano	princess
Godzilla	cougar	grizzly bear	love bird
Rhamphorhynchus	jaguar	army tank	marriage
Rodan	the red lynx	Australia	teacher
Pteranodon	mountain devil	Viking ship	Minnie Mouse
Ankylosaurus	Indian tiger	king cobra	my grandma
Monster X	Siberian tiger	pollution	Baby Jesus
I guanodon	golden cat	computer	
Gamera	king tiger	Heavenly Father	
Brachiosaurus	ocelot	carniverous animals	
blue whale	cloud leopard	Golden Retriver	
crocodiles	serval cat		
sawfish	mountain screamer		
alligators			
Styracosaurus			
Stegosaurus			
Protoceratops			
Monoclonius			

Resource K: Sample Page From *It's a Tangram World*

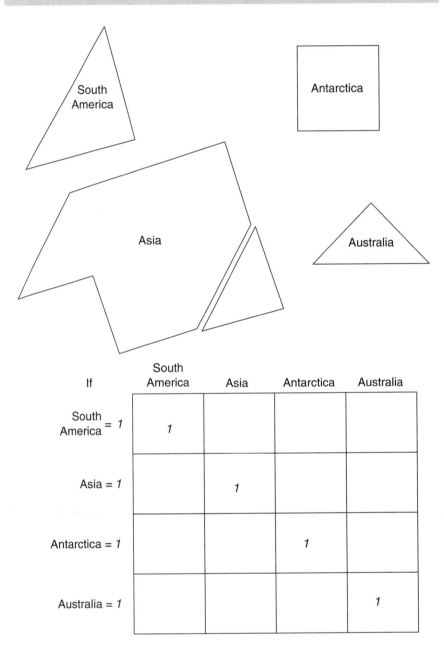

If	South America	Asia	Antarctica	Australia
South America = 1	1			
Asia = 1		1		
Antarctica = 1			1	
Australia = 1				1

Resource L: Geoboard Recording Sheet

Resource M: Science Stabilization

Secondary School Science Stabilization

The Massac County High School science teachers have created a PowerPoint based upon Rhonda Johnston's work in Lloydminster, SK. First, they aligned their concepts removing duplicates. Second, they stabilized the curriculum with the LtoJ® quizzes. Each teacher has a color-coded PowerPoint presentation showing the periodic table. The first ten elements are colored red and are for Grade 7 science. Elements 65–77 are colored pink and are on the scientific method. Seventh-grade students are quizzed on nine Grade 7 questions and one scientific method.

Skip ahead to physics. Students are quizzed on five physics questions, one biology, one chemistry, one physical science, one Grade 7 general science, and one scientific method. Permission to Forget prior science courses is gone.

Tongue Depressors – 1 bucket per teacher

Red – 7th-Grade Science

Green – Physical Science

Blue – Biology

Yellow – Chemistry

Orange – Earth Science

Black – Physics

Pink – Scientific Method

Science Review PPT

Elements	Subject Matter	# Concepts	# Questions	Color	Stabilization Formula: Number of questions from each subject.
1–10	7th-Grade Science	10	30	Red	9 Red, 1 Pink
11–28	Physical Science	18	54	Green	6 Green, 3 Red, 1 Pink
29–46	Biology	18	54	Blue	5 Blue, 2 Red, 2 Green, 1 Pink
47–64	Earth Science	18	54	Orange	5 Orange, 1 Blue, 1 Yellow, 1 Red, 1 Green, 1 Pink
65–77	Scientific Method	13	24	Pink	
78–90	Physics	13	54	Black	5 Black, 1 Blue, 1 Yellow, 1 Green, 1 Red, 1 Pink
91–113	Chemistry	23	69	Yellow	5 Yellow, 2 Blue, 1 Green, 1 Red, 1 Pink

Resource N: Radar Chart Directions

Creating a Radar Chart

Below is a sample radar creation with fewer vectors than the example in Chapter 8. The directions that follow will assist educators in creating a radar chart for their own school or school district. In the data below, note that the percent sign has not been added after each numeral; it is unnecessary. All that is in each cell of the Excel spreadsheet is the percentage of students that met standards for each subject and each grade level.

The ** and the * have been typed into the spreadsheet by looking across each row to determine if there was an all-time-best (ATB) or a tie for an ATB. Each year this data must be updated. Note that on the second half of the list the ** are placed at the left of the subject title. This makes the radar chart consistent with all the asterisks on the outside edge.

	2010	2011	2012	2013
3rd Reading**	59	64	78	79
4th Reading**	60	71	72	81
5th Reading**	55	67	73	75
6th Reading	62	78	76	74
7th Reading	62	72	80	78
8th Reading**	62	73	64	81
10th Reading	61	64	58	60
3rd Math*	63	64	72	72
**4th Math	70	71	67	74
5th Math	77	78	80	78
6th Math	70	72	71	65
7th Math	72	60	77	75
**8th Math	68	66	73	85
10th Math	41	44	50	43
**Science 4	60	63	67	68
**Science 8	60	63	62	77
**Science 10	61	62	60	69

Once the data are completely entered into the spreadsheet, you are ready to create the radar chart. Highlight all the data and then in Excel click on the label "Insert," and then "Other Charts," and finally "Radar Chart." Click on the middle radar chart.

Your radar chart will look like the one below and in great need of cleanup.

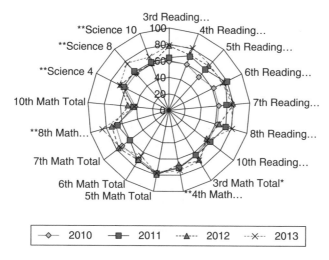

The default radar chart in Excel shows the lines for each year and is thus very hard to read. You will need to remove the lines for 2010, 2011, and 2012. This is done by clicking on the years inside the legend. It takes at least two clicks. The first click selects the whole legend, and then you click again to highlight only the year. It takes a little practice to click only on the year. Once this is done, then right-click the year to bring up the command "Format Data Series." Click here and you have many options. Select "Line Color" and then click on "No Line."

Repeat for all three years.

Next, you will probably want to make 2013 stand out more. Follow the same process by clicking on 2013, then right-click, then "Format Data Series." This time click on "Line Color." I selected red for the example. Last of all, click on "Line Style." I did this and typed "4" into "Line Width."

The last step is placing the legend for *ATB* and *tied ATB* in the bottom right of the graph. This is done by clicking on "Insert" at the top of Excel, then inserting a text box and entering the two symbols for ATB and tied ATB.

Step by step, the radar chart is created as follows:

1. Complete the spreadsheet with data for all years.

2. Look for ATBs and type ** by the subject/grade level. Be sure to type ** in front of the grade level/subject on the second half of the spreadsheet.

3. Look for tied ATBs and place * after or before the grade level/subject.

4. Highlight the data in the spreadsheet.

5. Click on "Insert" on the Excel ribbon and select "Other Charts."

6. Under "Other Charts" select the middle radar chart.

7. Clean up the radar chart by selecting each year, other than the final year, in the legend. This is done one year at a time. After the year is selected, right-click and select "Format Data Series."

8. This brings up a menu—select "Line Color" and then "No Line."

9. Repeat this for every year except the most recent year.

10. Select the most recent year, then right-click to obtain "Format Data Series."

11. Select "Line Color" and choose a bold one.

12. Select "Line Style" and choose 4 for width.

As you become more comfortable with the radar chart, feel free to spruce it up according to your likes and dislikes.

Resource O: Old Ironsides

The US frigate, the *Constitution*, called "Old Ironsides" because her crew insisted that the shot of the enemy rebounded from her sides, was first commissioned in the US Navy in 1798. In 1804, she first became distinguished as leader of the brilliant attack on Tripoli. But her deathless glory rests on her signal victories in the War of 1812, chief of which was the complete destruction of the *Guerriere* in a fierce thirty-minute engagement, August 19, 1812. For this victory, Captain Hull was given rousing ovations in New York, Boston, and Philadelphia. Congress awarded him a gold medal and appropriated fifty thousand dollars as a reward to him and his brave crew. Other victories followed in rapid succession, and the *Constitution*, became a veritable "eagle of the sea."

In 1828, after a glorious career, the old frigate was pronounced unseaworthy, and the naval authorities ordered she be dismantled. This order met with a general murmur of disapproval, which burst into a storm of indignant protest after the fiery heart of the youthful Oliver Wendell Holmes had dictated the following remarkable lyric. His poet's eye sees the heroic old vessel sweeping proudly into port, her tattered flag at top mast, seemingly conscious of having lent herself to the protection of the bodies of heroes and to the preservation of human liberty, but all unconscious of her impending fate at the hands of those who should be her friends. This impassioned appeal so charged the national heart that the poem was printed as a handbill and scattered broadcast in the streets of Washington, DC. It is not remarkable that the order was rescinded, and that after being rebuilt, in 1833, "Old Ironsides" kept her stately course as the historic queen of the US Navy until 1855. Now, full of honors, revered and loved, she rides in a safe anchorage in the Charlestown Navy Yard.

OLD IRONSIDES

Ay, tear her tattered ensign down!
    Long has it waved on high,
And many an eye has danced to see
    That banner in the sky;
Beneath it rung the battle shout,
    And burst the cannon's roar; —
The meteor of the ocean air
    Shall sweep the clouds no more.

Her deck, once red with heroes' blood,
    Where knelt the vanquished foe,
When winds were hurrying o'er the flood,
    And waves were white below,
No more shall feel the victor's tread,
    Or know the conquered knee,—
The harpies of the shore shall pluck
    The eagle of the sea.

Oh, better that her shattered hulk
    Should sink beneath the wave;
Her thunders shook the mighty deep,
    And there should be her grave;
Nail to the mast her holy flag,
    Set every threadbare sail,
And give her to the god of storms,
    The lightning and the gale!

                  —Oliver Wendell Holmes

EXERCISES

1. What called forth this poem and in what spirit was it written?

2. Why not call the vessel her real name?

3. What feeling seems to possess the soul of the poet in the first stanza? In the second?

4. What characteristic is given the ship in the first stanza?

5. How are you led to think of the ship—as a mass of spars and rigging, or as a living, feeling thing?

6. To what does the second stanza refer?

7. Why should the poet call her an "eagle"?

8. Is a "tattered ensign" one affected merely by action of the wind?

9. In what sense was the frigate's flag a "meteor"?

10. What kind of burial place is the sea?

11. Why is a flag ever "nailed" to the mast?

12. Why does he call the flag "holy"?

13. Why not capitalize the word "god" in the last stanza?

14. What feeling inspired Holmes as he wrote the last stanza?

15. What substitute for *dismantling* is suggested?

16. Why should such an alternative be preferred?

17. What in this protest has endured in the American heart?

18. What higher patriotic sentiment pervades the poem?

Source: From *Studies in Reading, Eighth Grade,* J. W. Searson and George E. Martin, The University Publishing Company, Lincoln, NE, 1910, pp. 5–9.

Resource P: Student Run Chart for Reading Fluency

Name _____

	August	September	October	November	December	January	February	March	April	May
100 WPM										
90 WPM										
80 WPM										
70 WPM										
60 WPM										
50 WPM										
40 WPM										
30 WPM										
20 WPM										
10 WPM										
0 WPM										

Resource Q: Science Dichotomous Rubric

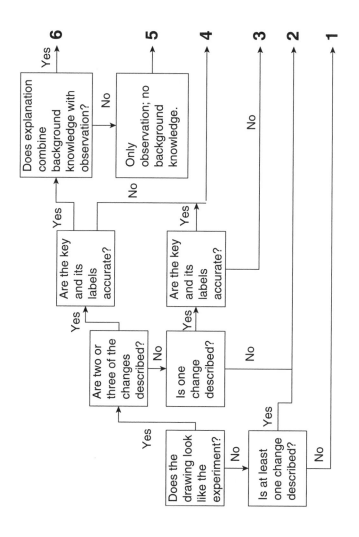

Source: Created by Traci Wierman.

Resource R: Dichotomous Rubric Student Run Chart

Dichotomous Rubric Student Run Chart for _____

Rubric Score																														
6																														
5																														
4																														
3																														
2																														
1																														
0																														

Assignment

Resource S: Teacher Feedback Form

My Teacher . . .	Never	Sometimes	Always
1. Is a happy person			
2. Helps me look at the good side of issues			
3. Is proud of my accomplishments			
4. Listens to what I have to say			
5. Really likes me			
6. Is easy to understand			
7. Is a person I like			
8. Encourages me to care about others			
9. Has a great sense of humor			
10. Comes to work prepared			
11. Helps me organize better			
12. Loves to learn him/herself			
13. Follows through on promises			
14. Treats students as individuals			
15. Remains calm when things go crazy			
16. Listens to my ideas			

Resource T: LtoJ® Seminar Feedback Form

Feedback From Seminar Participants

At the conclusion of this seminar, I am asking that you provide me feedback to assist me in planning for future workshops. Often seminar participants are asked to fill out an evaluation of the experience in order to assist administrators in decision making. Feedback, however, is different. It is to help me improve my seminars.
Thanks.

1. What was the most helpful to you?

2. Did you notice any written or spoken factual errors? If so, what were they?

3. This seminar is designed to blend theory, practical advice, application, practice, and activity. Was the seminar balanced? Were there "dead spots" in the seminar? If so, where?

4. What one concept or idea was the most provocative?

5. What activity was the least helpful to you?

6. How committed are you to beginning the LtoJ® process in your district, school or classroom? If highly committed, where will you begin?

7. Where are you on this scale?

   Confusion _____ Clarity

8. How did I do in these four essential elements of successful seminars? (5 is highest and 1 is lowest score.) Place an "X" on each line.

   Providing HUMOR   1_____5
   Speaking to your HEART   1_____5
   Giving you HOPE   1_____5
   Providing enough HELP   1_____5

Resource U: Sample Timed Math Fluency Quiz

Name _____ Grade 7   Week 1

$\begin{array}{r} 30 \\ \times 7 \\ \hline \end{array}$
$\dfrac{1}{3} = .$
$\sqrt{4}$
$72 \div 9 =$
$\dfrac{1}{3} = \dfrac{5}{-}$
$\begin{array}{r} 16 \\ +16 \\ \hline \end{array}$
$4 \cdot 4 \cdot 4 = 4^{\bigcirc}$

$\begin{array}{r} 56 \\ -38 \\ \hline \end{array}$
$\sqrt{\dfrac{121}{144}}$
$6\overline{)120}$
$\begin{array}{r} 38 \\ +14 \\ \hline \end{array}$
$\begin{array}{r} 8 \\ \times 8 \\ \hline \end{array}$
$1\dfrac{1}{2} = \ \%$
$2^4 =$

$\dfrac{2}{5} = \dfrac{4}{-}$
$\sqrt{25X^2}$
$40\% = .$
$\begin{array}{r} 4 \\ \times 6 \\ \hline \end{array}$
$(7^2)^3 = 7^{\bigcirc}$
$\begin{array}{r} 30 \\ -16 \\ \hline \end{array}$
$\dfrac{6}{7} = \dfrac{\ }{14}$

$\dfrac{45}{9} =$
$\sqrt{64}$
$\begin{array}{r} 41 \\ +29 \\ \hline \end{array}$
$(-3)(-3)(-3)(-3) =$
$\begin{array}{r} 64 \\ -7 \\ \hline \end{array}$
$\dfrac{1}{5} = \dfrac{\ }{10}$
$9\overline{)81}$

$\sqrt{\dfrac{4}{25}}$
$\begin{array}{r} 3 \\ \times 3 \\ \hline \end{array}$
$3^4 =$
$0.1 = —$
$\dfrac{36}{6} =$
$\sqrt{16X^2}$
$\begin{array}{r} 73 \\ +8 \\ \hline \end{array}$

$101\% = .$
$\begin{array}{r} 40 \\ \times 2 \\ \hline \end{array}$
$\dfrac{10^7}{10^4} = 10^{\bigcirc}$
$\begin{array}{r} 80 \\ -53 \\ \hline \end{array}$
$\dfrac{2}{9} = \dfrac{10}{\ }$

Resource V: Organization of Essay

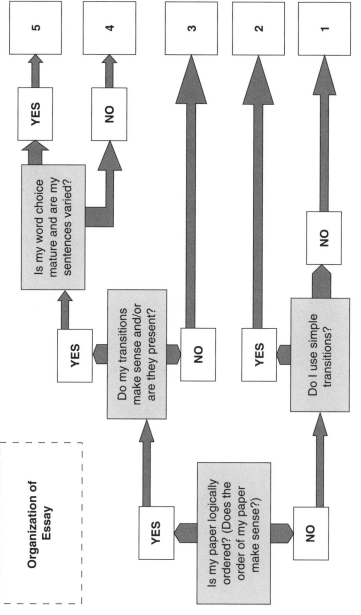

Organization of Essay

Is my paper logically ordered? (Does the order of my paper make sense?)

YES → Do my transitions make sense and/or are they present?

YES → Is my word choice mature and are my sentences varied?

YES → 5

NO → 4

NO → 3

NO → Do I use simple transitions?

YES → 2

NO → 1

Source: Created by Nicole Trovillion.

Resource W: Correlation Directions

1ST INITIAL	PROCESS (LtoJ® FINAL QUIZ)	STATE TEST
G	60%	419
Z	80%	439
S	88%	454
H	60%	413
L	76%	451
K	72%	428
T	92%	486
J	86%	413
H	66%	422
S	60%	431
A	74%	416
T	92%	478
D	44%	400
G	90%	466
S	62%	422
J	42%	378
I	86%	461
J	88%	459
J	80%	432
S	86%	449
R	90%	507
E	52%	414
K	74%	436
B	74%	405
J	66%	400
L	84%	449
R	62%	414
M	82%	455

The Pearson Correlation

The three columns in Excel are the student name, the process data, and the results data. In this example, the second column is the percentage correct on the final LtoJ® quiz in a Grade 5 classroom and the third column is the raw score on the state assessment. Correlation is calculated in Pearson by clicking on Formulas, More Functions, Scientific, and then Pearson Correlation. Place cursor in a blank cell when following this sequence and the pop-up below will appear.

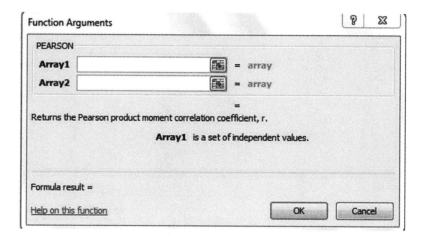

Enter into Array 1 the range of data for the second column separated by a colon. For example, the data above has data for 28 students. So, probably the data is located in cell B1 to B28, so B1:B28 is entered into Array 1. Then the results data is entered into Array 2. It will most likely be C1:C28. Click OK and a number between 0 and 1 will appear on the screen.

.3 is a little correlation

.5 is moderate correlation

.7 is high correlation

.9 is very high correlation

Resource X: Dichotomous Reading Rubrics

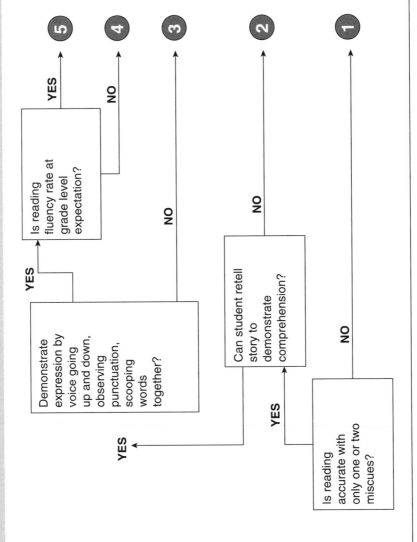

Resource Y: Pareto Chart Directions

Go on a search engine and enter "Pareto chart template." One of the possible templates to download is from the American Society for Quality. Below is the first portion of the download with an example Pareto chart.

Pareto Chart From American Society for Quality

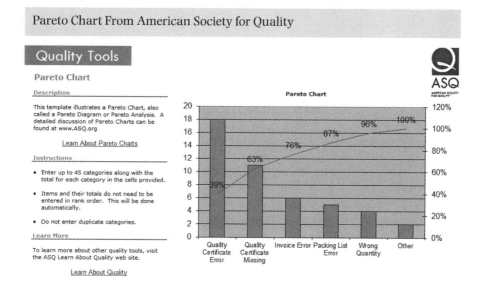

As you move down the page you downloaded, you will see the spreadsheet used by ASQ to create the Pareto chart.

ASQ Spreadsheet for Pareto Chart

Category	Total
Invoice Error	6
Wrong Quantity	4
Quality Certificate Missing	11
Packing List Error	5
Quality Certificate Error	18
Other	2

To use this template, you replace their data and labels with your data and labels. Below is the same spreadsheet with mathematics errors. The hard work of determining the number of errors is still necessary, but the graph is completed automatically. Further, you do not need to calculate the percentage of errors nor do you need to sort the data in descending order; the template you downloaded does this automatically for you.

Math Data Inserted Into ASQ's Pareto Chart Template

Category	Total
Algebra	146
Algorithms	182
Data	109
Estimation	73
Geometry	73
Measurement	155
Operations	300
Number Sense	146
Patterns	55
Probability	36
Systemic Listing	109

The Pareto chart created by the ASQ template is shown below. I did shorten the labels and change the font size to 5 for this chart.

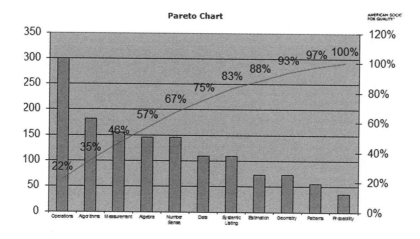

Histograms for One Year

Glossary

Adequate yearly progress (AYP): The name of the quota and results many states provide their schools and school districts.

Alignment: The process of assuring that grade level/course content is properly connected to content elsewhere. The most common alignment in schools is alignment with state standards. The emphasis in continuous strategic improvement is alignment internally, grade by grade, and course by course.

All-Time-Best (ATB): The best result ever. In the classroom, this is the best so far this year, but for many measures such as state exams, this is the best year ever.

Bottom-up: The employees or students, determine the direction of the organization. Decentralization is one example of bottom-up decision making.

Celebration: A "thank you" fun activity with a class, grade level, department, or whole school when the group has an all-time-best. All students in the group participate. No food or trinkets are given to the students.

Class run chart: The total points for the whole classroom (or grade level, department, or school) for each assessment. This can be the total words read in a minute by all the students, total rubric points, or total questions correct.

Composite chart: The "bottom line" for education. All grade levels, all subjects are compacted into one score. The question, "Did we improve" can be answered; the question, "Where did we improve?" is answered with the radar chart. The line is the percentage of exams in the total school district where the result was meeting or exceeding standards.

Cost per student: Calculating for each set of school expenditures the cost per student, with the goal of reducing costs for expenses that do not impact student learning.

Countermeasure: A countermeasure is a hypothesis based upon root cause analysis. When attempting to solve a problem, people can select a hypothesis to test, or they can conduct a root cause analysis; and then when the hypothesis is based upon the root cause, it is called a countermeasure.

Depleted curriculum: Significant aspects of curriculum missing, such as elementary geography, history, science, art, and music, or curriculum is only background knowledge with no performance expectations.

Dichotomous rubric: A scale of quality. The final score on the rubric is obtained by answering a series of yes/no questions. It is very similar to a tree diagram.

Dual composite chart: The same as the composite chart except two lines on the graph instead of one line. The two lines are usually percentage of exams with "exceeding standards" and percentage of exams with "below standards."

Evaluation: Information provided by your boss.

Exchange: A management tool that says, "If you do this for me, I'll do this for you."

Feedback: Information provided by "customers." For teachers, this information comes from students and parents. For administrators, this comes from direct reports.

Firefighting: The common term for addressing a problem but never solving it permanently. Thus the same problem occurs over and over.

***J* curve:** A histogram skewed to the left. Almost all of the results are stacked up at the right of the histogram. The bell curve is the best known histogram in education. The bell curve should be for the middle of a course; the *J* curve is for the end of the course.

Key concept list: A numerical listing of the background knowledge students are to know by the end of the course.

***L* curve:** A histogram skewed to the right. Almost all of the results are stacked up at the left of the histogram. The bell curve is the best known histogram in education. The bell curve should be for the middle of a course; the *L* curve is for the beginning of the course.

LtoJ®: A classroom formative assessment process with four distinctive features: (1) Students are assessed twenty-eight times a year on randomly selected items from end of the year expectations; (2) results are graphed for individuals, classrooms, and schools; (3) students create all the graphs rather than a computer; and (4) the quizzes are not graded.

Optimization: When all aspects of an organization are working together for the good of the organization.

Pareto chart: An analysis graph that (1) displays errors from most errors to least errors and (2) displays the cumulative percentage of errors until all 100 percent of the errors are accounted for.

Pearson correlation coefficient: Two aspects of an organization are compared to determine if they are going down the same path, that is, correlated. A commonly quoted education correlation is the comparison of students' reading fluency rate with their reading comprehension rate. The correlation will always be a numeral between 0 and 1. The higher the correlation, the more inclined the two variables are to go together. Correlation is not cause and effect. However, without a high correlation, one cannot even ask cause/effect questions.

Perfect: The process of identifying for every aspect of an organization, the ideal. The space between perfect and current reality provides the opportunity for continuous strategic improvement.

Permission to Forget®: The process which starts with Grade 1 spelling and continues throughout all of education with chapter tests and finals that communicates to students they do not need to know the content beyond the current assessment. Students, for example, in geometry are seldom asked to remember middle school math or Algebra I.

Preview questions: Questions asked about content not yet taught on non-graded quizzes.

Process data: The data collected throughout the school year. Its purpose is to advise teachers and others about adjustments that can be made to improve the final results data. The more common education terms are *formative* and *summative*, but *process* and *results* are the more common terms outside of education.

Radar chart: A graph with a vector for every evaluated aspect of an organization. It has the advantage of displaying multiple years' data for each aspect of an organization that is measured. It appears similar to a wheel with many spokes. All data is entered as percentage of accomplishment toward the elusive 100 percent attainment.

Results data: The data from finals, state assessment exams, any end-of-the-year data such as percentage of students participating in extracurricular activities, and results from college entrance exams.

Root cause analysis (RCA): The process of digging deep into organizations to determine what is really at the root of the problem. Sometimes this is called the *5-Whys* because people ask why something occurred, then why did that situation occur, then why again until they come up with the real root cause of the problem.

Scatter diagram: A graph, usually in classrooms, with one dot per student per assessment. The purpose is to observe the closing of the achievement gap over the course of a school year.

Scatter overlay: A graph, usually prepared for IEPs, which combines the scatter diagram and the student run chart onto one graph. Observers are able to see one student's progress compared the progress of the class as a whole.

Servant leader: A leader whose primary purpose balanced between setting the parameters for organizational success and assisting employees as they work together to meet the organization's priorities.

Stabilization: Creating systems so that students are required to remember course content from prior years' curriculum. Every assessment, for example, can include 30 percent questions from prior grade levels.

Student run chart: A graph of an individual student's progress completed after each assessment. This can be words per minute read, rubric scores, number of correct answers, and so on.

Sub-optimization: When one aspect of an organization wins at the expense of the whole organization.

Top-down: The boss decides and directs.

Top-down/bottom-up: The boss determines the overall direction and the employees (or students) are able to determine how this direction is accomplished.

Vector: The lines on the radar chart that display data between 0 percent and 100 percent. Each vector has data for one aspect of a school system or school.

Waste: Any activity requiring money or time that does not improve student learning. Also, any activity that diminishes students' kindergarten level of enthusiasm is a waste of enthusiasm.

References

Ackoff, R. L. (1994). *The democratic corporation.* New York, NY: Oxford University Press.

Albert, S. (2013). *When.* San Francisco, CA: Jossey-Bass.

Bakke, D. W. (2005). *Joy at work.* Seattle, WA: PVG Press.

Bogle, J. C. (2009). *Enough.* Hoboken, NJ: John Wiley.

Brady, D. (2010, June 21). *Bloomberg Businessweek,* 96.

Burgard, J. J. (2010). *Continuous improvement in the science classroom.* Milwaukee, WI: ASQ Quality Press.

Burlingham, B. (2005). *Small giants.* New York, NY: Penguin Group.

Collins, J. (2009). *How the mighty fall.* New York, NY: HarperCollins.

Deci, E. L. (1995). *Why we do what we do.* New York, NY: Penguin Books.

DeNeff, S. (2011). *More than forgiveness.* Indianapolis, IN: Wesleyan Publishing House.

Deming, W. E. (1986). *Out of the crisis.* Cambridge, MA: MIT Press.

Deming, W. E. (1992). Presentation at the Deming Conference, Alexandria, Virginia, January 21, 1992.

Deming, W. E. (1994). *The New Economics.* Cambridge, MA: MIT Press.

Drucker, P. F. (2009, Winter). Managing oneself. *Harvard Business Review,* 32–42.

Eichenwald, K. (2005). *Conspiracy of fools.* New York, NY: Broadway Books.

Fullan, M. (2011). *The moral imperative realized.* Thousand Oaks, CA: Corwin.

Gilbert, D. (2012, January). The science behind the smile. *Harvard Business Review,* 79, 86–87.

Gladwell, M. (2000). *The tipping point.* New York, NY: Little, Brown.

Godin, S. (2010). *Linchpin.* New York, NY: Penguin Group.

Ha, W. T. (2002). *The book of statistical process control.* Cincinnati, OH: Zontec Press.

Hattie, J. (2009). *Visible learning.* London, UK: Routledge.

Hirsch, E. D., Jr. (2006). *The knowledge deficit.* New York, NY: Houghton Mifflin.

Hirsch, E. D., Jr. (2010–2011, Winter). Beyond comprehension. *American Educator,* 30–43.

Hubbard, D. W. (2010). *How to measure anything.* Hoboken, NJ: John Wiley.

Jenkins, L. (1978). *The relationships between cognitive development, language development, and reading ability in children ages six-to-nine* (Doctoral dissertation). Claremont, California, Claremont Graduate School.

Jenkins, L. (2003). *Improving student learning: Applying Deming's principles in classrooms.* Milwaukee, WI: ASQ Quality Press.

Jenkins, L. (2008). *From systems thinking to systemic action.* Lanham, MD: Rowman-Littlefield.

Jenkins, L. (2013). *Permission to forget: And nine other root causes of America's frustration with education.* Milwaukee, WI: ASQ Quality Press.

Kelley, L. (2011, February). Refresh and revitalize. *Quality Progress,* 18–23.

Killian, C. (1992). *The world of W. Edwards Deming* (2nd ed.). Knoxville, TN: SPC Press.

Kirschenbaum, H., Napier, R., & Simon, S. B. (1971). *Wad ja get? The grading game in American education.* Oxford, UK: Hart Publishers.

Klein, G. (2013). *Seeing what others don't.* New York, NY: Public Affairs.

Lewis, M. (2003). *Moneyball.* New York, NY: W.W. Norton.

Liker, J. K. (2004). *The Toyota way.* New York, NY: McGraw-Hill.

Liker, J. K., & Convis, G. (2012). *The Toyota way to lean leadership.* New York, NY: McGraw-Hill.

Liker, J. K., & Franz, J. K. (2011). *The Toyota way to continuous improvement.* New York, NY: McGraw-Hill.

Liker, J. K., & Hoseus, M. (2008). *Toyota culture.* New York, NY: McGraw-Hill.

Liker, J. K., & Meier, D. (2006). *The Toyota way fieldbook.* New York, NY: McGraw-Hill.

Liker, J. K., & Meier, D. (2007). *Toyota talent.* New York, NY: McGraw-Hill.

Liker, J. K., & Ogden, T. N. (2011). *Toyota under fire: Lessons for turning crisis into opportunity.* New York, NY: McGraw-Hill.

Martin, R. L., & Riel, J. (2010, January 25). Innovation's accidental enemies. *Bloomberg Businessweek,* 72.

Marzano, R. J. (2004). *Building background knowledge.* Alexandria, VA: ASCD.

Maxwell, J. C. (2002). *The Maxwell leadership bible.* Nashville, TN: Thomas Nelson.

Maxwell, J. C. (2007). *Talent is never enough.* Nashville, TN: Thomas Nelson.

Maxwell, J. C. (2013). *Sometimes we win; Sometimes we learn.* New York, NY: Center Street Press.

McCaulley, Daniel. (2010). *Continuous improvement in the social studies classroom.* Milwaukee, WI: ASQ Quality Press.

Murphy, M. (2012). *Hiring for attitude.* New York, NY: McGraw-Hill.

National Assessment of Educational Progress. (2013). *Mathematics assessment.* Washington, DC: U.S. Department of Education, Institute of Education Sciences.

Orsini, J. (Ed.). (2013). *The essential Deming.* New York, NY: McGraw-Hill.

Pink, D. (2006). *A whole new mind.* New York, NY: Riverhead Books.

Pink, D. (2009). *Drive.* New York, NY: Riverhead Books.

Porter, M. E. (2011). What is strategy? In Harvard Business Review, *On Strategy* (pp. 2, 16). Boston, MA: Harvard Business Review Press.

Ripley, A. (2013). *The smartest kids in the world.* New York, NY: Simon & Schuster.

Roam, D. (2010). *The back of the napkin.* New York, NY: Penguin Group.

Savary, L. M., & and Crawford-Mason, C. (2006). *The nun and the bureaucrat.* Washington, DC: CC-M Productions.

Searson, J. W., & Martin, G. E. (1910). *Studies in reading, eighth grade.* Lincoln, NE: University Publishing Company.

Schmoker, M. (2011). *Focus.* Alexandria, VA: ASCD.

Tucker, M. C. (2012, September). Benchmarking the world's best. *School Administrator, 8*(69), 26.

Webber, L., & Wallace, M. (2007). *Quality control for dummies.* Hoboken, NJ: John Wiley.

Wheeler, D. J., & Chambers, D. S. (1992). *Understanding statistical process control.* Knoxville, TN: SPC Press.

Index

Rubrics. *See* Dichotomous rubric
Rutowski, R., 63

Savary, L. M., 24
Scatter diagrams, 183–184
Scatter overlays, 187–188
Schools
    A-F grades for, 96
    as one of four levels of leadership, 3–4
Science
    dichotomous rubric, 263 (figure)
    review PPT, 255
    stabilization, 254
Searson, J. W., 73
Self-reported grades, 123
    time for measuring, 123–125
Servant leadership, 3, 9, 38, 200–201
    addition tool in, 193–195
    versus fear, 10
    optimization and, 223
Shewhart, W., 214
Skeptics, 54–56
Social studies preview, 82–83
Spaced and massed practice, 137–138
Spanish vocabulary, 233–237
Special education teachers, 128
Special problems, 37
Spreadsheets, finance, 176
Stabilization, 110, 210–211
    importance of, 110–111
    science, 254
    student experts and, 119–120
Staff development, 116–118
Standards, 63, 64
    academic vocabulary and, 78–79
    alignment with, 69
    collaboration and, 74–75
    creativity and, 73–74
    critical thinking and, 76–77
    digital literacy and, 79–80
    informational texts and, 78
    key concept lists for, 114–115
    mathematics preview and, 81–82
    preview of future learning and, 80
    problem solving and, 75–76
    rigor and, 72–73
    social studies preview and, 82–83
    specific, 69–70
Statistics, formal, 16–17
Strategic (as noun)
    added to continuous improvement,
        20–21, 26, 59
    continuous strategic planning, 37

countermeasures, 24, 35–36
respect for people in, 21
root causes analysis, 19, 23–24, 35
somewhat successful, 22
teamwork, 25
top-down/bottom-up, 25–26
unsuccessful, 21–22
See also Continuous strategic
    improvement
Strategic plan
    countermeasures and, 104–105
    as difficult, yet essential and vital, 103
    digging deeper in, 103–104
    no perfect solution and, 105–106
    no quotas in, 106
    optimization for everybody and,
        106–107
    outline, 100–101, 101–102
    radar chart transition to, 98–100
    role of senior leaders in, 107–108
    See also Radar charts
Student achievement strategies, 122–123
    acceleration, 132–133
    classroom management,
        133, 134 (figure)
    feedback, 135–136
    formative evaluation, 129–130,
        131 (figure)
    incentives as, 195–197
    microteaching, 131–132
    Pearson Correlation Coefficient,
        143–144
    Piagetian research and, 125–129
    prior achievement, 138–141
    repeated reading programs, 143
    self-reported grades, 123
    spaced and massed practice,
        137–138
    teacher clarity, 134–135
    teacher-student relationships,
        136–137
    time for measuring, 123–125
    vocabulary programs, 142–143
Student experts, 64, 212
    aim for each academic subject and,
        66–67
    aim for educators, 64–66
    in mathematics, 66, 68
    in reading, 67, 68–69
    specific grade-level expectations and,
        67–68
    stabilization and, 119–120
    very specific standards for, 69–70

CORWIN

A SAGE Company

CORWIN HAS ONE MISSION: to enhance education through intentional professional learning.

We build long-term relationships with our authors, educators, clients, and associations who partner with us to develop and continuously improve the best evidence-based practices that establish and support lifelong learning.